The Democratic Party Heads North, 1877–1962

This book examines the dynamics of the American party system and explores how contemporary American politics was formed. Specifically, it asks how the Democrats, a party that had its main area of support in the South, could become sufficiently competitive in the American North as to be able to construct a national political majority. It rejects the conventional account, based on "realignment theory," that between the end of Reconstruction and the Civil Rights Revolution, the base level of support for the Democratic Party varied greatly from one era to another. Instead, by distinguishing between the "building blocks" available to the Democrats in coalition formation and the aggregation of those "blocks" into an actual coalition, the author shows that there was much less variation over time in the available "blocks" than is usually argued. Neither the economic depression of 1893 nor the New Deal had the impact on the party system that most political scientists claim.

Alan Ware is a professor and tutor in Politics at Worcester College, Oxford University. He has authored seven previous books and edited six books. He has written numerous articles that have appeared in scholarly journals. His most recent book, *The American Direct Primary*, was published in 2002, and *Political Parties and Party Systems* was recently translated into Spanish. He serves on the editorial boards for *Party Politics*, *Democratization*, and *Government and Opposition*.

The Democratic Party Heads North, 1877–1962

ALAN WARE

Oxford University

CAMBRIDGE
UNIVERSITY PRESS

CAMBRIDGE UNIVERSITY PRESS
Cambridge, New York, Melbourne, Madrid, Cape Town, Singapore, São Paulo

Cambridge University Press
40 West 20th Street, New York, NY 10011-4211, USA

www.cambridge.org
Information on this title: www.cambridge.org/9780521858274

First published 2006

Printed in the United States of America

A catalog record for this publication is available from the British Library.

Library of Congress Cataloging in Publication Data

Ware, Alan.
The Democratic Party heads north, 1877–1962 / Alan Ware.
   p.   cm.
Includes bibliographical references and index.
ISBN 0-521-85827-5 (hardback) – ISBN 0-521-67500-6 (pbk.)
1. Democratic Party (U.S.) – History.   I. Title.
JK2316.W373   2006
324.2736′09 – dc22   2005018254

ISBN-13   978-0-521-85827-4 hardback
ISBN-10   0-521-85827-5 hardback

ISBN-13   978-0-521-67500-0 paperback
ISBN-10   0-521-67500-6 paperback

To the memory of Michael Nast
and
For three other friends who have also discussed American politics
with me over the years:
Joseph Chytry
Nelson Polsby
Art Shartsis

Contents

List of Tables

Preface

Much of what we learn about politics in political science books is either wrong or highly misleading. I had reached this somewhat depressing conclusion long before I completed my previous book, *The American Direct Primary*, but my research for that book confirmed that my judgement was largely correct. The problem lies at the heart of how political science is conducted, especially in the United States, and is not the result of political scientists being either fools or knaves. In my experience the vast majority of its practitioners fall into neither of these categories. Rather, the problem is caused by the role played by fashion, especially fashions in methodology, which has two adverse consequences for the development of our knowledge about the political world.

First, the obsession with making one's research compatible with the latest fashion in methodology, together with changes in those fashions, means that research is often conducted without any knowledge of similar work that was undertaken years ago. Thus, the equivalent of the wheel *is* often reinvented by political scientists about every quarter of a century.[1] Secondly, as fashion changes, so do some conceptions and arguments go unchallenged and become part of the "evident truths" of the profession; they are held to be true because previous generations of political scientists believed them to be true. This was what I had discovered about the origins of direct primary elections in America – the events that led to their introduction actually bore no relation to the standard account that was found in every reference to the subject. Yet the last time anyone had done

---

[1] I make this point in "Old Political Issues and Contemporary Political Science", *Government and Opposition*, 38 (2003), 526.

extended research on the subject was in the 1920s. In the absence of continuing research on a particular topic, once the political science agenda has moved on, there is every possibility that highly contentious arguments become embedded as part of the received wisdom that is handed down from one generation of students to the next. That is what happened in the case of the direct primary.

In part, the origins of this book lie in work I undertook on the *American Direct Primary*. That book was focussed on party structures and not on the American party system, but, when writing it, I came to realize that much of the accepted view about long-term change in the party system did not seem to fit with what I was learning about the working of that system in the years between 1890 and 1915. Fortunately, during the later stages of the research I became aware of David Mayhew's critical analysis of the idea of "realigning elections" – work that was first published in the *Annual Review of Political Science* and then in more extended form as a book.[2] The idea that the American party system was transformed periodically by massive shifts in the pattern of voter alignments had been proposed in the 1960s, and had been accepted universally since then by those writing on American parties – including the present author. If, as Mayhew was arguing, realignment theory was seriously flawed, it might be doubted how much it really could contribute to our understanding of the American party system. Reinforcing my own doubts about how we should explain change in the party system, Mayhew's work provided the intellectual "spark" that started me thinking about how party systems change over time.

The central theme of the book is that, as institutions, parties are much better at managing change than is usually claimed. It is wholly inadequate, in asking the question "how and why did the party system change," to look just at voting behaviour in national elections. Yet this has been the dominant approach of those who have written on the subject. It is not the voters, acting as an exogenous variable, whose changed behaviour transforms the party system; it is the actors in political parties, whose decisions about strategy (and their failure also to take such decisions) shape the likely responses from voters. Given the resources available to parties, it should not be surprising that they can react to adverse circumstances, and can rebuild coalitions of support that are capable of winning

---

[2] David R. Mayhew, "Electoral Realignments", *Annual Review of Political Science*, 3 (2000), 449–74, and *Electoral Realignments: A Critique of an American Genre*, New Haven and London, Yale University Press, 2002.

elections later. Consequently, this book finds that over a very long period – 85 years – there was both a high degree of continuity in the coalitions that the American parties constructed and much less of an imbalance in relative strength between the two parties than has been usually claimed.

The data sources used in the research are specified in the Appendix to this book.

I commenced research on the book during a year of sabbatical leave in 2000–2001, and I am grateful both to Worcester College and to the University of Oxford for granting me that leave. I also wish to thank:

(i) the Moncrieff Fund (of Worcester College) for several small grants that helped me to finance some research trips to the United States;

(ii) Jane Roberts, who helped me utilize the Statistical Package for the Social Sciences (SPSS) in examining the data on American state legislatures that were acquired from the Inter-University Consortium for Political and Social Research;

(iii) Joni Lovenduski and Desmond King for their comments on some early drafts of the material that eventually made its appearance in this book;

(iv) Nigel Bowles, David Mayhew, Nelson Polsby, and Jack Reynolds for so kindly reading the manuscript and making helpful comments on it;

(v) two (anonymous) reviewers for Cambridge University Press for their most useful comments;

(vi) Jonathan Bernstein, Casey Dominguez, and David Hopkins for their helpful critiques of the manuscript at the panel at the Western Political Science Association Annual Convention held in Oakland in 2005; Mark Oleszek for helping me sort out the design for the book's cover;

(vii) Ildi Clarke for creating the index, Phyllis Berk for her work in copyediting the manuscript, and Regina Paleski who acted as my production editor for Cambridge University Press; all of them greatly improved the final version of the book.

As always, my deepest thanks are to Joni for her continuing support for my writing – which can be a most anti-social activity.

Alan Ware
Worcester College, Oxford

The South and the Democratic Coalition

1. The Democrats' Road from 1877

The presidential election of 2000 was not only one of the most closely contested in American history, but it was also an election that displayed significant regional differences in voting patterns. The Democrats won the popular vote by 0.5 per cent of the total, lost in the Electoral College (EC) by five votes, and yet won 79 per cent of the EC votes in (what might be called) the "Old North" and 66 per cent of those votes in the "West". The Democratic defeat resulted from their winning a mere 29 per cent of EC votes in the Border states and not a single vote in the South.[1] Not the least of the remarkable features of this pattern of voting is that it is almost a mirror image of the result in 1880. That earlier election produced an even closer contest for the popular vote with the Republican plurality being a mere .0002 per cent of the total, although they won the EC by 59 votes. In 1880, however, the Democrats won only 5 per cent of the EC votes in the Old North and 20 per cent in the West, while at the same time they won every EC vote in both the Border states and the South.

---

[1] See Chapter 2, Section 5, for a discussion of regional divisions in the United States. The "Old North" consists of those 13 states to the north of the Mason-Dixon line that had achieved statehood by 1840. The "West" is the non-slaveholding states above the Mason-Dixon line that achieved statehood after 1840 – with the exception of Oklahoma, which is classified as a "Border" state. (Both its physical location and the pattern of immigration there during its years as a territory – primarily from the South – prompt its re-classification in this way.) The Border states category comprises the four states below the Mason-Dixon line that did not rebel in 1860, together with Oklahoma and West Virginia. The "South" is the 11 states that formed the Confederacy in 1860.

Nor is this regional difference between the two eras merely a manifestation of the peculiarities of the EC system itself; similar, though rather less pronounced, differences are evident when looking at congressional elections in the two years. Ninety per cent of all southern congressional districts and 81 per cent of all Border districts were held by Democrats in 1881, compared with 43 per cent and 39 per cent, respectively, in 2001. Above the Mason-Dixon line the parties' fortunes had moved in the opposite direction: In 1881 the Democrats held 28 per cent of congressional districts in the Old North and 16 per cent in the West, but in 2001 they now held 56 per cent and 43 per cent, respectively. To put the matter another way, in 1881 the Democrats' congressional delegation was dominated by those from south of the Mason-Dixon line – only 36 per cent of them came from north of it – while in 2001 it was the northerners who dominated, for they now formed 68 per cent of the entire Democratic contingent in the House.

This movement of the Democrats from being a party that had the core of its support in the South to one that was mainly northern oriented is perhaps the most important long-term change in American electoral history. Paralleling it, of course, is the shift in the Republican Party – a party that originally had hardly any base south of the Mason-Dixon line, but which now counts that region as one of its most reliable areas of support in presidential elections, and from which it presently obtains over 40 per cent of its entire congressional delegation. It is a transformation of party politics that has several different components – most especially, the electoral realignment in the South since the 1960s, a realignment that made it possible for the Republicans to control both chambers of Congress in the 1990s, something the party had not done in successive Congresses since the 1920s. There is an impressive (and growing) literature both on the political strategy of Barry Goldwater that helped to stimulate Republican activism in the South and on the subsequent growth of Republican voting strength in that region; the current study makes no effort to replicate that work.[2] Rather, this book is about the earlier stages of the transformation

---

[2] On the rise of conservative political activism in the 1950s and early 1960s, and on the role in facilitating this, see Robert Alan Goldberg, *Barry Goldwater,* New Haven and London, Yale University Press, 1995; Rick Perlstein, *Before the Storm: Barry Goldwater and the Unmaking of the American Consensus,* New York, Hill and Wang, 2001; Lisa McGirr, *Suburban Warriors: The Origins of the New American Right,* Princeton and Oxford, Princeton University Press, 2001. On the growth of Republican voting strength in the South, see, for example: Alexander P. Lamis, *The Two-Party South,* New York, Oxford University Press, 1984; Earl Black and Merle Black, *Politics and Society in the*

(up to the end of 1962), and it deals with the question of how a party that was so rooted in southern rebellion could come to be a sufficiently strong electoral force in the North that was capable of forming a national political majority.

The book begins in 1877 – the year after the famous compromise that facilitated the final episode in the "normalization" of post-war American politics. From then on, the Democrats could contest national elections unhampered by the disenfranchisement of some of their potential voters or by the disputed status of the South in the national polity. For the first time since the beginning of the Civil War, the Democratic Party could begin the construction of a national coalition with all the southern states formally re-integrated into the national polity on the same basis as other states. Of course, the problem the party leaders faced was one of which they had been acutely aware since at least the time of the Union Army's military victory in 1865. How could the Democrats forge a national coalition that was large enough to win national elections yet still contain some unpopular (if relatively large) minorities: the defeated Confederate states, their pro-slave allies in the Border states, and those northerners who had been ambivalent about the war?

In the minds of many political scientists, the question of how, during the next 80 or so years, the Democrats succeeded in constructing coalitions that could do this has already been answered satisfactorily, but the aim of the present author is to provide a different explanation from the conventional account among political scientists. I will argue that much of that received wisdom is, at best, only partially correct and, at worst, misleading or wrong. So what is the received version in the political science community? There are three main elements to it:

(1) Despite the apparent evidence of electoral dominance in the North by the Republicans after the Civil War, much of the country was exposed to highly competitive electoral politics until the early 1890s. As a result, neither Democrats nor Republicans had secure electoral bases that embraced most of the country.

South, Cambridge, MA, Harvard University Press, 1987; John R. Petrocik, "Realignment: New Party Coalitions and the Nationalization of the South", *Journal of Politics*, 49 (1987), 347–75; Harold W. Stanley, "Southern Partisan Change: Dealignment, Realignment, or Both?", *Journal of Politics*, 50 (1988), 64–88; Norman V. Bartley, *The New South, 1945–1980*, Baton Rouge, Louisiana State University Press, 1995; Earl Black, "The Newest Southern Politics", *Journal of Politics*, 60 (1998), 519–612; Byron E. Shafer and Richard G. C. Johnston, "The Transformation of Southern Politics Revisited: The House of Representatives as a Window", *British Journal of Political Science*, 31 (2001), 601–25.

(2) That competition largely ended in the 1890s when the country became divided into two regions in each of which one party predominated – a South where the Democrats reigned supreme and a North where the Republicans won most elections. Under these conditions, with the Democrats a minority party nationally, usually only the Republicans could build a national political majority – that is, until the New Deal made the Democrats competitive again in the Old North and the West.

(3) Between 1932 and 1936 (or, on some versions, between 1928 and 1936), the Democrats acquired a political advantage nationally because while they remained dominant in the South, they became competitive again throughout most of the North. By the later 1930s, the New Deal had led to the creation of Democratic Party superiority in the nation, a superiority that was challenged successfully only when the Democrats lost their electoral stranglehold on the South.

Common to all three elements is the idea that the underlying strength of the two parties varied greatly over time. Parties won or lost at the national level because they either possessed or lacked the necessary "building blocks" from which to construct a winning coalition. National politics was merely the sum of local politics; from time to time the size of the "blocks" that each of the parties could mobilize would change, for reasons largely beyond the parties' immediate control, and that change affected the long-term prospects of a party's success in presidential and congressional elections.

The arguments presented in this book differ from the version just outlined in six main ways. Underpinning these arguments is the claim that the parties' "building blocks" varied much less over the 86 years covered by this book than is usually realized. The main changes in the party system had less to do with the strength of the parties in particular states than with their ability to get the "blocks" potentially at their disposal to cohere. Coalition building is not just about which potential members may be available for constructing an electoral alliance but also about how they can be made to coalesce (see Chapter 2). Various problems in uniting potential allies were to become evident to both parties over the years – problems of leadership, of internal party division, and so on – and these factors created radically diverging election results, even while the underlying strength of the parties changed much less. In brief, the book does not deny that there were major discontinuities in the way the American party system operated, nor does it deny that the problems of coalition building varied significantly over time, but it does argue that there was also much greater continuity in the dynamic of the system, over a period of more than eight decades, than is often claimed.

The six main respects in which the argument presented here differs from the conventional wisdom are as follows:

(i) The state of competition between the parties in the years between 1877 and the beginning of the 1890s was peculiar. Throughout the country one party was dominant in most states, in that it normally won elections during years of presidential contests. This imbalance in the parties was evident both in the South, where the Democrats were the dominant party, and in the North, where the Republicans usually held the advantage. Only five to seven states provided for a more even balance between the parties. The *appearance* of more extensive competition than this in the North largely stemmed from the problems of managing the internal relations of a majority party, because that management depended on the distribution of patronage, of which there was a limited supply. The losing party at the national level – normally the Democrats – could thereby win elections in the intervening years in these northern states. (See Chapter 3.)

(ii) Until at least 1910 (and arguably later), the underlying dynamics of the party system in the North remained unchanged in many respects. The main changes in these years after the early 1890s were the emergence of a largely one-party South; the consolidation of Republican advantage in a number of non-southern states, where earlier the Democrats had sometimes been able to win elections in non-presidential years; and the growing complexity of the potential Democratic coalition. That the Democrats appeared now to be a minority party in much of the North was mainly the result of difficulties, until after 1908, in recruiting suitable presidential candidates; this distorted the operation of what had earlier seemed to be a party system that did generate a kind of self-equilibrium. (See Chapter 4.)

(iii) Arguably there was an opportunity to re-configure the Democratic coalition after the 1912 victory, and it was missed. Unlike the later, successful attempts by Franklin D. Roosevelt to create long-term adherents to the party throughout the North, Woodrow Wilson

failed to exploit the chance to expand his party's coalition in the
West. (See Chapter 5.)

(iv) This missed opportunity notwithstanding, there were already factors undermining the basis of the old, 19th century, party balance. The growing diversity of the country made coalition building more difficult nationally for both parties, but, in particular, it had created problems for the Democrats. Cultural divisions – between old-stock Americans and newer immigrants – created political cleavages over particular issues such as prohibition, and these, too, made the process of coalition formation far more difficult. The Democratic Party was not a minority party nationally between the 1890s and the 1930s, but rather, at times, the more badly divided of two divided (but potentially evenly balanced) parties. It was that factor that was to contribute to its seemingly weak electoral performance nationally in the 1920s. (See Chapter 6.)

(v) Although Democratic gains in most major cities in the 1930s did make the party a more effective competitor in a number of non-southern states, the Republicans were far from becoming a minority party in these states. To the contrary, once the initial impact of the New Deal programmes had waned, Republicans were remarkably successful at containing the Democrats at the state level in the North. Between 1938 and 1952, the Republican Party enjoyed considerable electoral success in all regions except the South. (See Chapter 7.)

(vi) During the 1950s, the conditions that produced this relative Republican advantage in the North started to be undermined, and by the early 1960s there was evidence that the Democrats were in a position to improve their share of elected public offices in that region. At the same time, though, the Civil Rights Revolution was starting to destroy their hegemony in the South, and thereby opportunities were provided for the Republican Party to become a more southern-oriented party. (See Chapter 8.)

One of the main arguments in this book, therefore, is that while it was a hugely important turning point in helping to make the Democrats the party of the North, the New Deal did not bring into being a fully formed northern-oriented party. For more than 20 years after 1938, there was a serious struggle for political control of the North, and it was only afterwards that the transformation of the Democratic Party into a largely northern-oriented party came closer to completion. Moreover, the struggle by the Democrats to compete on at least equal terms with the Republicans in the North was not something that had, somehow, been interrupted by the political upheavals of the early 1890s, as the conventional political science accounts allege. The entire period from 1877 to 1962 can be characterized as one in which a party that started at a disadvantage in the regions that embraced a majority of the population, and also of the states, sought to establish the kind of electoral strength that would enable it to construct a national majority on a regular basis. How it tried to do that altered, and indeed had to alter, in light of major changes in American society and its economy. Nevertheless, the fight for sufficient political control in the North was at the centre of American politics until the 1960s. Only when the South became less "solid" and also a dynamic sector of the American economy did the electoral geography change. By 2000, of course, both parties had long been fighting for control of the South, as well as of the North. A more national party system had emerged eventually.

The position of the South in the party system was the reason that competitiveness in the North was so important for the Democrats. Throughout the period under consideration here, the South was both the Democratic Party's greatest asset and its greatest liability. It was its greatest asset in that it generated nearly a quarter of the Electoral College votes and a similar proportion of members of Congress. It was a liability in two respects. First, at various times, southern interests made coalition building more difficult for the party. In the 19th century, its very existence made it possible for Republicans to "wave the bloody shirt" in election campaigns; after 1948 it complicated the Democrats' continuing attempts to mobilize black voters and placate its urban, liberal wing. Secondly, throughout the period, though, the presence of such a large interest tended to reduce the flexibility of the party in aggregating interests at the national level. For example, until 1936 the South had its own protection built into the system for nominating the Democrats' presidential candidate, in the form of the two-thirds rule – a rule intended to ensure that anyone hostile to its interests could not be nominated. Although it was not the fault of southerners, the application of those rules in successive elections in the 1920s, for example, contributed to the party's problems in constructing a winning coalition.

But what had the South done to the American party system in the years before 1877? Historians and political scientists are divided in the answer they provide to this question, and there are three main kinds of answer – all of which provide a different interpretation of long-term change in that party system. As we see, each provides a useful insight into the position of the South in the Democratic Party in the post–Civil War period, and each has its limitations.

2. The South and the Party System After the 1850s: Three Accounts

The Majority Party Account

This account, which is more commonly given by historians, is that the growing conflict over race in American politics, from about 1850 onwards, followed by the Civil War, transformed the basis of the party system by creating a majority party, the Republicans, whose dominance persisted until the Great Depression. According to this view, the price the Democratic Party paid for siding with the South over slavery in the 1850s was a lack of influence over the country's policy agenda for 70 years. The years after 1865 saw a combination of Republican administrations and the courts facilitate the growth of industrial capitalism; the primary producing interests that supported the Democratic Party, and the limited role for government that formed the core of that party's ideology, counted for relatively little in the development of public policy. Only exceptionally could the party win a presidential election – it won only 4 out of 17 contests between 1868 and 1932 and only 2 elections consecutively (1912 and 1916).

What is undeniable about this interpretation is that, in general, the course of public policy did favour the interests that tended to support the Republican Party. However, the age-old mistake of confusing "luck" with "power" should not be made here.[3] It could be the case that the interests of industrial capital would have triumphed irrespective of how many (or few) elections the Republicans actually won, or, alternatively, it might be that it was the courts who were the primary agent in their success. The issue of concern to us is whether the electoral position of the Democratic Party after the Civil War was that of a minority party, and we shall see that it is far from evident that it was. It was not until after 1876 that the full complement of white southern voters were restored to the electoral rolls, and in the five presidential elections between 1876 and 1892, the Democrats won a popular plurality in every one except 1880. Moreover,

---

[3] For a formal analysis of some aspects of the relationship between power and luck, see Brian Barry, "Is It Better to Be Powerful or Lucky? Part II", *Political Studies*, 28 (1980), 338–52.

as we have seen already, that exceptional election (1880) produced an extremely close result in the popular vote. Of course, the distribution of the vote across the nation *could* provide a slight, but significant, advantage to the Republicans, but that advantage was not always decisive in this period. With only a 0.3 per cent plurality in 1884, for example, the Democrats could still win in the Electoral College.

The Changing Party Systems Account

Another account, popular with political scientists rather than historians, holds that there was electoral parity between the major parties after the Civil War – just as there had been from the mid-1830s until the early 1850s. However, it was not a restored party system that was evident after the Civil War but an entirely new system. Moreover, that system itself would break down and be replaced by a yet different system in the 1890s. The leading scholar of this view is Walter Dean Burnham, who argues that a so-called third party system was formed by 1860; organized initially around the issue of slavery, that system replaced the "second party system", the one that had started in the Jacksonian revolution of the 1830s. Thus, the Burnham analysis focusses on disjuncture, and on rather sudden changes in how the parties constituted themselves.[4] The alignment of the Jacksonian-era parties started to change from 1850 onwards as the debate about the extension of slavery into the territories, and the related issue of the admission of additional states to the Union, substituted a new line of division between the parties for a pre-existing party cleavage that centred on the scope of government activity. The result was a more pronounced regional split, although the proponents of this view usually concede that it did not produce a major change in the broader ideological divisions between the parties. Throughout the 19th century, the Democrats remained a party committed to a limited role for the federal government, and to "small government" more generally. The Whigs – and later the Republicans – championed a more active role for the federal government in opening up the country to trade and industry. By 1856 the new political alignment was largely in place, although the collapse of the remnants of the Whig Party would not occur until after the presidential election of that year.

---

[4] Walter Dean Burnham, *Critical Elections and Mainsprings of American Politics*, New York, Norton, 1970, and Walter Dean Burnham and William N. Chambers (eds.), *The American Party Systems*, Second Edition, New York, Oxford University Press, 1975. The "first" party system on this schema was the one that emerged in the 18th century in the dispute between Federalists and Democratic-Republicans.

But if the distinction between the second and the third party system hinges on different patterns of regional support, just how different was the third system? Was it really a "third" system? That is, how was it linked to the politics that preceded it, and was it, perhaps, merely a modification of the existing party system rather than an overturning of the older political order? For Burnham, there was, in Barbara Sinclair's words, a "cataclysmic event", to which the parties could not respond adequately and which thereby prompted new forms of electoral behaviour.[5] His analytic framework sees the move from one so-called party system to another as being marked by the inability of the parties to respond to mounting conflicts in American society and economy. However, this is a misleading account of the pre-1853 period in three important respects.

First, the issue of the expansion of slavery was not a cataclysmic event in the way that a major war or an economic depression might be; it was not an exogenous variable that had a sudden impact on the political process. Rather, it was an issue that had cross-cut party lines earlier because the structure of American political institutions had made it impossible to change the status quo.[6] The balance between slave and non-slave states in the U.S. Senate provided the former, in effect, with a veto over any policy change that threatened their interests. Consequently, divisions between the two major parties developed over other issues, ones that were suitable for party mobilization. This would have been a stable institutional solution but for three incompatible factors:

(1) Virtually all American political elites accepted as an objective the creation of new states once the population sizes of territories warranted it.

(2) The territories in which settlement was occurring were generally areas for which a slave economy was unsuitable, and hence there was little prospect of many new slave states being admitted to the Union, while there was growing pressure to admit new "free" states. Inevitably, that would end the South's veto in the Senate.[7]

[5] Barbara Sinclair, *Congressional Realignment, 1925–78*, Houston, University of Texas Press, 1982, p. 5.

[6] See, for example, Barry R. Weingast, "Political Stability and Civil War: Institutions, Commitment, and American Democracy", in Robert H. Bates et al., *Analytic Narratives*, Princeton, NJ, Princeton University Press, 1998, pp. 148–93.

[7] To many southerners, part of the attraction of a policy of American imperialism in the Caribbean and in Central America was that it would have brought land into the United States that could have supported a slave economy.

(3) The U.S. Constitution prohibited the sub-division of existing states, so that there was no possibility of creating new slave states artificially, and thereby preserving the balance in the Senate.[8]

Population expansion into the territories in the West thereby increased the politicization of the slave issue, and that politicization drew the parties in. The Compromise of 1850 was the symbolic end of a brief period of party politics, but neither it, nor any other event, can be recognized as "cataclysmic". Rather, party strategies had to change as the context in which the issue had been handled was changing.

Secondly, one of the two parties of the early 1850s – the Democrats – was all too capable of responding to the need for a new strategy. Its ideology of limited government fitted well with the needs of many southern whites (in relation to the slave issue), including those whites who had previously supported the Whig Party. Non-interference by the federal government in areas that would affect their interests adversely was a clarion cry to which they could respond, given that it appeared as if that government might eventually weaken the bargaining power of slave interests. Consequently, the Democratic Party could solidify its electoral base in the slaveholding states. That those states controlled 120 of the then-254 Electoral College votes put immense pressure on a Whig Party divided between its northern and southern wings. By 1854, the anti-Democratic opposition had three competing alternative organizations: the Whig Party itself, the nativist American Party, and the new Republican Party. John Aldrich has shown that political ambition – individual politicians throwing in their lot with the party that seemed most likely to succeed – decided that contest in favour of the Republicans.[9] But the important point is that with the exception of its stance on slavery, the Republican Party took over the political agenda of the Whig Party. Once the Civil War and the emancipation of slaves ended the salience of that issue, except as a valence issue with the Republicans "waving the bloody flag", the Republican Party really was little more than the former Whig Party operating under a different name. As John Gerring notes in his study of political ideology in

---

[8] Of course, in the Civil War this did not prevent the creation of the state of West Virginia in precisely this way. In this context it is also important to note the Texas Annexation Act of 1845, which made provision for Texas to be divided in future into five different states. Because of Texas's secession from the Union in 1861, the constitutionality of this provision was never tested, although it could be argued that it was incompatible with Article IV, Section 3.

[9] John H. Aldrich, *Why Parties? The Origin and Transformation of Political Parties in America*, Chicago, University of Chicago Press, 1995, pp. 140–56.

TABLE I.I. *Classification of States by Size of Democratic Plurality in Presidential Elections for Both 1840–1852 and 1880–1892*

	Heartland 1880–1892 (12 + 3)	Contested Territory 1880–1892 (7 + 2)	Foreign Parts 1880–1892 (6 + 8)
Heartland 1840–52 (9)	*Alabama* *Arkansas* *Mississippi* *Missouri*	Illinois Indiana New Hampshire	Maine Michigan
Contested Territory 1840–52 (11)	*Delaware* *Louisiana* *Georgia* *Maryland* *Tennessee* *Virginia*	Connecticut New Jersey New York Ohio	Pennsylvania
Foreign Parts 1840–52 (5)	*Kentucky* *North Carolina*		Massachusetts Rhode Island Vermont
States not included in data for 1840–52 (13)	*Florida* *South Carolina* *Texas*	California West Virginia	Colorado Iowa Kansas Minnesota Nebraska Nevada Oregon Wisconsin

Heartland is defined as a Median Plurality for the Democrats of more than 5 per cent of total vote over the Republicans (in 1880–92) and over Whigs in 1840–8; Contested Territory is defined as a plurality of less than 5 per cent for the Democrats, but no more than 5 per cent for the Republicans or Whigs; Foreign Parts is defined as a plurality of more than 5 per cent for the Republicans or Whigs.
Slave-owning states are shown in italics.

America, "a fairly consistent view of the political world was carried over from the party of Clay to the party of Lincoln to the party of Calvin Coolidge, the last bearer of American Whiggism".[10]

Thirdly, there was considerable continuity, as well as change, between how states voted in presidential elections in the 1840s and how they voted later (see Table 1.1). Nearly half of the states were in exactly the

---

[10] John Gerring, *Party Ideologies in America, 1828–1996*, Cambridge, Cambridge University Press, 1998, p. 57.

same category (Democratic Heartland, Contested Territory, or Foreign Parts) in the period 1880–92 as they had been in 1840–52. Predictably, most of the movement from one category to another was with southern and Border states moving into the Democratic Heartland category after the Civil War. Among the northern states, slightly more than half of the 13 states were in the same category in the two periods; of the 6 that changed categories only 3 (Maine, Michigan and Pennsylvania) moved into the Foreign Parts category (for the Democrats) during the Gilded Age. Whatever else it did, the transformation of the 1850s did not create an overwhelmingly Republican North. This point is compatible with the conclusion that the emergence of slavery as an issue dividing parties in the 1850s grafted onto the existing division an explicitly southern dimension, but it did so without replacing an important component of the earlier cleavage between the parties.

It is worth comparing the change from the so-called second party system to the third party system with the change in the British party system between the First World War and the 1930s. There, too, a new party replaced an older one as the major party in a predominantly two-party system. Furthermore, in the British case, too, there were some changes in the electoral base: The Labour Party took over much of the Liberal vote in the industrial cities, but in many rural areas it failed to attract the kind of support that had gone to the Liberals earlier. However, much more than in the United States in the mid-19th century, the rise of the new party saw a long-term shift in the kinds of issues that divided the two parties. British politics was radically different in 1945 than in 1910; this is not true when comparing American politics in 1856 with that of 1891. Yet, curiously, although all political scientists acknowledge change in the British system, hardly any of them has argued that a different party system had arisen. Yet in American political science, it has been widely accepted that the change in the American political agenda at the end of the 1840s and the beginning of the 1850s prompted the birth of an entirely new party system. Obviously, following Humpty Dumpty, we can call that change in party politics what we like, but the language of "second" and "third party systems" conveys the idea of a much sharper break with the past that is at odds with what actually happened.

The Political Continuity Account
This brings us to the third account of party change, and to the answer to the question of what, if anything, the South had done to the party system. Associated with historians such as Joel Silbey, this account rejects the

idea that the Civil War changed very much about party politics.[11] Instead, Silbey emphasizes the continuity in party politics between the ante-bellum period and the Gilded Age, and, accordingly, has characterized the United States in the entire period from 1838 to 1893 as "a political nation". In a number of respects it is clear that Silbey is correct in arguing that the practice of party politics was very similar in the two periods; the demise of the Whig Party, and the rise of the Republicans, produced only a limited change in the organization of politics around the mid-1850s. How parties related to mass electorates was much the same in the 1880s as it had been in the 1840s. Moreover, as we have just seen, many of the important strands in the respective electoral coalitions of the Democrats and Whigs before 1850 were still evident 40 years later. For example, some southern states (Alabama, Arkansas, Mississippi, South Carolina, and Virginia) had leaned to the Democrats for most of the 1840s and had been joined by Texas on its admission to the union. Similarly, parts of New England (notably Massachusetts, Maine, Rhode Island, and Vermont) were centres of Whig support. Both regions were to show similar patterns of support in the 1870s and 1880s.

However, with respect to the issue of the role of the South, the limitation of the Silbey account is that in focussing on how politics was conducted and on the issues that divided politicians, it does not take into account sufficiently the mechanics of constructing a winning national coalition. The creation of the Republican Party in 1854 produced a party that was perceived as antagonistic to the interests of white southerners – something that the Civil War could scarcely be said to have dispelled. Once disloyal rebels were re-enfranchised during the 1870s, the prospect diminished that Republicans could aggregate their pockets of southern voting strength into statewide victories there that could contribute to presidential election success. As we shall see, Democratic dominance in the South did not become a Democratic monopoly until the 1890s, but the "solid South" was largely in place by 1880; not only did the Democrats win all of the Electoral College votes from south of the Mason-Dixon line that year but, as noted earlier, they also won 91 per cent of southern House seats and 86 per cent of House seats from the Border states.

---

[11] Joel H. Silbey, *The American Political Nation, 1838–1893*, Stanford, CA, Stanford University Press, 1991. See also Richard L. McCormick, *The Party Period and Public Policy: American Politics from the Age of Jackson to the Progressive Era*, New York, Oxford University Press, 1986.

Of course, had the Democrats been able to retain their entire pre-1856 electoral base, the advent of the "solid South" would have made them a strong majority party. The Civil War changed that prospect, though. In a few states – Maine, Michigan, and Pennsylvania – voter support shifted decidedly in the Republicans' direction, and these states accounted for 13 per cent of all Electoral College votes. Moreover, the western states that joined the Union after the mid-1850s had been settled mainly by Yankee immigrants, and most leaned Republican – quite heavily in some cases.[12] They accounted for a further 8 per cent of the Electoral College. The 80 Electoral College votes that the Republicans thereby gained more than offset the 75 votes they lost in the Border states and the South, as a result of previously competitive states or Whig-leaning states becoming Democratic.[13] The long-term prospects appeared no better for the Democrats. Economic stagnation in the South meant that this would not be an area of growing population, while northerners were continuing to move into the West. The price of having a "solid South" might have been high indeed for the party.

What is abundantly clear, and was clear to politicians at the time, was that a winning Democratic coalition depended heavily on success in certain non-southern states. If the party could carry all of the South and the Border states, it needed to win about 21 per cent of the Electoral College votes in the Old North and the West. To take control of the House, the Democrats required victory in about 30 per cent of districts above the Mason-Dixon line. To do that they had to construct a party whose symbols and ideas could appeal both to its large base of southern voters and to particular kinds of northerners. Under changing circumstances, that was to remain the party's main task throughout the period under consideration here.

---

[12] These states were Colorado, Iowa, Kansas, Minnesota, Nebraska, Nevada, and Oregon.
[13] Delaware, Kentucky, Louisiana, Georgia, Maryland, North Carolina, Tennessee, and Virginia (see Table 1.1).

2

The Dynamics of Party Coalition Building

1. Electoral Realignment: How Are Parties Constrained in Coalition Building?

An underlying premise of this book is that parties are able to engage in activities that enable them to construct a national winning coalition in the long term: They are actors in a process that can influence electoral outcomes, and they are not merely institutions that respond to conditions in the electorate. They are constrained in numerous ways, but they are not reduced to mere reaction to an exogenously determined partisan electorate. This involves a rejection of the argument, often associated with those who analyze American parties in respect of "critical elections" or "realigning elections", that interest aggregation by parties is an activity that is always circumscribed by periodic (but major) shifts in the distribution of partisanship within the electorate.[1] That I do not use these terms in this context is significant because it reflects my rejection of an entire way of thinking about the situation of both victorious and defeated parties, a way of thinking that has dominated the study of American political parties since the 1960s. To understand this, it is necessary to begin by explaining the intellectual origins of the "realigning election". It represents a coming together of two principal sets of ideas about America's parties.

The first, which in its origins constituted little more than some informed observations by Samuel Lubell in the early 1950s, was that normally,

---

[1] For an excellent critical analysis of the realignment literature, see David R. Mayhew, "Electoral Realignments", and his *Electoral Realignments: A Critique of an American Genre*.

America had a majority and a minority party. According to Lubell:

My own study of American politics shows that the normal political condition in this country is not that of two evenly competing parties. Usually we have one dominant majority party – currently the Democrats – whose main function is to serve as the arena in which the issues of the time are fought out.[2]

Thus, for Lubell, imbalances in the party system were not just short term, corrected by the impact of competition at the next election or the one after that; rather they persisted over long periods. The majority party was a "sun" to which the minority party played the role of "moon" in that it was reactive, rather than itself being a source of issue formation.

The second set of ideas came out of the "Michigan School" of election research; on this view, parties were constrained to a considerable extent by long-term patterns of party identification among mass electorates.[3] Voters acquired identification with a party through the process of political socialization – in which family, workplace, and so on were key factors – and that identification tended to persist throughout a person's life. Moreover, party identification was linked directly to how a person actually voted – in all kinds of partisan elections.[4] Consequently, in interpreting an election, the analyst would look first at the underlying distribution of party identification. If there were more identifiers for Party A than Party B, then the normal election result (a "reaffirming election") would be one that was won by Party A. Obviously, opportunities existed for Party B to win some elections – because of external events that made administrations unpopular, because of temporary schisms within Party A, and so on – but to a large extent they were not the authors of their own fate. Elections that they did win were "deviating" elections, according to the Michigan School.

The conjoining of these two ideas was the work of, primarily, Walter Dean Burnham, although his analysis also drew on that of V. O. Key, who had discussed the idea of critical elections in a seminal article in 1955.[5]

---

[2] Samuel Lubell, *The Future of American Politics*, Third Edition, New York, Harper and Row, 1965, p. 12; first published 1951.

[3] Angus Campbell, Philip E. Converse, Warren E. Miller, and Donald E. Stokes, *The American Voter*, An Abridgment, New York, John Wiley, 1960.

[4] As David Brady and his collaborators said of the Michigan School approach in relation to congressional elections, "House elections focused on voter traits such as political interest and party identification that left individual candidates little responsibility for their own fates"; David W. Brady, John F. Cogan and Morris P. Fiorina (eds.), *Continuity and Change in House Elections*, Stanford, CA, Stanford University Press, 2000, p. 3.

[5] Walter Dean Burnham, *Critical Elections and the Mainsprings of American Politics*; V. O. Key, Jr., "A Theory of Critical Elections", *Journal of Politics*, 17 (1955), 198–210.

In the Burnham version, a realigning election occurred during a period of social and economic upheaval, and it was often characterized by the rise of third parties. The major parties were unable to cope with the new demands emanating during this upheaval, and the result was a disturbance of existing voting patterns. In the aftermath of the realigning election, key groups of voters would shift their voting identification permanently (or new groups of voters would identify with a particular party), and a new electoral order would become established. Realignment might well result in – though did not necessarily result in – the emergence of a majority and a minority party. Thus, after 1896, the Republicans became the majority party nationally, while they acquired minority status with the New Deal realignment following the 1932 election. According to Burnham, there was a regular pattern of realignment. The inability of the American political system to respond effectively to changed social conditions meant that realignment was not a pathology that became evident only infrequently, but something that revealed itself about every 36 years. (The limited capacity of the political system to respond meant that the party in power in Washington at these critical junctions might well be more exposed to voter reaction than its opponent; that made it more likely that it would emerge with minority status subsequently.) Thus, there had been major shifts in the American party system in the late 1820s, the early 1860s, the early mid-1890s, and the early mid-1930s. In between these realigning eras, the parties had to operate within the constraints imposed by a distribution of party identification over which they had relatively little control. Minority parties could devise strategies for winning particular elections, but they could do little to change the underlying pattern of voter identification that disadvantaged them.[6]

Realignment theory had the dual advantage of being elegant and of seeming to short-circuit many of the apparent complexities of American electoral politics. Unfortunately, there are a number of serious objections to it that undermine any claim that it helps to explain long-term party change throughout American history. The first problem emerged at the time of the publication of Burnham's pathbreaking book. On his theory, a party realignment should have occurred after 1968, but instead, voter attachments to parties seemed to be weakening. There appeared to be electoral dealignment, rather than realignment. Widespread ticket

---

[6] For the argument that there is no single optimal strategy for American parties that are out of office, see Kenneth Finegold and Elaine K. Swift, "What Works? Competitive Strategies of Major Parties out of Power", *British Journal of Political Science*, 31 (2001), 95–120.

splitting from the 1960s onwards, and switches in party voting from one presidential election to another, suggested that realignment theory might be able to explain the more distant American past but not the recent past and the present. However, even this more restricted role for it has been called into question now, and this brings us to the second problem; to introduce that problem, it is necessary to look slightly more closely at the "successive party system" view propounded by Burnham.

According to realignment theory, up to the 1960s there had been five quite separate party systems. The first, in the 1790s, had divided Federalists from Democratic-Republicans over issues of the power of the national government; it had dissolved and been succeeded by a period of partyless politics, which in turn was followed by the second party system. As we have seen, that second system, in which Democrats competed against Whigs, lasted from the 1830s to the 1850s and dissolved over the issue of slavery. Out of the Civil War era came another highly competitive system, in which Democrats were pitted against Republicans. That third system ended in the 1890s and was followed, it was argued, by a period of restricted competition in which Democrats were dominant in the South and Republicans dominant in much of the North, with the latter being the majority party nationally. Finally, the "fourth party system" collapsed in the Great Depression, and a broad coalition created by the Democratic Party became a majority nationally; the uncompetitive North of the years from the 1890s to the early 1930s gave way to a much more competitive electoral regime in that region. But are these party systems as separate as realignment theory indicates? Two points have been noted already, in Chapter 1. The transition from the second to the third system involved at least as much continuity as a break with the past. Moreover, contrary to the idea of successive party systems, we have seen from Silbey's argument that there was a quite distinct political era lasting from 1838 to 1893 – a period that spans the second and third party systems.[7]

These points might conceivably be embraced within a modified version of realignment theory, but more devastating has been evidence about the creation of the so-called fourth party system. The conventional wisdom has been that a massive shift in voting patterns (and in party identification) occurred during the years from 1893 to 1896, with northern urban voters deserting the Democratic Party. The result was a transformation in the North, with highly competitive party systems in most states there being replaced by Republican dominance, while in the South the Republican

---

[7] Joel H. Silbey, *The American Political Nation, 1838–1893*.

Party collapsed. The political equivalent of the Dark Ages began, with low levels of electoral turnout and restricted party competition. The parties retreated into their regions of strength, and nationally that meant majority status for the Republican Party. This electoral regime was even given a name (by E. E. Schattschneider) – "The 1896 System".[8] Unfortunately, recent analyses of voting data suggest that no major shift in voting support occurred in 1896, or in elections around that time.[9] This evidence confirms studies of electoral behaviour in some states – for example, New Jersey – that the local Democratic Parties were not destroyed by the election that year.[10] Whatever happened to produce change in the conduct in party politics after 1896, it was not the product of an electoral realignment.

Indeed, one of the consequences of using the idea of the 1896 system is that it conflates medium-term disruptions to the balance of the party system with long-term transformation. The American party system did develop features not evident earlier, but it did so from about 1890, and the period of instability lasted until after the election of 1908. As is shown in Chapter 4, much of the pattern of pre-1890 political competition resurfaced at that later date, so that far from there being a new, and distinctive, party system in place from 1896 until 1932, there was an interregnum between about 1890 and 1910 in which the party system behaved very differently from the years preceding and following it. A similar, but much shorter, interregnum was to be evident later, between 1932 and 1938.

This brings us to the system that supposedly succeeded the 1986 system. Of all the alleged electoral realignments, the one that most closely conforms with the theory is that of the New Deal. There is considerable evidence that with the introduction of popular programmes of economic and social interventionism, the Democrats were able to attract the support of sectors of the electorate (especially in large cities) that had previously been unmobilized or had (possibly) voted Republican. The collapse of many Republican urban machines in the 1930s was, perhaps, the most significant manifestation of this transformation. However, even in the case

---

[8] E. E. Schattschneider, *The Semisovereign People*, Hinsdale, IL, Dryden Press, 1975, Chapter 5; originally published 1960.

[9] Peter F. Nardulli, "The Concept of a Critical Realignment, Electoral Behavior, and Political Change", *American Political Science Review*, 89 (1995), 18; John E. Chubb and Paul E. Peterson, *The New Direction in American Politics*, Washington, DC, Brookings Institute, 1985; Larry M. Bartels, "Electoral Continuity and Change 1868–1996", *Electoral Studies*, 17 (1998), 316.

[10] John F. Reynolds, *Testing Democracy: Electoral Behaviour and Progressive Reform in New Jersey, 1880–1920*, Chapel Hill and London, University of North Carolina Press, 1988, p. 86.

of the New Deal, it is far from clear that the supposed minority party was quite so constrained by the weight of party identification opposed to it as the conventional wisdom postulates. By the 1930s, the link between party identification and voting behaviour was very different than 40 years earlier. Until the 1890s, ticket splitting was a phenomenon that occurred frequently, but at lower levels of elected office, and it reflected breakdowns of organizational control, rather than weak partisanship among voters. Contested nominations might result in rival candidates (from the same party) subsequently distributing ballot papers at the general election that offered a different list of candidates for some local offices than the "official" list. The introduction of the Australian ballot from 1889 onwards seems to have reduced the level of split-ticket voting in the 1890s and led to a reassertion of party control.[11] Nevertheless, split-ticket voting started to rise again in the early 20th century, but this time it occurred in relation to offices at the head of the ticket, and it reflected the growing importance of both individual politicians and personality in election campaigns. Consequently, the meaning of party identification was not the same in the 1930s as it had been from the 1830s to the 1890s. A smaller proportion of party identifiers now behaved as loyal party voters, and party strategy could no longer be about the efficient mobilization of those identifiers.

There is a more general point about the constraints of pre-existing party alignments, however – one that challenges directly realignment theory's assertion that electoral realignments are an exogenous factor that affect the nature of a party system. As Kenneth Finegold and Theda Skocpol argue: "Party alignments are not just manifestations of social cleavages, exogenous to the policy process, but products of ongoing interaction of social groups, state organizations and public policies".[12] Mobilizing groups of voters in support of a party is something that parties can do most effectively through the use of public policy, and they are best able to do that when they control public offices. The main feature of FDR's creation of a new kind of Democratic Party in the 1930s was his use of public policy to attract supporters; that voters were less attached to parties than they had been some decades earlier helped him to do that, but by itself their mere "availability" would not have made possible successive victories for his party.

[11] John F. Reynolds and Richard L. McCormick, "Outlawing 'Treachery': Split Tickets and Ballot Laws in New York and New Jersey, 1880–1910", *Journal of American History*, 72 (1986), 856.

[12] Kenneth Finegold and Theda Skocpol, *State and Party in America's New Deal*, Madison, University of Wisconsin Press, 1995, p. 51.

In part, therefore, this book involves, indirectly, criticism of a major strand of political science, namely, electoral studies. However, it is important to be clear about the nature of the criticism being made. It is most certainly not an attack on what studies of the U.S. electorate have told us about *voters*. Rather, the claim here is that not too much should be made of what those studies tell us about the dynamics of the American *party system*. Underlying this point is the argument that party systems are not, to use Marxist terminology, mere "superstructure"; as institutions, they are not just the consequences of a particular set of identities and behaviours found within mass electorates. Whilst parties are constrained by those factors, they are not reducible to them; a party system is an interaction between specific types of institution (parties), and those interactions are affected by many other factors – not least, the choices made by their leaders.

By contrast, an important assumption of the early voting studies – an assumption that has continued to influence our understanding of the working of the party system – was that there was a direct connection between the distribution of party identification among the major parties and election results.[13] Unfortunately, subsequent analyses have indicated this is not true. Fifteen years after the publication of *The American Voter*, Norman H. Nie and his colleagues published *The Changing American Voter*, which, among other things, used 1950s data to extrapolate what the distribution of partisan identifiers had been in earlier decades.[14] They showed that from at least 1920, self-identifying Democrats had outnumbered Republicans in the electorate and that this gap between the parties had started to grow during the 1920s itself. Nie et al. did not comment on this finding, but one of its consequences is that it drove the proverbial "coach and horses" through the application of the original Michigan analysis to the study of the American party system. Although there were more Democratic identifiers than Republicans in the 1920s, the Democrats had lost all three presidential elections that decade, and all had been heavy defeats. Indeed, between 1920 and 1956 (inclusive), only 5 of the 10 presidential elections had been won by the party that had more identifiers – and in 4 of those contests, that party had enjoyed the advantage of running an incumbent. In explaining the underlying position facing major parties in advance of a presidential election and the strategies available to them

---

[13] Angus Campbell et al., *The American Voter*.
[14] Norman H. Nie, Sidney Verba, and John R. Petrocik, *The Changing American Voter*, Cambridge, MA, and London, Harvard University Press, 1976, pp. 83–4.

in coalition construction, therefore, partisan identification could not be nearly as significant as the original Michigan analysis had suggested.

This finding by Nie and his colleagues generated little comment because, both in their book and more generally in political science, attention was focussed on evident contemporary change in the electorate. As noted earlier, after the 1960s, voters were becoming even less connected to their parties, so that party identification was of reduced significance in predicting the outcome of particular elections. In this new focus on the limited role of party, the issue of whether party identification had really constrained parties in coalition building in the decades up to the 1960s, in the way voting studies tended to indicate, was largely forgotten. Consequently, the role of party identification, and the supposed role of realigning elections in changing distributions of partisan identification, continued to dominate studies of the behaviour of the American party system.

If this approach is rejected as inadequate, what should be the focus of analysis? The argument presented here is that it is appropriate to focus on how a party can attempt to aggregate the interests that might conceivably be brought together in support of its presidential candidate. For example, was the way in which aggregation had been attempted in an election that had been lost heavily (or in elections preceding that) still a viable way of constructing a majority in the Electoral College? Were the interests that a party was seeking to aggregate compatible – had they, perhaps, become less compatible? Were there new strategies – involving the detachment of support from states that had frequently backed the other party – capable of offering the potential for victory? Did the party's strength at other levels of election in such states indicate that those strategies might succeed?

These last two questions raise important points about the options open to both victorious and defeated parties in the peculiarly American context. The construction of coalitions of social groups in presidential elections takes place in the context of an indirect election in the United States. Thus, even if a coalition of social groups $a \ldots n$ constitutes 50 per-cent-plus-one of the total vote, the party that has constructed that coalition may not win. The distribution of that coalition among the states may produce an Electoral College victory for the other party, and minority presidencies are not just hypothetical, as the instances of 1876, 1888, and 2000 demonstrate. Within any broad electoral strategy about, say, the mobilization of *groups a, b,* and *c,* a party has to determine how that can be made compatible with winning *states p* or *q.* (An obvious example of this consideration in practice was George W. Bush's early (and successful) targeting of West Virginia in 2000 – a state that had been a core part of the Democratic coalition in recent decades.) This is one of the ways in which how a party goes about aggregating interests at the presidential level must be linked to the strength that party has at its constituent state levels. Consequently, this book focuses on how successful coalitions might be constructed on the basis of party strength in the states during the years 1877–1962. But this, in turn, prompts questions about the nature of interest aggregation by political parties. In what does this bringing together of different interests by a party consist?

2. The Idea of Interest Aggregation

In the days when political science was much influenced by theories of structural functionalism that had been imported from sociology (the 1950s and early 1960s), accounts of political parties would often list supposed functions that all parties performed within a political system.[15] Often the first to be cited on such lists was interest aggregation. Leaving aside the more contentious point of whether this really is an activity that all parties necessarily undertake, it is certainly one in which many parties engage. However, there are two matters that the phrase "interest aggregation" obscures: What is covered by the term "interest", and is it literally just their "aggregation" in which parties are engaged?

Some of the interests that are brought together are indeed really *interests*. That is, they are groups of people who have the same kind of material stake in the economy.[16] They may be farmers or wage labourers, for example. That shared stake may be restricted to just some farmers – for example, those living in a particular region of the country (for whom, say, the cost of transportation is especially important), or those engaged in particular forms of production (growing cereals rather than raising cattle). How complex the pattern of these kinds of interest is will depend on the structure of the markets in which they operate – so that in some countries (or at some periods), farming might be a relatively unified single interest, while elsewhere it may be sharply divided into a series of different (and possibly competing) interests. Famously, orthodox Marxism argued that

---

[15] The classic discussion that expresses scepticism about parties actually performing these functions, or being the only institutions that perform them, is Anthony King, "Political Parties in Western Democracies", *Polity*, 2 (1969), 111–41.

[16] Brian Barry, for example, argued that something is in one's interests if it increases the opportunity to get what one wants; interests are resources for achieving goals. See *Political Argument*, London, Routledge and Kegan Paul, 1965.

in capitalist societies, complex patterns of interest reduced to just two (capitalists and wage labourers), even when more complex patterns of interest appeared to be present, though few political scientists would now claim that this was anything other than an extreme oversimplification of such patterns.

However, interests can also include "identities" – groups whose members may have different (or conflicting) material interests but who share the same cultural heritage, values, or language. In some regimes, particular parties are concerned exclusively with either mobilizing particular interests or particular identities, but not with both. However, such parties can thrive only if the political system provides no incentive for broader aggregation than this. Given that its institutions, and most especially an elected presidency, have provided an incentive for electoral mobilization around only two parties throughout its history, the United States has always had major parties that have produced a complicated mix of interest and identity aggregation. Part of what brought groups into the 19th century parties was "tribalism"; particular culturally defined groups (such as the Irish) gravitated to the party opposite to the one in which their traditional enemies were predominant. Both immigration (especially from outside Protestant northern Europe) and the Civil War generated further conflicts that were important in shaping who supported which party. However, there were considerable local variations in this tribalist basis of American parties. Some immigrant groups – and this was true of the Italians, for example – were recruited by the Democrats in some cities and by the Republicans in others. Again, in the South (and more importantly in the border states), there were also pockets of Republicanism that derived from opposition to the Confederacy – usually among hill farmers who had had no use for slavery.

Nevertheless, despite its importance, tribalism was only one component of interest aggregation in American parties. In the 19th century, parties tended to recruit different sectors of the economy into their ranks – the Whigs and Republicans being far more supportive of commerce and industry (and of federal government promotion of those interests) than Democrats. That is why the tariff so frequently divided the parties in that century, and why it is possible to find evidence of a consistent ideology in the two main parties, despite the frequent assertion that they have always lacked ideology.[17]

---

[17] On the ideological basis of America's parties, see John Gerring, *Party Ideologies in America, 1828–1996*, Cambridge, Cambridge University Press, 1998.

If interest aggregation by parties was just *aggregation,* though, politics would scarcely be rendered more manageable than in the absence of parties. Adding together the various demands of different groups would still create an impossibly complicated political world. It would amount to Rousseau's "will of all" and could be practised only in huge legislative assemblies, where the intermediation of parties would impose little order on attempts to resolve conflicts. Rather, interest aggregation" actually involves two further activities beyond mere aggregation – *filtration* and *transformation.* Both in election campaigning and in representing interests when in public office, parties have to filter out demands – partly because there will be so many of them, and partly because in any coalition there will be conflicting demands from different groups. Successful coalition building involves finding ways of not bringing to prominence in public debate demands that would likely fragment the coalition. It is only certain interests that can be aggregated; others have to be filtered out of the political process if a coalition is to be maintained. In this process of filtering, one of the most successful techniques is to transform demands, such that different groups can all accept a policy (or a set of values and ideas) as being one that protects each of their own separate interests. In the 19th century, Democrats advocated a minimal role for the federal government, a policy that a variety of groups could accept. For white southerners, it was a way of protecting their region from attempts to claim rights for African Americans; for ethnic groups in the large cities, it was a device for ensuring that Yankee Protestants did not try to interfere with their own customs – such as by restricting drinking on Sundays; for those engaged in agriculture, mining, and forestry, it was the basis of a "principled" rallying cry against tariffs – policies that benefited industrial production but not primary producers.

The aggregation of interests, then, is not just a relatively passive process in which political leaders do no more than articulate demands that their supporters are articulating already. Leadership has to play a more positive role than that – failing to articulate some demands because they are less important, as well as others because they are sources of conflict within the coalition, and devising ways of uniting disparate demands into a coherent agenda. However, in the processes of filtration and transformation, party leaders are not trying to unite followers around policies, principles, or ideas that are alien to the latter; that approach would be suicidal. Rather, they are attempting to downplay the importance of some social conflicts – conflict displacement, in Schattschneider's words – and to find means of uniting seemingly different sorts of conflict.[18] The efforts by leaders to impose order on the political world, through the activities of filtration and transformation, do not usually produce the appearance of coherence:

Political conflicts are waged by coalitions of inferior interests held together by a dominant interest. The effort in all political struggle is to exploit the cracks in the opposition while attempting simultaneously to consolidate one's own side. Inevitably this results in many people saying many different things simultaneously.[19]

But, leaving aside this "fog" that necessarily accompanies political conflict, does interest aggregation amount to a process of preference *shaping*?

As always, it all depends on what is meant by "shaping".[20] At one extreme, shaping could be taken to mean that party leaders can move beyond the original demands of their supporters to create political divisions that are not grounded in those demands. Were this to happen, the political market would not be one in which the demands to which politicians were responding could be said to be determined exogenously. What they would have done, in effect, would be to replace one set of demands with another (their own). However, this is not what those (such as Schattschneider) who discuss the transformative role of party leaders normally have in mind. There are many different "shapes" (or patterns) that political conflict can take because there are so many different conflicts at any given time, so many different ways of defining each conflict, and so many different ways of combining the conflicts together into a political coalition. On this view, political leaders are still constrained by the kinds of conflicts in the political world that they are seeking to organize, but there are many alternative ways in which they can attempt to aggregate the interests engaged in those conflicts. Some of those ways will surely be unsuccessful for them, though there are likely to be a number of alternatives, between which they can choose, that do hold the prospect of electoral success. The demands articulated by politicians are, in a real sense, determined exogenously, but they are not a unique reflection of the

---

[18] E. E. Schattschneider, *The Semisovereign People*, Chapter 4.

[19] Ibid., p. 67.

[20] Patrick Dunleavy, for example, distinguishes preference-shaping behaviour by parties from preference-accommodation behaviour, where the latter occurs within a world of exogenously determined preferences. But he does not discuss the point that this distinction may be too rigid to embrace the range of actions covered by "shaping". See *Democracy, Bureaucracy and Public Choice*, Hemel Hempstead, Harvester Wheatsheaf, 1991, Chapter 5.

demands evident at the mass level; there are many possible such reflections. That is why the distinction in economics between endogenous and exogenous determination of preferences is often so unhelpful in politics.

3. Interest Aggregation Failure

The period under consideration in this book, 1877–1962, included many years (more than half of the total number) when one or the other of the two main parties suffered at least three defeats in a row in presidential elections – 1896–1912, 1920–32, and 1932–52. For such periods especially, it is clear that attempts at interest aggregation had failed: A coalition of interests that had been constructed was insufficiently large to bring the party close to victory. What, if anything, was making it difficult for the defeated party to compete with its opponent? Perhaps nothing was. Consecutive defeats could be the product of a number of unrelated factors that might make this sequence of defeats appear in hindsight to be little more than bad judgement by particular candidates or even just bad luck. However, it is also possible that there were more basic factors that made coalition building especially difficult for the defeated party, and that may account for Democratic weakness (in two of the periods) and strength (in the remaining one).

The problem facing defeated parties, of course, is that their attempts at interest aggregation have failed. They have not aggregated sufficient interests to make victory possible. Such parties are interesting because they often shed particularly good light on the possibility of coalitions that were not constructed, thereby helping us understand the stability of those that were. Understanding the options open to parties in defeat involves, in part, understanding why a particular form of interest aggregation became unsuccessful, and what were the alternative forms of aggregation that might have been attempted. For these purposes, it is useful to discuss two different ways in which we might approach aggregation failure.

One way was mentioned in Chapter 1. We can distinguish between failure that results from having too few potential members with whom to ally oneself ("too few building blocks") and failure that stems from an inability of the potential to come together as a coalition. This analytic framework focuses on the *type* of failure that has been experienced. However, a second approach is to focus on the *causes* of the failure, distinguishing between failure that has its origins in the interests themselves and failure that originates in leadership. All interest aggregation failure for which leadership is responsible is about an inability to combine an adequate supply of potential members into a winning coalition, but not all failure that has its origins within the interests derives from there being insufficient potential members. It may be that incompatibility of some interests has made it unlikely that some potential allies could ever come together, irrespective of what political leaders did. For our purposes here, it is more useful to use the second approach because it focusses on causes, and the two aspects of aggregation failure it identifies are now considered in turn.

Aggregation Failure Originating in Interests Themselves

With this kind of aggregation failure, a further distinction can be made between failure that stems from change within the party's own coalition of interests and those originating in outside interests or in the external political environment.

Intra-coalition problems may be of three kinds:

(i) Interests that had been compatible previously now become incompatible;

(ii) The interests are so disparate that uniting them behind a single leader, policy programme, or set of principles becomes difficult.

Assuming we are concerned with parties that had been successful previously, we are dealing with change here. Changes in society or economy may have altered the perceptions that groups have of each other, of how their interests relate to each other, and what it is that they want for themselves. Both (i) and (ii) may be the result of long-term changes – changes that eventually have a significant impact on the party at a particular election. However, (i) may result from short-term factors – a major economic depression, a war, and so on – that pits one component of a party's coalition against others. In this case, a party's "civil war" may be short-lived and a return to the previous coalition arrangements feasible.

(iii) The supply of resources that have been used by leaders to manage potential conflicts of interest among supporters may decline, making reconciliation between different elements of a coalition more difficult. For example, patronage may be reduced either as a result of institutional reform, or because major electoral defeat has deprived the party of the minimum supply needed for purposes of party management, so that rebuilding the coalition becomes more difficult than it was earlier.

An inability to construct a winning coalition for a party that originates in interests other than those mobilized by the party, or in the external environment, may also take three forms:

(iv) New, and previously unmobilized, interests emerge in the society, and initially these interests are mobilized by other parties. Victory becomes defeat (perhaps only temporarily) because the balance of interests has altered.

(v) A change in external political structures is introduced, with consequences for the translation of electoral majorities into the occupation of public office. For example, electoral boundaries may be redrawn radically or new sub-units (states or provinces) introduced into the political system that affect adversely a party's ability to win an election, even though there is no fundamental change to its own electoral coalition or that of its opponents.

(vi) Interests that previously were open to conversion by a party at particular elections now become committed to its opponents. The loss of "fluidity" in the electoral market makes it far more difficult for the one party than for others. Electoral realignment arguments that posit an imbalance in the size of party coalitions following a realigning election are one version of this kind of argument, but they are not the only kind. For example, the reduced fluidity may not be so much because of stronger voter identity with a given party by some social groups, but may be the result of stronger party organization that establishes closer links with these groups than was possible earlier. A more efficient means of reaching such voters, an increase in the ability to offer them individual benefits, and so on may be the means by which a party's opponents gain the upper hand. Consequently, some aspects of (vi) correspond to (iii), in that both involve new differentials in the supply of resources for managing coalitions.

Aggregation Failure That Originates in Leadership

The other source of problems in aggregating interests successfully lies in leadership. The problems may be of three rather distinct kinds:

(vii) Following an electoral defeat caused by other factors, subsequent defeats may ensue because the original defeat has denuded the parties of a supply of "suitable" leaders. "Suitability" in this context refers to leaders who are likely to be attractive to those interests that may have defected in the first defeat, as well as to others. A party that has endured a major defeat may be left with party diehards who represent only one set of interests in the party's original coalition. Even if those leaders recognize the need to restore the original coalition, their efforts to do so may not be recognized as such by defectors who believe that they will not obtain the concessions they want from such leaders. The absence of a large pool of such leaders may make it difficult for a party to recover from defeat. Of course, that a party lost tells us nothing, in itself, about the "pool" of leaders; for example, the Democrats between the late 1960s and late 1980s lost frequently in presidential elections but on many occasions had a good supply of suitable potential candidates.

(viii) Even in parties that have not suffered a defeat for other reasons, the balance of power of different interests may have shifted, such that one group, or set of groups, in a party exercises disproportionate power over the selection of a party's leader, policies, and principles. An apparent omission of concern for some other interests may be the result of a misjudgement about the likelihood of their defection or of whether they are actually necessary for a winning coalition, or it may be the consequence of attempting to display power within the party (in ways that George Tsebelis has demonstrated in the case of the British Labour Party).[21]

(ix) Even if there are not problems of supply of the kind discussed under (vii), a third leadership factor affecting the selection of leaders and policies may emerge – changed rules for selection. Changing the rules changes the game, and some rules may make it more likely that a "balanced" leader or programme will not be selected. If, for whatever reason, selection rules change, a previously defeated party may find that its capacity for aggregating its supporting interests in the future has been hampered. Just as changed external political institutions can bring this about – (v) above – so can changed internal institutions.

One or more of the nine factors identified here may have contributed to the original electoral defeat, but even when they have not, it may be one or more of them that subsequently prevents the defeated party from

---

[21] George Tsebelis, *Nested Games: Rational Choice in Comparative Politics,* Berkeley, University of California Press, 1990, Chapter 5.

either rebuilding its original coalition or building a rather different winning coalition. Of course, it is not only defeated parties that may have problems of aggregation; indeed, those problems may be more severe in the party that won – Herbert Hoover's Republicans after 1928 and (in Britain) John Major's Conservatives after 1992 both illuminate that point. Nevertheless, particularly in a presidential system like that in the United States, where an administration cannot fall between elections and thus cannot be deprived during those four years of many of the resources for managing interest aggregation, it is often in parties that have suffered major electoral defeats that these problems are most apparent.[22]

This framework for understanding the coalition-building strategies open to defeated parties is employed in three chapters in this book (in Chapters 4, 6, and 8). Chapter 4 uses it to consider the causes of the Democrats' poor performance at many levels of electoral competition in the years between 1896 and 1910. Similarly, in Chapter 6 it is used to explain why the Democrats performed disastrously in presidential elections in the 1920s, while their performance in other elections indicated that the party had not become a permanent minority party in the two-party system. However, the framework can also be employed to explore problems in a party's long-term coalition building that have not been revealed previously in repeated electoral failure. It is used in this way in Chapter 8 with respect to both the Democratic and Republican strategies in the 1950s; this was a period in which the ability of both parties to construct viable coalitions came under stress. As in the case of parties experiencing serial defeats, it can help expose why the parties seemed to have encountered difficulties in constructing alliances that could endure.

4. Aggregating State Parties into a National Coalition

One of the peculiarities of the American system is that it is possible for the same party to have both a victorious and a losing coalition at the same time. A winning coalition may be constructed at the presidential level, but the party may fail to win a majority in Congress – or, indeed, may be losing control of a majority of state governorships and state legislatures at the same set of elections. In this sense, creating a "national majority" is not a single, unambiguous, aim for a party but a complex one. One context in which such complexity would be apparent in a system of separated

---

[22] Leaving aside the cases of impeachment, or of the death of both president and vice president.

powers is if there were two different kinds of issue dimensions of concern to voters; in expressing their views in voting, voters could display support for one position on one dimension in one set of elections and support for another on the second dimension in other elections. Indeed, this is the basis of the so-called Two Majorities explanation of divided government, with Democratic Congresses and Republican presidents, that was common in national politics between 1968 and 1992.[23]

Nevertheless, "Two Majorities" do not necessarily have to be formed around two different sets of policy issues, nor is divided government the only important manifestation of the effect of two such majorities. For example, there might be only one issue dimension of concern to voters, but they express their views on that mainly in voting for one kind of public office; in respect of other offices, factors such as sub-cultural group loyalties might be important in accounting for voting choices. To the extent that there is complete overlap between views held on issues and group loyalties, there will not be two majorities. However, to the extent that there is divergence, there is the possibility of two majorities – one majority (for one kind of office) reflecting majority opinion on that issue, and another majority (found in elections for another office) that consists of a coalition of different sub-cultures. The result might be divided government, or it might not – there might be an even balance between the sub-groups whose members engaged in ticket-splitting behaviour. In any case, though, even when there is undivided government in such circumstances, there could be different kinds of majorities in the executive and legislature. A legislature whose composition is the product of group members' voting for their "tribe" might leave individual legislators from the chief executive's party free to pursue a policy agenda different from his or hers, or it might leave them more exposed to the pressures of fellow legislators who oppose that agenda.

How parties are organized can also play an important role in the emergence, or not, of two majorities. When, as in the United States, parties have been highly decentralized, it is to be expected that organizational power will be a more potent factor at lower levels of office. To put the matter crudely, electorally attractive issue positions may be more effective at generating victory at the presidential level than, say, in House elections where there is more at stake for local party organizations. Thus, to the

---

[23] See, for example, Byron E. Shafer and William J. M. Claggett, *The Two Majorities: The Issue Context of Modern American Politics,* Baltimore and London, The Johns Hopkins University Press, 1995.

extent that an issue encounters opposition from within the party locally, it may weaken the chance that candidates who support the party's national position will either be nominated or elected; yet at the same time, and with much the same electorate, the presidential candidate may be able both to be nominated by the party and to win. The impact of decentralized party structures in the United States is reinforced by the Electoral College. State parties matter to a national party not just because of their contribution to the overall electoral coalition, but more importantly because it is states that have to be won in order for the presidency to be won.

Building a winning presidential coalition, therefore, is not just a matter of developing positions on issues that can command majority support; it is also about winning majorities within particular states. Consequently, the pursuit of a national majority can be conceived as having three elements. First, there is the construction of a series of beliefs, ideas, symbols, and values that can be used to attract a majority of voters nationally. Secondly, there is the attempt to fuse this framework of ideas with the interests and values of party elites and their voters in particular states. Thirdly, between elections there is the problem of managing relations between a national level of politics (essentially presidential-level politics) and local- and state-level politics (that may be manifested in Congress, as well as within the states themselves) – when that framework and those interests do not cohere. Important though it is, therefore, studying party ideologies take us only so far in understanding how national majorities are constructed and managed. Moreover, we already know quite a lot about those ideologies in America. Recent studies, particularly John Gerring's, have demonstrated not only that American national politics has always been infused by ideology but additionally how those ideologies changed over time.[24]

There would be little point in seeking to duplicate this kind of work. Rather, the present study seeks to complement it by examining the opportunities and constraints facing the national Democratic Party in winning *states* in the North. Given the presence of the solid South, and of a (frequently) loyal group of Border states, it was the Old North and the West that held the key to Democratic prospects. But, as just noted, it was states in the North that had to be won – states with their own organizations loosely connected to the centre – and it is on the question of how they could come to control a sufficient number of these units that this book focusses. To a large extent, of course, the opportunities and constraints

---

[24] Gerring, *Party Ideologies in America*.

can only be understood by examining the situation simultaneously facing the various Republican Parties; for that reason, there is necessarily considerable discussion here of the Republicans and their strategic position.

Looking at the building blocks, as distinct from how the "blocks" are put together into a coalition, requires an examination of sub-national politics, as well as the politics evident in presidential contests. For that reason, evidence from gubernatorial, congressional, and state legislature elections is cited throughout this book. Consequently, it is worth examining, at this stage, a possible objection to that approach. Might not sub-national candidates in states that are unfavourable territory for their party simply be "copying" their opponents just to win an election? "Copycat" victors of this kind would tell us nothing about the potential for national coalition building because, in a real sense, particular blocks were not ones that could actually be used in that process. The main problem with this objection is that it presupposes that a copycat could position himself or herself in relation to the other party without consideration of his or her own party's activists or financial backers. Independently wealthy candidates can sometimes do so today, but in the era discussed here, there were few who sought nomination *outside a party framework*. In other words, would-be candidates were usually constrained by other elements of their party.

If, then, the objection were to be modified in light of this, so that it becomes a claim that local or state parties in some areas might themselves have traditions or values that run counter to those of the party nationally, the riposte is quite easy: That is precisely what a distinction between "building blocks" and "aggregation" is intended to illuminate. Especially when the balance between different elements in a party changes nationally, some state parties may then become more difficult to embrace in a national coalition because some of their views are out of line with a larger faction. Examining, for instance, how successful a party is in winning governorships can help inform us about the available building blocks; by itself it cannot tell us whether particular blocks can actually be put together. Of course, understanding the former is as important as understanding the latter when examining the constraints facing a party.

This reference to governorships is not accidental. Perhaps the single best way of analyzing the underlying position of the Democrats in the North is to examine their success in winning state governorships. By comparison with presidential elections, and for an era when parties and party organizations still mattered, these elections have two advantages. They were usually held more frequently than presidential elections, and they demonstrate how a party might perform absent the particular issues and personalities present in a presidential campaign. U.S. Senate nominations are not a possible alternative for any study that begins before the introduction of direct elections to the chamber in 1914. Moreover, for two reasons, gubernatorial elections also provide a better guide to party strength than elections to the House – arguments that are relevant also in the case of state legislatures. First, electoral boundaries cannot be manipulated to advantage one party in the way that single-member constituencies can be so manipulated. Secondly, there is no "seniority" advantage accruing to incumbents that can result in an overestimation of underlying party strength in a given legislative district.

What pattern or trend might we expect to find in the success rate of Democrats in the North over this 90-year period? As we have seen, the conventional wisdom, derived from realignment theory, holds that the Democrats were reasonably competitive in much, though certainly not all, of the North until the mid-1890s, then became uncompetitive there until the 1930s, when, once more, the party became competitive in the North.[25] On the basis of this interpretation, therefore, we might expect to find a relatively high level of success in the holding of governorships in the years after 1876 – perhaps, on average, between 35 per cent and 40 per cent of governorships would have been in Democratic hands. This would have been followed by a long period with a much lower rate of success – from the 1890s until the 1930s – perhaps they usually held around 20 per cent of governorships. Then, after 1932, we would expect to find much greater success – with the Democrats typically holding, say, 50 per cent, or more, of governorships from the mid-1930s onwards.

The success rate of Democrats in holding governorships is shown in Table 2.1, and it should be clear immediately that the pattern of results bears little relation to the conventional wisdom about the changing nature of Democratic party competitiveness over the 86-year period.

The point becomes clearer still if we exclude consideration of two exceptional eras. The first comprises the years between the elections of 1890 and 1910. During that time, the Democrats initially performed far better in elections than they had earlier (1890–2), and then suddenly their success rate in winning public offices plummeted. It was not until 1910 that the status quo ante was restored. The second exceptional era was

---

[25] One example of this sort of account is Malcolm E. Jewell and Sarah M. Morehouse, *Political Parties and Elections in American States*, Fourth Edition, Washington, DC, Congressional Quarterly Press, 2001, pp. 23–4.

TABLE 2.1. *Proportion of Northern State Governorships Held by Democratic Party in the February of Years Following Presidential Elections or Mid-term Elections, 1877–1973 (as Percentage of Total Northern Governorships)*

1877	27	1903	17	1929	16	1955	39
1879	27	1905	14	1931	39	1957	45
1881	14	1907	24	1933	71	1959	63
1883	45	1909	31	1935	74	1961	55
1885	36	1911	45	1937	71	1963	58
1887	27	1913	61	1939	42	1965	52
1889	18	1915	48	1941	42	1967	36
1891	46	1917	32	1943	29	1969	27
1893	43	1919	19	1945	32	1971	52
1895	21	1921	6	1947	26	1973	58
1897	24	1923	42	1949	42		
1899	21	1925	32	1951	23		
1901	17	1927	26	1953	10		

TABLE 2.2. *Median and Mean Proportions of Northern State Governorships Held by Democratic Party in the February of Years Following Presidential Elections or Mid-term Elections for Selected Periods, 1877–1973 (as Percentage of Total Number of Northern Governorships in Each Year)*

	Median	Mean
1877–89	27	27
1911–31	32	33
1939–57	36	33
(1939–53)	(28)	(31)
1959–73	54	50

that of the New Deal – that is, the elections of 1932–6 – when Democratic successes were far greater than they had been before or since. These two eras are excluded from Table 2.2, which shows the proportion of northern governorships the Democrats typically held in four periods – 1877–89, 1911–31, 1939–57, and 1959–73. Contrary to the popular view, the kind of competitiveness associated with the party system in the late 19th century did not yield the Democrats many governorships; both the median and mean for their share of northern governorships is a mere 27 per cent of the total. Moreover, the data for 1911–31 show that far from having

TABLE 2.3. *Median Share of Northern State Governorships Held by Democratic Party in the February of Years Following Presidential Elections or Mid-term Elections for Selected Periods, 1877–1973, and by Type of Election (as Percentage of Total Number of Northern Governorships in Each Year)*

	After Democratic Candidate Wins Presidency	After Mid-term Elections During a Republican Presidency	After Republican Candidate Wins Presidency	After Mid-term Elections During a Democratic Presidency	Mean for All Four Types of Election
1877–89	36	36	18	27	29
1911–31	47	41	16	34	35
1939–57	42	39	28	28	34
1959–73	54	58	43	47	51

declined even further after the early 1890s, both the median and the mean were actually higher in this second period. The conventional wisdom is also unreliable in relation to the immediate post–New Deal era: There was no large increase in the Democrats' share of northern governorships. Although the median is slightly higher for 1939–57 than for 1911–31, the mean is not. In any case, the increase in the median is the result of a much better performance by the Democrats in the two elections at the end of the period, 1954 and 1956. If they were to be excluded, the Democrats can be seen to have done slightly worse post–New Deal than they did between 1911 and 1931. It was only after the mid-1950s, and especially with the 1958 landslide, that the Democrats made much of an advance over their performance (in the North) in the late 1870s and 1880s. To put the matter crudely, it appears that the Democrats had no larger a base in the North from which to construct a winning coalition in the 1940s than they had had 30 or 60 years earlier.

It might be questioned whether this pattern of stability in the extent of Democratic penetration of northern states is a mere artefact of the *kinds* of elections that the party happened to face in different periods. It is to be expected that it would have greater success in years when it won the presidency and in the mid-term year following a Republican presidential victory than it would in a year when a Republican was elected to the White House or two years after a Democratic presidential success. Table 2.3 shows the different success rates of the party in these four types of election

TABLE 2.4. *Northern State Governorships Weighted by Number of Electoral College Votes Attached to Each State: Proportion of Total Held by Democratic Party in the February of Years Following Presidential Elections or Mid-term Elections, 1877–1973*

1877	27	1903	6	1929	18	1955	51
1879	39	1905	7	1931	38	1957	55
1881	8	1907	17	1933	72	1959	66
1883	53	1909	25	1935	73	1961	63
1885	52	1911	46	1937	77	1963	54
1887	30	1913	69	1939	47	1965	45
1889	23	1915	35	1941	43	1967	29
1891	63	1917	19	1943	16	1969	16
1893	62	1919	24	1945	21	1971	37
1895	24	1921	5	1947	10	1973	43
1897	13	1923	37	1949	39		
1899	11	1925	30	1951	31		
1901	8	1927	29	1953	14		

for each of the four periods. If we assume that each period had one election of each type, would the pattern of Democratic success be any different? The evidence of Table 2.3 suggests that the answer to that question must be no. Here, too, it is clear that the Democrats did somewhat better in 1911–31 than in 1877–89, did not improve their situation in the post–New Deal years of 1939–57, but were much more successful in controlling northern governorships in the era that began more than 20 years after the New Deal.

Of course, as the foundation stones of a national majority coalition, winning the governorships of small states would be much less useful to the Democrats than winning large states. If we weight states according to their Electoral College vote, does the pattern of change in Democratic success more closely resemble the conventional view of the party's fortunes over the 86-year period? Table 2.4 shows the share of northern governorships held by the party for each two-year period (four months after a presidential or mid-term election), while Table 2.5 aggregates the data into the four periods used in Table 2.2.

The first point to note is that Table 2.4 exposes the problem of aggregating data over time when exceptional periods, during which the political system was behaving very differently, are included. For example, including the three New Deal elections of 1932, 1934, and 1936 with the elections of

TABLE 2.5. *Northern State Governorships Weighted by Number of Electoral College Votes Attached to Each State: Share of Total Votes Held by Democratic Party in the February of Years Following Presidential Elections or Mid-term Elections for Selected Periods, 1877–1973 (as Percentage)*

	Median	Mean
1877–89	30	33
1911–31	30	32
1939–57	35	33
(1939–53)	(26)	(28)
1959–73	45	45

the years 1938–56 (inclusive) increases the median share of the "weighted" governorships held by the Democrats from 35 per cent to 51 per cent of the total. The restored Republican advantage in much of the North, after the initial shock of the New Deal, is thereby concealed. A similar distorting effect, to that generated by including 1932–6, is created for the earlier period by including the years 1890–1910 in an analysis that comprises the pre-1890 years or the years from 1911 onwards. After 1889, a previously finely balanced party system started to provide much more pronounced biases towards first one party and then the other. By 1910, a more balanced party system was evident again – one in which there were clear similarities with the pre-1890 system. However, if, following the orthodox approach, the years 1877–1931 are divided into two periods, rather than three, with the 1894 election as the turning point, it is possible to show that the Democrats' share of the weighted governorships fell from 39 per cent of the total to 24 per cent. Yet the two categories, 1877–93 and 1894–1931, are essentially empty ones – in that each includes eras that are dissimilar. Competition between the parties in 1890 and 1892 was rather different than it had been at any time since the end of Reconstruction. Similarly the elections from 1894 to 1908 (inclusive) featured a still different kind of competition than was to be evident later between 1909 and 1931. What unites the years 1890–1910 is that throughout the two decades, one party or the other struggled to retain core elements of its potential electoral base. That is why the data presented in Table 2.5 provide a more complete picture of long-term change than would a table presenting the standard account, with 1894 as a hinge between two supposed eras.

The pattern seen in Table 2.5 is slightly different from that evident when just the number of governorships that the Democratic party typically held is considered, but once again it does not come close to confirming the conventional wisdom. The performance in 1911–31 is virtually identical to that of 1877–89, further disconfirming the idea of a "system of 1896" in which the Democrats were largely excluded from office in the North for nearly 40 years; it was actually only in the years from 1893 to 1909 that they struggled to win office statewide. However, their median share of weighted governorships post–New Deal does suggest an improved position compared with the two earlier periods. Nevertheless, not only is the mean similar to that in the earlier periods, but if the elections of 1954 and 1956 are again excluded, the Democratic Party also seems to be doing worse after the New Deal than it was earlier. Once more, it is only from the middle to late 1950s onwards that the party's underlying strength in the North appears greater. Until then, the size of the party's building blocks in the North seems to have been remarkably stable over eight decades when the distorting effects of the two exceptional periods are taken into account.

5. What Was the North?

But what was the American North? It was never just a geographical entity. From the beginning of the Republic, most of the inhabitants of states north of the Mason-Dixon line had a shared set of views – a belief in the virtues of a free-labour economy. Unlike the southern states, there had been no potential for the development of a slave economy in the North, and not surprisingly in a society with a shortage of labour, free labour was a powerful idea. As is well known, later on the Civil War helped to create an American identity – the states as a source of personal identity subsequently declined relative to that of national identity. However, it was a national identity that was very much formed in the image of the victors – the northerners. In the 30 or so years after 1865, the bonds of having fought together provided a further source of shared identity for the inhabitants of the northern states. Consequently, at the beginning of the period under discussion, there is no question that "the North" was something more than just a collection of states that shared merely the fact that they were geographically not in the South.

Nevertheless, at the beginning of the era under consideration in this book, America did not consist simply of a North and a South. The regional composition of the country was more complicated than this – for two reasons. For all the traditions and beliefs that united it, the North consisted of two parts that have been mentioned already – an Old North and the West. The former states had been settled earlier, often had more diverse economies, and had longer established traditions of political competition. For the purposes of this book, statehood attained by 1840 is taken as the dividing line between the "two Norths". The West would continue to expand as new states were included in the Union, and the impact of this region's different history would make the distinction between the Old North and the West significant for much of the period covered by the book. The other factor complicating a regional analysis of the United States was the Border states. These were states in which slavery had been legal before 1860, but which, for a variety of reasons, had not formally taken up arms on the side of the Confederacy in 1861. There is no doubt that the Border states constituted a distinct political region at the end of the Civil War, but over the next century, they were to become a political equivalent of the Cheshire Cat. In their case, the "cat" that disappeared was a distinctive socio-economic basis to politics, while the pattern of support given to the two parties remained distinctive. As will be seen later, the Border states were to behave rather differently than both their northern and southern neighbours.

After the first decade or so of the 20th century, there is a further distinction within non-southern states that becomes important, especially because of its impact on the Republican Party. This is the distinction between coastal and interior states. With the emergence of a difference of both interests and opinion over the role the United States should play in international affairs, a clear cleavage would become evident between an essentially inward-looking interior and those states that bordered the Atlantic and Pacific Oceans, where internationalist causes had far more proponents.

Perhaps the most important point about regions in America is that increasingly after 1865, the North became much more diversified; new states were created in the West, while in the East, the growth of large, industrial cities created tensions both within particular states and between different kinds of states. Those changes were to complicate the strategies for national coalition building that form the subject of this book. However, for the Democratic Party, the North did not become a mere residual category, the "non-South". One of the distinctive aspects of the region is that the party nearly always faced strong opposition from the Republicans; in some states, this was opposition that the Democrats could overcome only occasionally, and throughout the region, there were few easy victories to be had by them at the state level of politics.[26] As the parties became more institutionalized in the late 19th century, the Republicans were able to convert their earlier, immediate post–Civil War, electoral advantage into a more long-term core of electoral support. Consequently, even though Civil War symbols of "northernness" declined in importance, with the passing of that generation, the Democrats' task became no easier. Their principal opponent had consolidated its organizational strength in nearly all the northern states, thereby sustaining a permanent opposition to the Democrats in the 20th century – an opposition with persisting links to many sectors of the northern electorate.

The absence of many Democratic-leaning states in the North in the years 1877–1962 can be illustrated in the following rather crude yet revealing way. Of the 21 presidential elections between 1877 and 1962, the Democrats won 10 (48 per cent of the total). In only one northern state was the success rate greater than it was at the national level – Nevada (where the Democrats carried the state on 62 per cent of all occasions).[27] Only in Idaho, Montana, and New Jersey did the Democrats have the same success rate in carrying the state as they did in winning presidential elections. Nor were these 4 states of great significance in presidential elections – typically they could yield only about 5 per cent of all Electoral College votes. In the remaining 27 states, the Democrats' success rate was lower than in the nation as a whole. This lack of a northern "core" is apparent throughout the eight and a half decades; even after 1932, the Democrats did not develop a really solid electoral core in the North. The party won 6 of the 8 presidential elections between 1932 and 1962, but no northern state was carried on more than six occasions – and only 6 states were won as many as six times in that era (Illinois, Massachusetts, Montana, Nevada, New Mexico, and Rhode Island). Moreover, even if the party won all these 6 states plus the entire South and the Border states,

[26] This was less true of two of the newest states, Oklahoma and Arizona, which leaned Democratic for the first few years after being granted statehood. The migration of southerners to these southwestern states provides one of the main explanations for regular Democratic successes there.

[27] In states, such as Arizona, that were granted statehood after 1880, the success rate at the state level is compared with the Democrats' success at the national level *for the period following statehood only*. If Oklahoma is counted as a northern state, rather than as a Border state, it, too, provided Democrats with more victories at the state level than the party achieved nationally. It carried Oklahoma on 9 of 14 occasions after 1907, compared with their 8 victories in presidential elections after that year.

it would still have been more than about 25 votes short of victory in the Electoral College. Nor is it surprising that the Democrats were unable to construct centres of Democratic loyalty at the state level in the North. Although voter-party links weakened after the end of the 19th century, the decades up to the 1960s were still ones in which parties were an important intermediary between voters and candidates. The institution-alization of the parties in the late 19th century had helped to perpetuate Republican electoral strength, so that throughout the period of this study, the Democrats would always lack a northern electoral base on which the party could rely – with the possible, and unimportant, exception of Nevada.

The contrast with the Border states – let alone the South – is instruc-tive in this regard, even though, as is shown later, it was growing com-petitiveness in the Border states from the 1880s that contributed to the Democratic Party's problems. The party did at least as well in all the Border states as it did nationally between 1880 and 1960, and in 5 of the 6 states, a state was carried more often than were presidential elec-tions won nationally. Furthermore, from the early 1930s, the Border states remained more consistently Democratic than the northern states. In 4 of the 6 states (Kentucky, Maryland, Missouri, and West Virginia), the Democrats were victorious on at least 6 of the 8 occasions between 1932 and 1962 – compared with only 6 out of 31 northern states that repli-cated this result. Furthermore, despite increased party competition in the Border states after 1880, they tended to remain more pro-Democratic than did most of the North. That is a measure of how much the north-ern states presented a special kind of problem to the Democrats: They were opposed there by a long-established, well-organized, and well-supported party in virtually all the states. The problem for the Democrats was to be sufficiently competitive in enough of these northern states that the party could win both presidential elections and majorities in Congress.

Achieving that objective meant that the party had to hold together its strongholds in the South and the Border states, whilst at the same time building on local support in particular northern states and devising an ideology and an image for the party that could unite its disparate ele-ments. While challenging, this task was far from impossible. Towards the very beginning of the era under examination, divisions between west-ern primary-producing interests and commercial interests in the Old North were already becoming apparent. The organizational strength of the Republicans would not necessarily withstand the strains in its coalition that this generated, and that presented Democrats with their own opportunities. How well they could exploit these kinds of opportunities, and how much their own electoral bases might come under threat, is the subject of the ensuing chapters.

3

The Unstable Party Equilibrium, 1877–1896

One important respect in which the task facing the Democrats after 1877 was similar to the one that had faced them in the 1840s was that the winning of majorities at the national level was primarily achieved by the mobilization of their own loyal voters. Both parties had large numbers of devoted supporters, while the number of potential voters who had no underlying party loyalty was relatively small. In a sense, therefore, both parties had viable electoral coalitions in place – what they had to do was try to prevent those coalitions from fragmenting. In part, this emphasis on "keeping their own troops together" was facilitated by the fact that the party coalitions were of similar sizes nationally – a point that is analyzed further during the course of this chapter.

Continuity between pre-war and post-war politics is also clear from an examination of the sources of the two major parties' support. It was not the Civil War itself that had modified the patterns of voter support but the earlier partisan division over the extension of slavery into the territories. When the Republican Party contested its first presidential election in 1856, the "shape" of the Democratic coalition that would have to be mobilized in the late 1870s was already revealed. The war and other factors subsequently changed it a little, but what is surprising about voter support in 1856 is just how much it corresponds with the pattern of support later.

Table 3.1 provides a rank ordering of the states in terms of the strength of voter support for the Democratic Party in the 1856 presidential election. (South Carolina is omitted because of the absence of data.) This was done by subtracting the combined vote share for the Republican and Whig-American Party candidates from the vote share of the Democratic

TABLE 3.1. *Rank Ordering of States by Plurality of the Vote Obtained by the Democratic Party over Other Parties in 1856*

1st Arkansas	11th Kentucky	21st Illinois
2nd Texas	12th Tennessee	22nd Wisconsin
3rd Alabama	13th Louisiana	23rd Connecticut
4th Virginia	14th California	24th Michigan
5th Mississippi	15th Indiana	25th Iowa
6th Georgia	16th Pennsylvania	26th Maine
7th Florida	17th New Jersey	27th Rhode Island
8th North Carolina	18th New Hampshire	28th New York
9th Delaware	19th Maryland	29th Massachusetts
10th Missouri	20th Ohio	30th Vermont

TABLE 3.2. *Rank Ordering of States by Median Plurality of the Vote Obtained by the Democratic Party over Other Parties, 1880–1892*

(South Carolina)	10th Tennessee	19th California	(Colorado)
1st Texas	11th Delaware	20th Ohio	(Nevada)
2nd Mississippi	12th Missouri	21st Illinois	28th Maine
3rd Louisiana	13th Maryland	22nd New Hampshire	29th Rhode Island
4th Georgia	14th North Carolina	23rd Wisconsin	(Minnesota)
5th Alabama	(West Virginia)	24th Iowa	(Nebraska)
6th Virginia	15th New Jersey	(Oregon)	(Kansas)
7th Arkansas	16th New York	25th Pennsylvania	30th Vermont
8th Florida	17th Connecticut	26th Michigan	
9th Kentucky	18th Indiana	27th Massachusetts	

candidate in each state. Table 3.2 provides a rank order derived in the same way for the years 1880–92; in this case, the median vote share of the four elections was calculated, and both South Carolina and new states are included in their place on the ranking, but so as to permit easy comparison, they are not denominated ordinally. It becomes evident that with only a few exceptions, the rank orderings in the two tables are similar: The states that leaned to the Democrats in 1856 generally did so 30 years later, just as the states where they were weak electorally were the same ones. Only three states moved more than six places in the rankings. Of these changes, one – Louisiana (13th to 3rd) – is not significant: It had been more Democratic in 1856 than the country as a whole, and relatively, it became far more Democratic after the Civil War.

The other large movements within these rankings were significant, though. Pennsylvania was the most Democratic of the non-slave states in

1856, but by the end of the Civil War it had become a solidly Republican state. This may seem scarcely surprising since unlike most northern states, it had been invaded during the course of the war and was the site of its most decisive battle, Gettysburg. After 1865, Pennsylvania voters tended to support the party identified with the Union cause. However, even in the case of Pennsylvania, the role of the war itself in harming the Democratic cause may be doubted. James Huston has argued that it was the Panic of 1857 that was crucial in transforming it into a Republican state, first in the 1858 mid-term elections and then in the 1860 election.[1] (Whatever the cause, Democratic strength relative to that of the Republicans in Pennsylvania was to be lower than that of the party nationally in all presidential elections between 1872 and 1952.)

Conversely, New York, which was the third least Democratic state in 1856, became one of the most fiercely contested states in the Gilded Age – as its ranking as the 16th most Democratic state (of the 30 states in 1856) in Table 3.2 illustrates. New York's changed position in terms of party competitiveness was the result of massive immigration into New York City, with the Democrats better placed than Republicans there to incorporate the newcomers into their party. This migration had begun in the mid-1840s, in the wake of the Irish famine, and within two decades had changed the political balance in the state.

With these two exceptions, the electoral coalitions available to the Democrats (and their opponents) from among the various states were remarkably similar in the Gilded Age to those available in 1856; this is noteworthy because it might have been expected that a devastating Civil War would have disrupted party politics far more than it did. That is one reason why Silbey is correct in emphasizing continuity between the two periods.[2] This continuity is illustrated also in Table 3.3, which uses three categories of states, distinguished by the size of the Democratic plurality. Heartland states were ones where the median plurality for the Democrats over the Republicans in the 1880–92 presidential elections was at least 5 per cent of the total vote; for 1856, they are states where the Democratic plurality over the Republicans and Whig-Americans combined was at least 5 per cent of the total vote. Contested Territory is those states where neither the Democrats nor the Republicans (plus Whig-Americans in 1856) had a plurality of more than 5 per cent, while Foreign Parts

---

[1] "...the economic issue of protectionism was absolutely essential in transforming Pennsylvania from a Democratic to a Republican state". James L. Huston, *The Panic of 1857 and the Coming of the Civil War*, Baton Rouge and London, Louisiana State University Press, 1987, p. 267.

[2] Joel H. Silbey, *The American Political Nation, 1838–1893*.

TABLE 3.3. *Classification of States by Size of Democratic Plurality for Both 1856 and 1880–1892*

	Heartland 1880–1892 (14 + 1)	Contested Territory 1880–1892 (8 + 1)	Foreign Parts 1880–1892 (8 + 6)
Heartland 1856 (13)	Alabama Arkansas Delaware Florida Georgia Kentucky Louisiana Mississippi Missouri North Carolina Tennessee Texas Virginia		
Contested Territory 1856 (4)		California Indiana New Jersey	Pennsylvania
Foreign Parts 1856 (13)	Maryland	Connecticut Illinois New Hampshire New York Ohio	Iowa Maine Massachusetts Michigan Rhode Island Vermont Wisconsin
States not included in data for 1856 (8)	South Carolina	West Virginia	Colorado Kansas Minnesota Nebraska Nevada Oregon

Heartland is defined as a Median Plurality for the Democrats of more than 5 per cent of total vote over the Republicans (in 1880–1892) and over Republicans and Whig-Americans combined in 1856; Contested Territory is defined as a plurality of less than 5 per cent for the Democrats, but no more than 5 per cent for the Republicans (plus Whig-Americans in 1856); Foreign Parts is defined as a plurality of more than 5 per cent for the Republicans (Republicans plus Whig-Americans in 1856).

are states where the Republican (plus the Whig-American vote in 1856) plurality was more than 5 per cent of the total vote.

Table 3.3 reveals that apart from New York and Pennsylvania, only 5 of the remaining 28 states are in different categories for the two periods.

Maryland had gone solidly for the Whig-American Millard Fillmore in 1856, but after the Civil War followed the other Border states in having a pronounced lean toward the Democrats. In addition to New York, four other states (Connecticut, Illinois, New Hampshire, and Ohio) were (relatively) more closely contested in 1880–92 than earlier. In fact, as will be discussed shortly, neither Connecticut nor Illinois was quite as competitive overall as this might suggest, and the same is also true of New Hampshire. But that discussion is reserved for later. The main point to be noted here is just how much of a link there was between late 19ᵗʰ century patterns of support for the parties and those evident in the mid-1850s. If, as proponents of realignment theory argue, there was a third party system, this provides evidence that Paul Kleppner is correct in arguing that it would have started about 1853 (and lasted until about 1892).[3] Even if we reject the successive-party-systems typology, it is clear that there is something quite distinctive about party coalitions in this era.

The argument developed in this chapter is that there were a number of peculiarities in the Gilded Age party system – a party system that seemed to be so evenly balanced at the national level. First, in most of the states, the parties were actually in imbalance, so that national competitiveness depended on a truly competitive form of politics in only a handful of states. Secondly, the different socio-economic interests of the West, and the potential for political mobilization around those interests, posed an increasing threat to this national balance. Thirdly, in the later 19ᵗʰ century, there were other dynamic factors in the polity that threatened the underpinnings of the balanced party system. Finally, in the early 1890s, a series of events made some of the political alliances from which the parties had been constructed increasingly unstable; the result was change in the party system, though not, as will be shown in Section 4, the kind of transformation that is sometimes assumed to have occurred. These points are examined further in the rest of the present chapter.

1. Party Coalitions from the 1850s to the 1890s

Understanding the nature of 19ᵗʰ century American politics is difficult because it involved the fusion of two very different ways of organizing. On the one hand, as was discussed in Chapter 2, party politics was partly "tribal": A person joined a particular party because of his loyalties to

---

[3] Paul Kleppner, *The Third Electoral System, 1853–1892: Parties, Voters and Political Cultures*, Chapel Hill, University of North Carolina Press, 1979.

a particular sub-culture in that society. David Thelen provides a good account of this for the Border state of Missouri, although what he says was broadly true of the northern states:

> Parties became the political arm of ethnic, religious and sectional cultures. Each new group from Europe joined the party opposite to the one that had attracted its most bitter enemy from their homeland. Irish Catholics became Democrats when they spotted their ancient enemies, English Protestants, in the Republican party and its forerunners.... German immigrants subordinated their religious differences to their desire to protect things German, particularly their language, and this led them to become the most important voting base for the Republican party in urban and rural Missouri alike.... Republican Henry Zigenhein won the mayor's office in St. Louis in the 1897 with the boast that he knew German better than English.... In the decades after the Civil War other Missourians voted for the political arm of the army in which their fathers had fought. Blacks repaid the Republicans with their votes for the next half-century.[4]

Reinforcing these tribal loyalties was a spoils system that had emerged rapidly in Andrew Jackson's presidency, but which had its origins in the personalized system of public appointment that the United States inherited from the British colonialists.[5] Party patronage helped to tie the elites and some voters to their party, thereby reinforcing the tribal basis of politics.

Tribalism was not quite as simple as Thelen's description makes it sound, however. Local circumstances could have a huge impact on how people identified themselves. For example, the German solidarity evident in Missouri was by no means common elsewhere. Often German Catholics tended to identify with the Democrats, as the party more likely to protect Catholicism from its Protestant enemies, while German Protestants headed towards the Whigs and, later, the Republicans. Italians often became Democrats for the same reason as did German Catholics, but in some cities, and most notably Philadelphia, many Italians became Republicans. Even the issue of the side on which a person, or his father, had fought in the Civil War did not produce a wholly clear pattern. Certainly, there were very few ex-Confederate veterans who were even closet Republicans, but the northern Democracy fared much better as a cross-sectional party. In 1876, the party received nearly 48 per cent of the total presidential vote in states outside the South and the Border states. Not all ex-Union soldiers and their families could have been staunch Republicans,

---

[4] David Thelen, *Paths of Resistance: Tradition and Disunity in Industrializing Missouri*, New York, Oxford University Press, 1986, p. 23.
[5] On how the systems of patronage diverged in the two countries, see S. E. Finer, "Patronage and the Public Service", *Public Administration*, 30 (1952), 329–60.

therefore. The overall result was that viewed from the national level, this pattern of group solidarities did not so much seem to divide the electorate into neat categories as to produce a mosaic of electoral support that could appear to be incoherent at first glance.

On the other hand, the major parties were by no means just conduits through which group solidarity could be expressed and the rewards of office distributed. They represented different interests, as well as different tribes, and aggregating those interests meant espousing ideas and images around which the various interests could cohere. Thus, as they had been before the 1850s, each of the parties was united by ideas and values that both gave a coherence to the myriad individuals they bound together, and helped to distinguish that party from its opponents. The Whigs and Republicans believed in social harmony, in the ultimate unity of the different economic interests in society, in the need for order to maintain that unity, and in a positive role for the state; within limits, the state could be used to promote national economic development and a distinct cultural order. In Gerring's words, "Despite the party's constant appeal to material interests, [Republican] party leaders could be found just as often touting the significance of morality, spirituality, and (nonmaterial) devotion to country".[6] If it was in some sense conservative, theirs was a nationalism very different in content from, say, the conservatism that Margaret Thatcher was to espouse in Britain a century later. Thatcher did not believe in society, which was for her a mere aggregation of individuals, whereas for 19th century Republicans, the older idea of a unified social order in which there were shared moral ideals was important.

The Democrats were united by a belief in the desirability of limited government, a value that had its origins in Thomas Jefferson's political ideas. This appealed as much to white southerners, who after 1876 wanted to be freed forever from the constraints placed on them during the Reconstruction era, as to Catholic immigrants, who feared the intrusion of a Protestant political order on their ways of life. But just as the Republican political world was far removed from the libertarian ideals of the later 20th century New Right, so, too, was the Democrats'. Theirs was not an ideology to attract industrial and commercial interests who favoured strict laissez-faire economics above all else. Certainly Democrats tended to oppose tariffs (which Republicans usually supported), but it was to an America of farmers, and not an America of manufacturers and traders, that they looked. In their own eyes, they were unlike the Republicans in

---

[6] Gerring, *Party Ideologies in America*, p. 108.

that they did not seek to impose a moral order on the individuals who made up the United States. But, equally, they did not want the United States transformed into something that it had not been at its founding. It should remain a nation in which agriculture predominated and in which political power would continue to rest ultimately with the people. The people were the final check on the power that government might use against sections of them, and they mistrusted the role for government that Republicans advocated.

While there was a significant ideological element to 19th century politics, there were two respects in which the conduct of politics was different from that evident in many parliamentary democracies in the 20th century. First, the complexity of the electoral coalitions that each of the parties had constructed precluded the specific application of their ideologies to more than a few policy areas. As Gretchen Ritter has observed: "Party leaders avoided taking clear stances on issues likely to divide the party membership. It was left to third parties and social movements to put forth clear programmatic alternatives."[7] This was especially important in relation to the key policy area Ritter herself examined, namely finance. Tariff policy was an exceptional issue therefore – the parties consistently did take up the issue in elections as a way of demarcating themselves from their opponents.

Secondly, even with a policy like tariffs, it was likely that local economic interests might dictate that the parties locally not follow the general line taken by the parties nationally, but instead mark out their own position. This affected party behaviour in Congress, where the predominance of local interests had always produced difficulties for those who sought to unite their entire party behind a given policy. Consequently, both at the level of party platforms in elections and over their behaviour in legislation and administration, neither party was programmatic. The decentralization of the political system meant that a key respect in which parliamentary-based parties were usually to behave several decades later was not present in the United States.

As with the three Democratic-Whig contests in the 1840s, the later competition between Democrats and Republicans was intense, and presidential elections generated close results. Or rather, they did so from 1876 onwards. In 1856 the Republican Party was still in the process of replacing the Whigs, in 1860 four parties contested an election that was fought on

---

[7] Gretchen Ritter, *Goldbugs and Greenbacks: The Antimonopoly Tradition and the Politics of Finance in America*, Cambridge, Cambridge University Press, 1997, p. 28.

sectional lines, and in the next three elections significant portions of the
eligible electorate could not participate. The election of 1876 was the first
contest since 1860 in which both major parties could hope to mobilize
all of their potential voters. That year the Democratic party's plurality in
the popular vote was 3 per cent, in 1880 the two parties had a nearly
identical share of the vote, in 1884 the Democrats enjoyed a 0.3 per cent
plurality, in 1888 they had a 0.8 per cent plurality, and in 1892 it was a
3.1 per cent plurality. In spite of usually having a narrow advantage over
the Republicans in the popular vote, the Democrats actually lost three of
these five elections in the Electoral College (1876, 1880, and 1888).

Nor was it just the Electoral College that tended to prevent wafer-thin
pluralities from being translated consistently into institutional majorities.
Control of Congress might go to the party that polled fewer votes overall, and several factors could be responsible for this. First, the localism
of much political activity meant that problems for a party in a particular
locality could result in losses that helped prevent the party from taking
control of the House, even while the presidential candidate was securing a popular plurality. Secondly, the apportionment of districts was a
politicized activity, and popular pluralities might fail to be translated into
control of a state's congressional delegation because of boundary-drawing
decisions made by the then-majority party a few years earlier. Thirdly, not
only was it the case that a mere one-third of Senate seats were up for nomination every two years, but it was still state legislatures who nominated
senators; divided control of state legislatures, for example, as well as too
few seats being available to be won, could lead to control of the Senate
remaining with the party that had failed to win a plurality of votes in the
presidential contest.

The five elections from 1876 show how these various institutional factors complicated the pursuit of a national majority in a party system where
support was so evenly divided. In 1876, the Democrats won a plurality
of votes in the presidential election (but lost in the Electoral College),
retained control of the House, but failed to gain control of the Senate (in
spite of making a gain of seven seats). In 1880, the Democrats lost an
exceptionally narrow plurality in the presidential election and lost more
heavily in the Electoral College; they lost control of the House and also
lost their recently acquired control of the Senate. In 1884, the Democrats
won both the popular presidential vote and the Electoral College; they
also retained control of the House but failed to take the Senate. In 1888,
they reverted to the earlier pattern of winning the popular vote but losing
in the Electoral College (despite the fact that their popular vote plurality

was larger than in 1884); they lost control of the House whilst the Republicans retained their hold on the Senate. Finally, in 1892, with their largest plurality in the popular vote since 1856, the Democrats won in the Electoral College, retained control of the House, and took control of the Senate.

When there was a strong national trend to one party, as in 1892, local variations in support for the parties mattered much less. However, in the close contests that were typical of the era, party control of the national polity could well depend on oddly divergent successes at the local level. Consider the cases of Illinois and Indiana in 1884 and 1888. Consistent with the national trend, Democrat Grover Cleveland lost the popular vote in Illinois slightly more narrowly in 1888 than he had in 1884; at the same time, though, the Democrats were doing worse in House elections than they had in 1884. (Both the major parties won 10 seats in 1884, while in 1888 the Democrats won only 7 to the Republicans' 13.) In Indiana, Cleveland's plurality over the Republicans in 1884 was overturned in 1888 – thus running counter to the slight national trend to Cleveland that year. However, at the same time, the Indiana Democratic Party won more congressional seats than it had in 1884 – it also made a net gain of 4 seats compared with 1886 – and it now controlled the state's delegation 10 to 3. Here we see that not only could party support in particular states move in opposite directions to that evident nationally, but the pattern of results might be different, depending on the level of office. In a polity of weak parties, this would not be surprising, but this was a polity of strong party attachments – although those attachments were mediated by local institutions, perhaps producing patterns of results that, initially, might seem to be inconsistent with strong partisanship in the electorate.

This returns us to the point made at the beginning of the chapter – the relevance of strong partisanship in middle to late 19th century America to the process of building a national coalition. The seeming intensity of party competition was magnified by one of the main features of party mobilization in that era. There were relatively few non-partisans, so that the main aim of a party was not so much to convert wavering or undecided voters but to make certain that all their own partisans went to the polls.[8] The winning party was likely to be the one that, overall, had fewer defections

---

[8] Even less common than the undecided were converts from the other major party. As Mark Wahlgren Summers notes, "converts from one major party to the other were a minority, and conversions possibly occurred among active politicians more than among the rank and file"; Summers, *Party Games: Getting, Keeping, and Using Power in Gilded Age Politics*, Chapel Hill and London, University of North Carolina Press, 2004, p. 23.

from its ranks. However the effort expended in winning contributed to a splintering of support for the winning party after an election – too few expectations of preferment could be satisfied, and the inability to satisfy the demand made it more difficult for that party to maintain its position. There were two consequences of this splintering. First, the advantage that one party had gained in the presidential election often would be nullified in mid-term elections. Not only did this tend to produce divided government after mid-term congressional elections, but it also made it possible for a party to win both the governorship and control of the state legislature in states that they could not carry normally in presidential years. As we shall see shortly, this made the party system appear far more competitive at the sub-national level than it really was. Secondly, disputes among political elites were often greater in the party that held the presidency because of the problem of frustrated ambitions, and incumbency carried few of the advantages that it would later. Just as in the 1840s, when the party holding the presidency lost it at four successive elections (1840, 1844, 1848, and 1852), parties in the Gilded Age encountered difficulties in holding onto the White House – failing to do so in 1884, 1888, 1892, and 1896.

Although the two major parties were at the centre of competition in this era, third parties and other candidates were also a crucial part of the system. As noted earlier, third parties tended to take up political issues that the two major parties did not; often these were ones that potentially cross-cut divisions between those parties. The share of the vote obtained by third parties exceeded, by some way, the plurality of the largest party over its main rival in all of the elections between 1880 and 1892; in 1880 this difference was 3.5 per cent of the total vote, in 1884 2.9 per cent, in 1888 2.8 per cent, and in 1892 7.8 per cent. In other words, third-party interventions were always likely to affect the overall outcome of an election. Moreover, generally, third parties took votes disproportionately from one of the two major parties – for example, the Greenbacks from the Democrats and the Prohibitionists from the Republicans. This prompted two strategies from the major parties. The party threatened by vote loss might try to come to a "fusion" agreement with that third party. It might agree to support the same candidate at the head of the ticket or, more extensively, agree on a shared ticket for that election. Conversely, the other main party had an interest in keeping the third party in business as an entirely separate operation, and there were a number of occasions on which third parties were funded by a major party during an election campaign, just for the purpose of helping their opponent's vote to splinter.[9]

All of these features made the party system in the Gilded Age highly competitive *in some respects*. Particularly because of the tendency of winning coalitions to fragment after an election, the smaller of the two parties in a state could win offices that would be well beyond its capabilities in a presidential year. This point is important because there is a tendency among scholars to think of these years as ones during which the parties were evenly matched in most states.[10] They were not. Consequently, it is important not to confuse the *intensity* with which elective offices were contested with the *balance* between the parties contesting them. As Mark Wahlgren Summers has shown so clearly, Gilded Age politics involved intense competition, but the argument presented here is that that intensity disguises underlying limits to the level of party competition present throughout the country.[11]

Late 19th century America exhibited the same feature as most polities that use territorially based electoral systems: Support for the major parties was unevenly distributed between the states. Consider a schema involving four categories that reflect the degree of competitiveness in presidential contests. These categories are:

(1) the Highly Competitive states, which happened to include some of the largest states in the Union. These were states for which, in the four presidential elections from 1880 to 1892, the gap between (a) the median difference between the Democratic and Republican share of the total vote in the state and (b) the difference between the two parties' share of the vote nationally was 4 per cent of the total vote or less. In order of competitiveness, these states were New York, Connecticut, Indiana, New Jersey, West Virginia, California, Ohio, and Illinois. Constituting only just over one-fifth of the states in 1880, they controlled nearly one-third of the votes in the Electoral College.

---

[9] See Alan Ware, "The Funding of Political Parties in North America: The Early Years", in Peter Burnell and Alan Ware (eds.), *Funding Democratization*, Manchester, Manchester University Press, 1998, pp. 33–4.

[10] E. E. Schattschneider claimed, for example: "Before 1896 the major parties contested elections on remarkably equal terms throughout the country". *The Semisovereign People*, 1975, p. 80.

[11] Summers, *Party Games*.

(2) the Moderately Competitive states. Here the difference between the parties' performance at the state and national level was between 4 per cent and 8 per cent of the total vote. In order of competitiveness, the states in this category were New Hampshire, North Carolina, Maryland, Missouri, Wisconsin, Delaware, and Tennessee. These seven states formed about 18 per cent of the states and controlled about 16 per cent of the Electoral College vote.

(3) the Not-Very-Competitive states. Here the difference in vote share at state and national levels is between 8 per cent and 12 per cent of the total vote. The states in this category, in descending order of competitiveness were Iowa, Oregon, Pennsylvania, Massachusetts, Michigan, and Kentucky. They formed 16 per cent of all states but controlled over one-fifth of the Electoral College vote.

(4) the Uncompetitive states. These were states in which the difference in the vote share between state and national levels was at least 12 percent, and in many cases it was considerably more – for example, in the case of Kansas it was 25 per cent, while in South Carolina it was 54 per cent. By far, this is the largest category, containing 17 of the 38 states. All were small or of medium size, though, so that they controlled under one-third of the Electoral College votes.

Using this definition of competitiveness, less than 40 per cent of the states in the Gilded Age were either Highly Competitive or Moderately Competitive. However, even these notions of "highly competitive" and "moderately competitive" are overly generous and somewhat misleading, especially in relation to the dynamics of presidential coalition building. The place of Illinois in the Highly Competitive category is a case in point. The Democrats did carry the state once in presidential elections (1892), and Republican pluralities over Democrats in national elections were typically quite narrow. But the gap between the parties was still a decisive one, with the state leaning to the Republicans; only splits in that party brought about their defeat. This was a pronounced feature of state elections in Illinois; as Thomas Pegram oberves: "Following the Civil War Illinois was essentially a one-party state. Democrats controlled the General Assembly for a total of only four years between 1880 and 1932, and all but three governors between 1865 and 1932 were Republicans."[12]

---

[12] Thomas R. Pegram, *Partisans and Progressives: Private Interest and Public Policy in Illinois, 1870–1922*, Urbana and Chicago, University of Illinois Press, 1992, p. 10.

The narrow margins of victory in presidential elections would have indicated a high level of inter-party competition if there had been a core of floating voters to whom both parties could hope to appeal in their pursuit of victory. There were relatively few of them, and the Illinois Democrats were actually much less of a force in state politics, and much less significant as potential members of a Democratic national majority coalition, than the size of the electoral pluralities indicates.

Connecticut is also interesting, but for different reasons. Provisions in its state constitution resulted in permanent Republican control of the lower chamber of the state legislature – in a polity in which the governorship was weak, and hence control of part of the legislature really mattered. Unlike Illinois, the underlying electoral position of the two parties was one of balance; however, the Republicans possessed an institutional resource that could possibly be used to their advantage. Until the beginning of the 1890s, though, they dominated politics only in relation to the state's public policy agenda; their permanent control of the lower chamber could not be converted into an electoral resource and provide regular success in presidential elections for the Republicans. (After about 1912, it was to be used in conjunction with centralization of the state party organization to entrench the Republicans' electoral position.) Thus, in this era and unlike Illinois, Connecticut was highly competitive at the presidential level. The Democrats could, and did, win the state. However, it should have been a matter of concern for Democratic strategists whether, under slightly different political conditions and with continuing Republican control of the state's policy agenda through its control of the lower legislative chamber, that kind of competitiveness could persist.

The "Moderately Competitive" category is also not quite what it might seem at first glance. With one exception (Wisconsin), all of these states were won by the same party – by the Republicans in the case of New Hampshire – at every presidential election between 1876 and 1892.[13] In other words, these were not states that were constantly changing hands from one presidential election to the next. Of course, the effect of coalition breakup between presidential elections was to make it possible for the minority party in these states to win congressional and statewide elections. Indeed, this was true even of states in the Not-Very-Competitive category. For example, during the Democratic mid-term landslide of 1890, the Democrats managed to win the governorship of Pennsylvania. However,

---

[13] Wisconsin was won by the Democrats only in the year of their largest national plurality, 1892.

this phenomenon of parties winning other elections in states where they were consistently losing presidential contests really reflected the temporary disintegration of the more dominant party, rather than providing evidence of an underlying even balance of party strength. In most states, there was actually an imbalance in the period between 1877 and 1896, so that the Democrats' ability to win in most of the North is exaggerated if we focus on these types of victories.

Evidence for this imbalance can be seen by looking at how many years the Democrats controlled state governorships between January 1877 and January 1891, at how many occasions on which a candidate of their party was nominated to the U.S. Senate following a general election in that period, and at their success rate in House elections.[14] (In this highly partisan period, gubernatorial elections provide direct evidence of partisan strength in the electorate, while Senate nominations largely reflect party strength in state legislatures at that time.)

At first glance, control nationally seems to be weighted towards the Democrats with respect to governorships. For all states, the mean number of years in which the Democratic Party held the governorships in this 14-year period is 8.57. But this is distorted by the inclusion of the 11 southern states in which the party held the governorships throughout the period. If the South is excluded, the mean is 6.37 years. Moreover, the impact of the Civil War was such that the Democrats controlled the governorships of the five Border states throughout the years 1879–91, and if they, too, are excluded, the mean decreases again to 3.72 years. The median for the northern states was just 2 years. Of these 22 states, only in 6 did the Democrats occupy the governor's mansions for more than 4 years: Ohio (5), California (7), Indiana (8), Oregon (9), New York (11), and New Jersey (12). Of course, the states in which the parties were more evenly matched included some of the largest ones, and it is the competitiveness of the Democrats there that prevented the party system nationally from being one of Republican dominance. If the proportion of the total years that the Democrats controlled each governorship (in the North) between 1879 and 1891 is weighted by the number of Electoral College votes attached to that state, the Democratic Party's share of gubernatorial control rises from 26.6 per cent (unweighted) to 32.6 per

[14] Senators appointed by states to fill an uncompleted term by an incumbent senator are omitted from these calculations; states that joined the Union in this period (Idaho, Montana, North Dakota, South Dakota, Washington, and Wyoming) have been excluded.

cent (weighted). Nevertheless, what is striking about the northern states is just how weak a force the Democrats were in most of them. Looked at from the perspective of success in gubernatorial elections, the seeming equilibrium of the late 19th century party system at a national level largely hinged on the Democrats' competitiveness in a mere 6 or 7 of the 38 states in the Union.

The dominance of the Republicans in much of the North is also apparent from a glance at U.S. Senate nominations following each of the six elections between 1878 and 1888 (inclusive). One of the problems of using Senate seats as a measure in this context is that during the Civil War and afterwards, the Republicans continued to grant statehood to territories with small populations, knowing that these states would likely lean Republican and, hence, bolster the party's position in the Senate.[15] So it is not surprising to find that while the Democrats occupied governors' mansions on 61.2 per cent of all possible occasions (between 1877 and 1891), nominees of their party entered the Senate on only 49.3 per cent of possible occasions following the six elections in this period. But the overall pattern is the same as with the governorships. Outside the South and the five Border states, a mere 13.6 percent of nominations went to Democrats. Five of the most competitive states (in gubernatorial elections) identified here (California, Indiana, New Jersey, Ohio, and Oregon) accounted for 11 of these 12 nominations, which meant that in the remaining 17 states, Democrats were nominated to Senate seats on less than 1.5 per cent of all occasions. (The single occasion was in Nevada following the 1880 election.)

Exactly the same pattern is evident in House elections, although care must be taken in using such evidence because the number of seats a party could likely win was affected by the impact of partisan districting by state

[15] Charles Stewart and Barry Weingast have argued that this stacking of the Senate changed the whole pattern of American political development after the Civil War: "[T]he particular pattern of American political development critically depended on the Republicans' use of statehood politics to secure their hold on the presidency and the Senate in the last quarter of the nineteenth century. This pattern of electoral success allowed them to protect their policies instituted during the Civil War and early Reconstruction, through the election of 1896.... [H]ad the Republicans followed the conventions about statehood in use prior to the Civil War, not only would the Democrats have played a more prominent role in government and policy choice, but the development of the American state would have followed a much different 'blueprint'". Charles Stewart III and Barry R. Weingast, "Stacking the Senate, Changing the Nation: Republican Rotten Boroughs, Statehood Politics and American Political Development", *Studies in American Political Development*, 6 (1992), 226. See also Summers, *Party Games*, pp. 125–34.

legislatures. As Summers explains: "Malapportioned legislatures helped assure congressional district lines that distorted the political will of the nation, North and South. Across the North, as of 1880, 1.8 million Republican votes elected ninety congressmen, and 1.6 million Democratic votes elected just twenty."[16]

Nevertheless, House elections do provide a useful, if crude, indicator of the variation over time in the disadvantage the Democrats had in the North, especially in presidential election years. Consider first presidential election years. In 1880, the Democrats were in a minority of 136–151, but they were outnumbered 49–138 in the northern districts. In 1884, they held a 180–141 majority, but the Republicans held a majority of northern districts, 128–75. In 1888, the Republicans had an advantage of 166–159 overall, but led the Democrats 147–57 in the northern districts. Moreover, only in Indiana (in both 1884 and 1888) and in Ohio (in 1884) did the Democrats ever control individual state delegations. The weakness of the Democrats outside the six most competitive states (as identified from gubernatorial elections) is evident if they are excluded from data on House elections. The proportion of House seats won by Democrats was 24 per cent, 29 per cent, and 18 per cent, respectively, in the three presidential election years (compared with 26 per cent, 36 per cent, and 28 per cent for the entire North).[17]

As might be expected, the pattern for mid-term elections is slightly different; in years when the Republicans held the presidency, the Democrats could expect to benefit from intra-party fighting amongst the Republicans. Thus, in winning control of the chamber in 1878, the Democrats won 28 per cent of all northern districts, and in 1882 they won 46 per cent.[18] (Excluding the six most competitive states, the Democrats' share of northern seats shrank to 21 per cent and 33 per cent.) Unless support for the Democrats collapsed completely when they held the presidency (as it was to do in 1894), Republican prospects for making major gains at the expense of their opponents were small. Thus, in 1886, the Democrats were still able to win 32 per cent of northern districts (and 28 per cent excluding the six "competitive" states). Yet even when they were doing relatively well, and in 1878, 1882, and 1886 they took control of the House on all three occasions, the Democrats controlled few

---

[16] See ibid., p. 131.

[17] With these data and in subsequent calculations made in this section, seats held by third parties are excluded.

[18] The House elections in California were held in 1879, not in 1878.

of the northern state delegations. After 1878 it had a majority in just Indiana's, Ohio's, and Oregon's, and after 1886 it controlled Connecticut's and Minnesota's. Only after its massive mid-term victory in 1882, when it controlled the delegations of California, Connecticut, Indiana, Nevada, New York, Ohio, Oregon, and Wisconsin, did the party look close to being the equal of the Republicans in the North. Moreover, what is apparent about this list is that it is composed mainly of the "usual suspects" – five of the six states were those identified as competitive in gubernatorial elections. The others on the list are Connecticut, which we have seen can be classified as competitive in presidential elections in this period, plus Nevada and Wisconsin. The key point is that before 1890, the Democrats remained very much a minority party in most northern states, even in years like 1882 when their opponents faced major difficulties. Only in 1890, when the dynamic of the party system started to change and much larger voter revolts against particular parties became apparent, was this mould broken.

This pattern, of the Democrats' ability to win when the Republican Party fragmented in mid-term years but inability to sustain that success, is apparent also in elections to the lower houses of state legislatures. In the 12 years from 1877 to 1889, 10 northern states had Democratic majorities for at least one term, but in only 4 states (California, Indiana, New Jersey, and Ohio) did they have a majority for more than one term.

Thus, when we turn to look at presidential elections, it appears as if the competitiveness of the national party system hinged largely on possibly seven or eight states, of which one (West Virginia) was not in the North, as defined here. However, taking into account other evidence, only five of these northern states actually had highly competitive parties at the state level (California, Indiana, New Jersey, New York, and Ohio). Connecticut (and to a lesser extent Illinois) could produce close presidential elections, but (for different reasons) the Republicans were much stronger (or potentially much stronger) than the Democrats in both states. Peculiarly, the Democrats did well in gubernatorial elections in Oregon in the 1880s but failed to convert this into support in presidential elections.

To conclude, the competitiveness of the party system nationally after 1877 depended on competitiveness within no more than seven states, of which only five – several of them large ones – featured competitive contests between two well-matched parties at most levels of office. Thus, the 19th century party system maintained a rather fragile balance. The word "fragile", rather than "even", is used deliberately here – and for two related reasons. First, part of the appearance of competitiveness outside of these five to seven states lay in the propensity of coalitions to break up after electoral success; this allowed the smaller party (and in all cases outside of the South and the Border states this was the Democrats) to win elections "on the return of the pendulum". If, for whatever reason, the disintegration of the governing party could be reduced in the future, alternation in office would also be much reduced, and a very different-looking party system might emerge. Secondly, the overall balance between the parties at the national level depended on the Democrats remaining competitive in the five states in which two evenly matched parties really were pitched against each other. Those states controlled 22.6 per cent of the Electoral College votes and were the key to victory. With the sole exception of the "stolen election" of 1876, in every election between 1876 and 1892 the candidate that won a majority of those five states won the presidency.[19] In theory, this was a party system that could become much less competitive as a result of change in a relatively small part of the polity; it would not take much to transform radically the behaviour of the entire system. In fact, there were already factors that were putting strain on that fragile system.

We shall examine these factors in turn, beginning with the diverging interests between the Old North and the West. First, however, we need to consider how party strength in the Old North and the West differed.

2. The Increasing Significance of the West

In the late 1870s, just under two-thirds of all House districts were in the North, of which only about 12 per cent were in the West – that is, in those states that had been granted statehood after 1840. With the exception of California, the Democrats were much weaker in the western states, many of which had been settled by Yankee immigrants who had brought their mainly Whig, and later Republican, partisanship with them. Consequently, the share of the vote the Republicans obtained in the western states was higher than in the Old North. In the three presidential elections of 1880–88, the median share of the vote obtained by the GOP (the "Grand Old Party") in the western states was 54.0 per cent, 54.2 per cent, and 53.8 per cent, while in the states of the Old North it was 51.5 per cent, 51.1 per cent, and 49.6 pert cent, respectively.

In a sense, therefore, the West was the Democrats' "northern state problem" writ large. In the 1880s, this mattered most in the Senate, where the

---

[19] In 1876, the Republican Rutherford Hayes carried only California and Ohio (28 votes), losing the other 59 votes.

nine western states possessed nearly a quarter of the seats. Yet increasingly, the West was to provide opportunities for the Democratic Party – simply because the Republicans were to have difficulty reconciling the interests of primary producers in the West with those of its commercial support-ers in the Old North. The former wanted low tariffs (so that they could buy equipment as cheaply as possible and sell their produce in the most extensive free trade area), wanted railroad companies to be constrained in relation to their shipping charges, and were attracted to cheap money policies. The latter often favoured tariffs to protect domestic manufac-tures, were the sources of finance for the railroads, and wanted to return to a gold-based currency that had had to be abandoned during the Civil War. Until after the 1888 election, the Republicans balanced these con-flicting interests quite well, with the party's share of the vote holding up slightly better in the western states than in the Old North. This changed after 1888, however.

The mid-term elections of 1890 saw a massive gain of seats by the Democratic Party, one that easily outstripped their performance in 1882. The reaction against the Benjamin Harrison administration enabled the party to win a majority of seats in both the Old North and in the West, but it was their performance in the West that was the more remarkable. In the Old North, the Democrats had held 33 per cent of House districts after 1888, and this increased to 61 per cent after 1890. However, in the West, they had held a mere 11 per cent of districts after 1888 but that increased to 57 per cent after the 1890 election.[20] For the first time ever, the party was doing nearly as well in the West as in the Old North; the weaker links between voters and parties in the newer states, compared with those further east, was working to the Democrats' advantage. Not surprisingly, as politics normalized to some extent at the 1892 election, the Democrats did less well than in 1890 – winning 47 per cent of the districts in the Old North and 38 per cent in the West. That their decline was greater in the latter than in the former is of less significance than the fact that the Democrats were now doing so much better in the West (relative to the Old North) than they had done in any of the three previous presidential-year elections. (In the West their share of House seats had ranged from 11 per cent to 16 per cent previously, while in the Old North they had obtained between 28 per cent and 42 per cent of the total.) Although the West was

---

[20] The result would have been even better for the Democrats in the West but for the addition of five new states before the 1890 election. They won 62 per cent of the seats in the western states that had had congressional representation in 1889.

still more pro-Republican than the Old North, by the early 1890s the gap seemed to be narrowing. However, as we shall see later, it was one thing for the Democrats to be able to exploit Republican divisions that reflected conflicting interests between East and West when there was a Republican in the White House; it was quite another for the Democrats to keep this new East-West alliance of their own together when they themselves occupied the White House.

3. Long-Term Change in the 19th Century Party System

Political discontent in parts of the western United States was only one of several factors that were changing the bases of party politics, and hence the potential for national coalition building. The apparent stability in party competition, which was evident until about 1888, was increasingly under threat from a number of sources. It is important to emphasize this point because too often the changes in American party politics towards the end of the 19th century are linked only to the specific events of the years 1892–6. No one should doubt the importance of those events, but even if the depression of 1893 had not been as severe as it was, or even if the Republicans had controlled the White House at the time, the American political universe was already changing in significant ways and would have continued to do so.

The first change to which attention should be drawn is that of its socio-economic composition. On the one hand, mass migration from Europe between 1880 and 1920 altered the ethnic composition of the United States – especially in the Old North; the numerical dominance of Protestants from northern Europe was much lower by 1920. On the other hand, settlement became increasingly concentrated in large urban areas, so that the role of rural America in the polity was challenged. In 1880, there were only 8 cities that had populations of more than 200,000; fewer than 8 per cent of members of the House of Representatives represented districts from these cities. By 1930 there were 30 such cities, and following the 1931 reapportionment, more than one-fifth of House members represented such districts. Even this does not quite capture the long-term relative decline of rural America, because at the same time there had been an equally important rise in mid-sized cities, leaving rural and small-town communities with less political clout than they had had. This affected the stability of the electoral coalitions in both parties, but especially in the Democratic Party.

A second change was in the South. In the 1890s, developments that were already well advanced in the previous decade were to become still more pronounced. The marginalization of African Americans in the southern states began with de facto racial segregation in public places in the 1880s and was transformed into the Jim Crow laws in the 1890s. Through a variety of devices, black Americans were increasingly excluded from the political process, with consequences for electoral turnout. In 1876, 75 per cent of eligible southerners had voted in the presidential election; by 1892, under 60 per cent were voting, and by 1904, under 30 per cent were to do so.[21] Rules and practices making it harder to vote made it more difficult to organize opposition through a competitor to the Democratic Party, and during the 1890s, the remaining vitality of the minority Republican Parties in the region was sapped. The South became not so much a one-party area as an area without organized parties. Because the possibility of mobilizing opposition to the Democrats had been removed, the Democratic Parties in most of these states became no more than a label for which rival candidates competed. Writing in 1949, V. O. Key was to claim that "[t]he South, unlike most of the rest of the democratic world, really has no political parties".[22] The Democratic share of the vote increased dramatically in the 1890s. States that had been heavily Democratic, like Mississippi, saw an eradication of effective Republican opposition; states like North Carolina that had been Democratic, but had retained an effective Republican presence, saw that opposition much weakened. As can be seen in Table 3.4, in Mississippi between 1880 and 1892, the median difference between the Democrats' share of the vote in presidential elections and the Republican share was 40.5 per cent of the vote higher than the corresponding difference between the vote shares nationally; in the period from 1908 to 1920, that difference was 91.5 per cent of the vote. In North Carolina, the corresponding differences were 5.0 per cent for the period 1880–92 and 23.0 per cent for the years 1908–20. The entrenchment of Democratic power in the South was happening at the same time as external factors were changing the dynamics of party coalition building elsewhere in the country, but it was not caused by those dynamics.

In the long term, Democratic monopoly in the South reduced pressure on the Republican Party to do anything about the position of African Americans in the American polity. The impossibility of a Republican South being part of a majority coalition for that party simplified its coalition-building strategy. For the Democrats, the problem of the South was that

[21] Walter Dean Burnham, "The Turnout Problem", in A. James Reichley (ed.), *Elections American Style*, Washington, DC, Brookings Institution, 1987, p. 113.
[22] V. O. Key, *Southern Politics*, New York, Alfred A. Knopf, 1949, p. 16.

TABLE 3.4. *Democratic Dominance in the South, 1880–1892 and 1908–1920: Comparison of Difference in Democratic Plurality in Each State and the Nation (Each as Percentage of Total Vote)*

	1908–1920			
	Under 10 Per Cent	Between 10 and 20 Per Cent	Between 20 and 50 Per Cent	Over 50 Per Cent
Under 10 per cent		Tennessee (7.5, 13.0)	North Carolina (5.0, 23.0)	
Between 10 and 20 per cent			Arkansas (17.0, 31.0) Virginia (17.5, 31.5)	Florida (13.5, 52.0)
Between 20 and 50 per cent				Alabama (27.0, 53.0) Georgia (32.5, 61.5) Louisiana (35.5, 70.5) Mississippi (40.5, 91.5) Texas (40.5, 61.0)
Over 50 per cent				South Carolina (54.0, 94.0)

(Row labels on the left side are grouped under the heading 1880–1892)

Dominance is measured by taking the median value of (Democratic plurality over Republicans as percentage of total vote in each state) minus (Democratic plurality over Republicans nationally) for 1880–92 and 1908–20.

The first figure cited is for 1880–92, the second for 1908–20.

it would always exercise a huge influence over the party's agenda; in the 1880s, that influence had not hurt the party in its search for support because the party had been able to unite its different elements behind an ideology of limited government. Difficulties would arise if that ideology was no longer a uniting force or if a satisfactory alternative to it could not be found.

Thirdly, the informal means of conducting political life that had been characteristic of the Jacksonian democracy were coming under pressure. As fewer Americans lived in the kind of face-to-face societies in which control could be exerted through peer pressure and the application of customary practices, so it became necessary to replace such practices with formal rules and laws, if control was to be possible at all. Customarily, the switch to formal methods of regulation has been associated with particular kinds of political activist – middle-class reformers who wanted to transform the basis of American politics; it has been seen as the product of Progressivism. However, as I have argued in the case of both the Australian Ballot and the direct primary, the demand for some types of reform came as much from inside the parties as outside. Party elites found that traditional methods no longer allowed them the kind of control over party politics that they wanted. I have shown that the direct primary was a reform that was "waiting to happen"; it was not imposed on the party by anti-party reformers but was a response to the problems of conducting politics under changed conditions.[23] However, these reforms had consequences that were not understood fully at the time. For example, ultimately the direct primary was to make it more difficult for party elites to provide for balance on party tickets, as power passed from party organizations to candidates. Moreover, in the long term, legal registration of voters was to have a depressing effect on voter turnout – by comparison with the turnout levels evident in the 19th century. It is interesting to note, though – and this is a point to be considered shortly – that the impact in the short term of this particular reform was not as great as is usually imagined. Overall, however, the "legalization" of party politics tended to make it more difficult for parties to conduct their internal affairs, and that in turn contributed to the problems of coalition building in the distant future.

Fourthly, by the 1880s the first stages of change in the relationship established in the Jacksonian era between parties and the state were apparent. The Pendleton Act of 1883 provided for the introduction of a civil service system of administration, to supplement the traditional method of patronage placements. It was many decades before the spoils system would be removed at the various levels of politics; for example, in some cities, employees were still serving "at the pleasure of the mayor" after the Second World War, and the last vestiges of "spoils politics" were not removed from the U.S. Post Office until the 1960s. As with the reforms of the party structures, the crucial actors in this transformation were not so

---

[23] Alan Ware, *The American Direct Primary: Party Institutionalization and Transformation in the North*, Cambridge and New York, Cambridge University Press, 2002. The Australian Ballot was the name given to a secret ballot in which the ballot papers were printed and issued by governments, and not the political parties; its name derives from the fact that such a system was first used in Australia.

much those outside of the parties as those inside who were pursuing their own self-interest. Filling all posts through patronage was time-consuming and caused division within a party; it suited the interests of party leaders to have some positions filled by a different means, and once the civil service system had been introduced, it proved difficult to reverse the policy in the changed political circumstances. In the long term, this transformation altered many aspects of the relationship between leaders and party activists, and also those between leaders and some voters. The slow erosion of individual self-interest as a basis for party loyalty meant that, indirectly, parties could no longer rely on core electorates in winning elections. The party strategy that had worked from the 1840s to the 1880s was under threat.

This links to a fifth point. Just as voters' ties to parties were gradually weakening, so, too, was the *method* of campaigning in elections changing. Much greater emphasis came to be placed on the personality of a candidate at the head of the ticket and on issues, rather than party loyalty, in communications with mass electorates.[24] One consequence was that by the early 20th century, the nature of ticket splitting had changed. As John Reynolds and Richard McCormick show in the cases of the marginal states of New Jersey and New York, ticket splitting declined in the 1890s following the introduction of the Australian Ballot. However, no sooner had the parties gained a much tighter grip over local forms of disloyalty in party organizations that prompted ticket splitting, than a new form of ticket splitting was to develop – at the head of the ticket, with voters now responding to the image and messages of high-profile candidates.[25] Once again, this change between the 1890s and the early 20th century was not the result of a particular sequence of political events in the early to middle 1890s but of longer-term factors. Yet it also complicated the task of coalition building in the parties, and would have done so even if politics had not been disrupted in the way that it was between 1893 and 1896.

Sixthly, from 1889 on, the introduction in most states of the Australian Ballot weakened considerably one of the factors that had contributed to the "pendulum swing" after a presidential election during the Gilded Age. The consequences of the intra-party splits that usually followed the

---

[24] Michael E. McGerr, *The Decline of Popular Politics: The American North, 1865–1928*, New York and Oxford, Oxford University Press, 1986.

[25] John F. Reynolds and Richard McCormick, "Outlawing 'Treachery': Split Tickets and Ballot Laws in New York and New Jersey, 1880–1910", p. 856.

winning of state governorships had included a reduction in the size of the party workforce available to distribute ballots at subsequent elections within a state; the withdrawal of disaffected party members, who had failed to gain the patronage rewards they believed they had deserved, from the task of distributing ballots had usually hampered vote maximization on election days. Under the Australian Ballot, in which ballots were no longer distributed by party workers outside the polling booths, the absent workforce now had much less effect on vote mobilization for the party on election day.[26]

Finally, party organization at the local and state level was becoming far more centralized than it had been. For all the talk of political machines, party organization during most of the 19th century was decentralized. Party bosses depended on complex series of alliances for exercising control, and most periods of supposed dominance by a single boss were either illusory or short-lived. Competition within a party between elites with strongholds in different parts of a city or county was the norm. By the 1890s, though, much greater centralization was possible. Ironically, the kinds of centralizing reforms in local government usually advocated by anti-party reformers often facilitated this change – by providing an incentive for party elites to co-operate with one another. Kenneth Finegold has explained the reason: "The structure of local party organization reflected the structure of local government. Governmental consolidation encouraged party consolidation, and governmental fragmentation encouraged party fragmentation".[27] Unwittingly, anti-party reformers often pushed for the very structures that would empower their opponents for the next three or four decades.

In some cases, the pressure for party centralization came from within the party itself. A late example of this was to be Connecticut, with the statewide machine established under J. Henry Roraback.[28] Another outstanding, but earlier, example was Philadelphia, of which Peter McCaffery has said:

[T]he emergence of a full-fledged political machine in Philadelphia came about as a result of a series of innovations initiated by state and local Republican party leaders, and those innovations transformed the way the Republican party organization

---

[26] I am grateful to Jack Reynolds for pointing this out to me.

[27] Kenneth Finegold, *Experts and Politicians: Reform Challenges to Machine Politics in New York, Cleveland and Chicago*, Princeton, NJ, Princeton University Press, 1995, p. 29.

[28] Roraback, whose machine was arguably the most powerful ever constructed, has been the subject of remarkably little study; see, however, Edwin McNeil Dahill, "Connecticut's J. Henry Roraback", PhD dissertation, Columbia University, 1971.

functioned at both the state level and the city at the turn of the century. This transformation ... was not simply a natural and automatic consequence of the monopolization of patronage distribution. It was also due to a number of changes in party methods, rules, recruitment, and finance implemented by the state and city party leadership in a deliberate attempt to centralize power within the Republican party.[29]

Thus, Burnham's earlier assertion about Pennsylvania, which is part of his overall claim about the significance of voter transformation in the 1890s – that a "political realignment centring on 1896 eventually converted an industrializing state with a relatively slight but usually decisive Republican bias into a solidly one-party GOP bastion"[30] – conveys a wholly misleading impression about political change in the state. It is misleading in two respects. One is that Pennsylvania did not have a "relatively slight Republican bias" before 1896; it was a solidly GOP state even then, as can be seen from Tables 3.2 and 3.3. The second way in which the Burnham claim is misleading is that the consolidation of that position may well not have stemmed so much from any supposed electoral realignment in the period 1893–6, but, as McCaffery shows in detail for Philadelphia, from organizational changes that enabled the GOP to establish that party's complete dominance. In other words, care must be taken in distinguishing long-term change in the party system from the alleged effects of short-term political destabilization.

The interaction between governmental reform and political factors that pushed in the direction of greater centralization in the parties could be driven by the emergence of individual leaders in the parties who wanted to develop their own power base. Pegram, for example, has analyzed the role of Democratic Governor John Peter Altgeld in the early 1890s in bringing about this kind of transformation at the state level in Illinois:

Altgeld's attempt to build a personal organization that was committed to his own ideological agenda but remained within the party became the model for gubernatorial leadership in progressive-era Illinois. ... Because Altgeld developed a mechanism that pursued reform without destroying party organization – close executive supervision of state services and centralization of decision making within government – progressive-era Republican leaders such as Governor Charles Deneen

---

[29] Peter McCaffery, *When Bosses Ruled Philadelphia: The Emergence of the Republican Machine, 1867–1933*, University Park, Pennsylvania State Univeristy Press, 1993, p. 78. Italics in original.

[30] Walter Dean Burnham, "The Changing Shape of the American Political Universe", in Walter Dean Burnham (ed.), *The Current Crisis in American Politics*, New York and Oxford, Oxford University Press, 1982, p. 34.

managed to build powerful organizations of loyal government insiders even as they publicly worked to streamline administration.[31]

But, irrespective of the particular circumstances that prompted greater party centralization in specific states, the important point is that in the years after the early 1890s, a massive change in the internal dynamics of many city and state party organizations was evident.

All of the factors just identified would have worked to undermine the finely balanced, and fragile, party system of the 19th century. In that sense, transformation in the party system was inevitable – irrespective of events, or which party happened to win particular elections. However, the precise form that change took, and how quickly it occurred, was something that both factors external to party politics and decisions made by party politicians would influence. Indeed, there was one factor that was always likely to have an *immediate* impact on the balance between the parties – the one discussed in the previous section, that of keeping divergent economic interests together within the same coalition. Under certain conditions, and these conditions were to be present during the early to middle 1890s, these coalitions would likely fragment. When that happened, the viability of the ideology that had held together at least one of the parties would come under threat, and, in turn, this would prompt a major *short-term* shift in political coalition building by the parties. The consequences were to create longer-term problems for the defeated party – problems that were different in kind from those that had faced a party in the preceding decades when it had happened to lose a presidential election.

4. The Destabilization of the Party Coalitions, 1889–1896

The election of 1888 was the last under the old political order, in its original form. Even before then, there was evidence of the potential for instability in the party system. Fundamental conflicts of interest between eastern commercial and financial interests, on the one side, and western agrarian and mining interests, on the other, had been a feature of politics for nearly two decades. By the later 1880s, this conflict intensified and was marked in the 1890 elections by the appearance of various farming-related parties. At the same time, the Democrats benefited from being the "out" party; the result, as Kleppner puts it, was that "[t]he tight partisan balance that had typified most of the stable phase of the third party system

---

[31] Thomas R. Pegram, *Partisans and Progressives*, p. 158.

gave way in 1890 to a surging Democratic majority."[32] The formation of the People's Party in 1891 marked a further stage in the conflict and in the destabilizing of the previously balanced party system. Potentially, this was a much larger party than any other third party of the Gilded Age. Indeed, in the 1892 election, the Populists won over 8.5 per cent of the vote nationally, a much better performance by a third party than any since the Civil War. Moreover, focussing on its national performance underestimates its strength in the West and in parts of the South; the Populists won at least 30 per cent of the vote in nine western states (Colorado, Idaho, Kansas, Nebraska, Nevada, North Dakota, Oregon, South Dakota, and Wyoming) and in one southern state (Alabama). Yet as the events of the next three years were to demonstrate, the People's Party faced enormous difficulties in holding its electoral base together, and even more difficulty in expanding that base without fragmentation.

For all the voting strength displayed by the Populists in 1892, between them the two major parties were always likely to repel the electoral threat posed. Their size, their increasing institutionalization, and their longevity all gave them huge advantages. The much greater problem for the major parties was how to handle the long-term economic conflict of interest that formed around one of the core issues that the Populists had taken up. Finance had been divisive ever since the Civil War, when the North had funded its war effort through the issuance of paper money (the so-called greenbacks). The question of whether gold should have a privileged position in America's financial arrangements, or whether a more inflationary financial policy involving some role for silver, had long divided commercial eastern interests, who favoured the former, from primary producers in the West, who favoured the latter. As Ritter observes of the years 1865–96:

Within both major parties the financial issue was regarded as a threat to their national electoral coalitions.... National party leaders tried to suppress, subvert and temporize on an issue that threatened the electoral base of both parties.... During most of this period ... rifts were avoided by short-term compromises in financial legislation ... and longer term plays at partisan loyalty.[33]

From the point of view of party management, no other approach made sense. Nevertheless, in response to the depression of 1893, the greatest economic depression thus far in America's history, Democratic President

---

[32] Kleppner, *The Third Electoral System*, p. 298.
[33] Ritter, *Goldbugs and Greenbacks*, p. 29.

Grover Cleveland broke with this strategy. It was to have far-reaching consequences for his party's attempts at interest aggregation.

The New Yorker Cleveland blamed the depression on the Silver Purchase Act of 1890, a compromise measure passed by a Republican president and Congress that had done enough to satisfy the inflationists within the GOP. In calling for the act's repeal, something that was achieved in the Senate only because of strong Republican support in an institution in which, as we have seen, the GOP had a major advantage, Cleveland split his own party. Discord within it was intensified by the party's disastrous performance in the 1894 elections, in which voters appear to have reacted to hard economic times by blaming the party that controlled the White House and the Congress. (In terms of offices lost, 1894 was a far more severe blow to the party of the President than 1930.) The result was that there was a civil war in the Democratic Party over the nomination of the presidential candidate for 1896. Party leaders and activists in the West wanted a candidate who would support an inflationist policy, while eastern leaders opposed this. In the event, the nomination went to the young westerner William Jennings Bryan, and the party adopted a bimetallic party platform. ("We demand the free and unlimited coinage of both silver and gold at the present legal ration of 16 to 1 without waiting for the aid or consent of any other nation," stated the party platform.) The party then fused with the People's Party for the presidential election, with Bryan being the presidential candidate of both parties. Few party leaders in the East were enthusiastic about the candidate or the platform, and many were actively opposed to both. This was to reduce the impact of the party's campaign in the East and contribute to a very different pattern of election results from those evident in earlier years.

The Republican strategy was driven by two considerations. First, with the Democrats controlling the presidency and Congress at the time of the depression, the Republicans could afford to pay less heed to the interests of the western states. Republicans would benefit from the electorate's backlash against the Democrats, and so it now mattered less if they alienated their own support in the West; given the disparity in the population sizes of the two parts of the North, they could more than make up for losses there by making gains at the Democrats' expense in the East. Secondly, the evidence from the Populists' success in 1892 suggested that the Republicans might have to go some distance, by way of policy compromise, towards making their formerly solid western states secure for the party at the next election. Such a compromise would be difficult to

reconcile with eastern commercial interests, so that ignoring the West electorally made sense – at least in the short term. Consequently, both parties
abandoned their previous coalition-building strategies in 1896, and a different pattern of election results was its product. The Democrats won a
number of western states that had been solidly Republican, and even in
states to the west of Wisconsin that they did not win, they still performed
relatively better than they had earlier. (Minnesota was one such state.)
However, their (non-southern) eastern political base cracked. They lost
three Border states that they had carried previously (Delaware, Kentucky,
and Maryland), and they were defeated heavily in the competitive northeastern states of New Jersey and New York, and also in Connecticut.
In addition, most of the New England states swung even more to the
Republicans than they did usually.

From one perspective, the 1896 election was a decisive defeat for one of
the two major parties, although, from another, it was still a rather closely
fought contest – one that resembles more the tightly fought battles of
earlier decades than it does all but a few of the elections in the succeeding
century.[34] It was the largest margin of victory in the popular vote since
1872, and the winning party enjoyed a rather larger plurality (4.3 per cent
of the total) than in even the most lopsided of the earlier contests, 1892,
when the Democratic plurality had been a mere 3.1 per cent. However,
given the closeness of the contest in the real battleground states in 1896,
Bryan could be said to have come near to victory, despite being heavily
outspent by his opponent. In Kentucky, the Republican William McKinley
won by less than 300 votes, in California by 0.6 per cent of the vote,
in Oregon by 2.0 per cent, in Indiana by 2.8 per cent, and in Ohio by
4.8 per cent. Had Bryan carried Indiana and Ohio and no more than two
of the other states, he would have won in 1896. (Of these states, one
was a previously solid state for the Democrats and the other four were
among the most competitive states in presidential elections in the previous
decades.) If fewer than 34,500 voters in these states – one-quarter of 1
per cent of the entire electorate – had changed their votes, Bryan would
have won.

What happened between 1893 and 1896 changed the direction
American party politics took, but the drama of that election should not
provide an excuse for overstating the significance of the events associated

---

[34] Of the 27 presidential elections after 1896, only 6 produced pluralities for the winning
candidate that were smaller (as a proportion of the total vote) than the plurality in 1896
(1916, 1960, 1968, 1976, 2000, and 2004).

with it. That it was the Democrats who were in control of Congress and the White House in 1893 shaped how politics could develop after 1896. Had the Republicans been in power, it is unlikely that they would have initiated the repeal of their own 1890 Act, and as the party out of power, the Democrats would have been more able to keep their coalition together. However, the very fragility of the party balance in the Gilded Age, together with the long-term changes in party politics already noted, meant that even if there had been no depression in 1893, it is unlikely that the 19th century party system would have survived long; the party equilibrium was already being undermined before 1893, and it would have changed further, irrespective of the precise chain of events. (As with the assassination in Sarajevo in relation to the First World War, the events of 1893–6 were a trigger, but not the only possible trigger, for a major political transformation.) Yet at the same time as the focus is on forces that were, or were likely, to bring about change in the party system, it must be emphasized that many aspects of the 19th century party system persisted after 1896. All was not swept away by early 1897. Americans had not woken up on William McKinley's inauguration in March to find themselves in unfamiliar political territory; for the Democrats, reconstructing a winning coalition would not be taking place in uncharted terrain. It is to that point we turn in the next chapter.

4

The Re-assembling of the Democratic Coalition, 1896–1912

Those who subscribe to the idea that there was a "system of 1896" point to the decline of both electoral participation and party competition after 1896 as evidence that that year (or if not that year, then more generally the years between 1893 and 1896) constituted a turning point in the American party system. However, much of the evidence for the view that, after 1896, the United States entered the political equivalent of the Dark Ages has been distorted.

We begin briefly with reduced voter turnout, with which the post-1896 era is often associated. It is true that nationally turnout declined after 1896, but much of that decline was the result of developments in the South. Moreover, the decline in the South had begun a decade earlier. Outside the South, turnout in the 1900 election was, indeed, lower than in 1896, but in 1900 it was still higher than it had been in 1892.[1] In fact, comparing turnout in the North in the 1900, 1904, and 1908 elections with that for the period 1840–96 reveals that there were several elections in which turnout had been lower in the earlier period: In 1848, 1852, and 1872 it was lower than in all three elections of the later period. Outside the South, turnout did decline dramatically, but it did not do so until 1912. It was to be much lower still during the 1920s, but it should be evident that the direct cause of this decline could scarcely have been the election of 1896.

Surprisingly, perhaps, this pattern of turnout decline is even more apparent from a glance at turnout in mid-term years. If voters' detachment from parties had been prompted by events in the mid-1890s, it might be

---

[1] These data are taken from Walter Dean Burnham, "The Turnout Problem", pp. 113–14.

expected that the clearest evidence would be found in mid-term elections after 1896 – elections where the stimulus to vote was less. However, at every election until 1918, turnout was at least as high as it was in the years with the lowest turnout in the mid–19th century. It is true that the very high levels of mid-term turnout found in the 1880s were not repeated after 1894, but for nearly 20 years after the mid-1890s turnout was not that far out of line with that of the 1840s. Certainly from 1918 it did decline seriously, but this suggests that if there was a great discontinuity in party politics, it was one that might have occurred then, rather than in 1896. Long-term turnout decline was the result of several factors but especially of the reduced centrality of party politics in people's lives, and also of the costs associated with annual voter registration. While these factors help to explain why turnout did not again reach the record levels attained in 1896, the more important point is that they did not produce a dramatic change in the short term, but rather contributed towards a long-term shift to lower turnout rates.

As regards party competition, the conventional wisdom about the entire period from the mid-1890s to the early 1930s is that the Democrats were a minority party in the nation. Moreover, many analysts argue that that status was a direct result of the events of the years 1893–6. Superficially, there is little to dispute in relation to such a view. The party won none of the three presidential elections that followed its defeat in 1896, and its share of the vote in those three elections was even lower than in 1896 itself. The party did not regain control of Congress until 1910. If the Civil War election of 1864 is excluded, along with the two succeeding elections in which many southern Democrats were disenfranchised, there is no comparable period of extended failure for the Democratic Party in American history. Yet, in part, this impression that 1896 represents a watershed in party politics is an illusion. There was change, and some of that change was important, but there was also a high degree of continuity as well. Coping with electoral defeat in 1896 was not quite the radically new departure for the party that might be imagined.

To illustrate this point, consider the immediate aftermath of 1896 – the years 1897 and 1898 – and compare it with the two years following the party's defeat in the 1880 election. Of the five highly competitive states (California, Indiana, New Jersey, New York, and Ohio) in the period up to 1890, four held gubernatorial elections in the three years following a presidential election. (Indiana was the exception.) In 1881 and 1882, the Democrats had failed to regain the governorship of Ohio (their candidate obtaining 46.2 per cent of the vote), but did capture California

(55.1 per cent), New Jersey (49.9 per cent), and New York (58.5 per cent). Although they did not win any of the gubernatorial elections in the corresponding period after 1896, their share of the vote was relatively high: Ohio (47 per cent), California (45 per cent), New Jersey (47.3 per cent), and New York (47.7 per cent). With the exception of California, the Democrats came close to winning those elections, suggesting that the "pendulum effect" so evident in post-presidential-election years in the 1880s had not disappeared completely. Moreover, in 1898 the Democrats did well with respect to their vote share in congressional elections – winning 1 per cent more of the total vote than the Republicans, though malapportionment in the North and the particular distribution of the vote at that election resulted in the Republicans obtaining 52 per cent of the seats. That politics might have been returning to "normal" in most of the competitive states is reinforced by Philip VanderMeer's account of Indiana:

[T]he election of 1896...caused relatively few voters to change parties. Within a few years the money question had receded, and other issues were defined in terms of traditional partisan views. The election is most important because of its impact on partisanship. Many were concerned about the bitterness, hostility and divisiveness the election had engendered. Fearing this might continue and perhaps expand beyond the bounds of electoral politics, and afraid of the apocalypse that each had predicted, members of both parties modified their rhetoric and lowered their voices.[2]

Yet if the political world after 1896 looked similar to that of pre-1892, it was not actually the same, and there were six crucial respects in which the equilibrium of 1877–89 had changed.

First, as can be seen from the voting data in the preceding paragraph, off-year and mid-term election years in the most competitive states were not producing quite the level of reaction to the party that held the White House that they had done earlier. The Democratic vote had not collapsed – their vote share was higher in New Jersey in the two years after 1896 than it was in the two years after 1880, for example – but the party was not actually winning governorships. Because the "swing of the pendulum" against an incumbent party that was so evident earlier was not quite as pronounced now, the Democrats would win fewer major offices. That was to have a crucial consequence for the Democratic Party – one that will be examined in more detail later in the chapter.

---

[2] Philip R. VanderMeer, *The Hoosier Politician: Officeholding and Political Culture in Indiana, 1896–1920*, Urbana and Chicago, University of Illinois Press, 1984, p. 31.

Secondly, though of less direct consequence for presidential coalition building by the Democrats, the party was doing much less well in gubernatorial elections in states that were previously part of the Republican coalition (as well as in Connecticut, which had been important for the Democrats at the presidential level). Excluding the southern and Border states and the 5 highly competitive states, 16 states had held gubernatorial elections in 1881, 1882, and 1883, and Democrats had won in 7 of them, replacing Republican governors in Connecticut, Colorado, Kansas, Massachusetts (but only in 1882, and not in 1881 and 1883), Michigan, Nevada, and Pennsylvania. By contrast in 1897, 1898, and 1899, 20 such states held gubernatorial elections and there were four Democratic gains – all with the Democrats being part of a Fusion ticket, and all in western states (Colorado, Idaho, Minnesota, and South Dakota). The issues of 1896 continued to be of significance in the latter, where the Democrats could benefit from those issues, but the pendulum effect, previously evident in a number of Republican-leaning northern states, was weaker, and this contributes to the overall impression that the Democrats were doing badly. Moreover, and this was one aspect of change whose effects persisted until the New Deal era, the Republicans were often able to consolidate their organizational strength in those states that had previously leaned Republican, with their greater party cohesion shutting out the Democrats in mid-term years.

Thirdly, full recovery for state Democratic Parties from the 1894–6 experience was not always as quick as it was in the Indiana party. Just as the Democrats benefited electorally in 1897 and 1898 from the lingering impact of the bimetallic controversy in some western states, so, too, were they harmed in some Old North states by this. For example, in New York State, the Democrats took a few years to recover completely at the state level, though in New York City they had already regained lost ground by 1898. In other cities the recovery would take longer. In Boston it was not until 1904 that the share of the vote the Democrats received in congressional elections reached the levels evident in the 1890s, and as in New York, the Democrats were not fully competitive at the state level until 1910.

Fourthly, although the margin of defeat in 1896 was not large by 20th century standards, it was large by comparison with pre-1892 elections, and this meant that the Democrats had more ground to make up in 1898 than had parties earlier. They had to do this in the absence of any major disruptive factor – such as another economic depression of the kind that had hurt them in 1894 – confronting the party of the president.

Fifthly, a gradual return to the "politics of the tariff", in place of the "politics of silver", would always be a mixed blessing for the Democrats. It did open up the prospect of further splits in the Republican coalition, and would help intra-party reconciliation for the Democrats. Nevertheless, the tariff issue would also work against the party that, in part, in 1896 had clearly traded its electoral base in the Old North for new support in the West. Yet it was the manufacturing industries of the cities in the former region that constituted the most dynamic sector of the national economy, and it was those interests that had tended to favour tariffs. Long-term demographic factors were not helping the traditionally low-tariff party, therefore, so that however closely the pre-1892 conditions came to being restored, there would now likely be a greater pro-Republican bias in the national electorate than earlier.

Finally, 1896 might be seen as marking the beginning of a period when the Border states became visibly more competitive than they had been earlier – and that competitiveness was sufficient to make it possible for the Republicans to win more elections in this region than they had done earlier. Until then, superficially, Border state election results had been more like those in the rest of the ex-slave states following the end of Reconstruction – they had gone Democrat. However, the margins of victory had been narrower in both presidential and gubernatorial elections in the Border states than in those in the South itself. Before the 1893–6 crisis, all five Border states had voted for the Democrat in every presidential election since 1876, all had had Democratic governors for the entire period, only one Republican senator had been nominated from the region, and the proportion of Republicans in their combined House delegations had ranged from just 3 per cent of the total to 27 per cent of the total. After 1896 this seemed to change. Having not lost a Border state since 1876, the Democrats could carry only two at each of the presidential elections between 1896 and 1908. In the 16 years immediately after 1896, the Republicans held the governorship of Delaware for 8 years, Kentucky's for 7, Maryland's for 4, Missouri's for 4, and West Virginia's for all 16. They enjoyed similar success in getting their candidates appointed to the U.S. Senate: Nearly one-half of all Senate nominations between 1894 and 1910 went to Republicans. Excluding the exceptional result in 1894, the Republicans won between 28 per cent and 46 per cent of House districts in the years up to 1908 (Table 4.1). Only with the Democratic victory in 1910 did this dip down again to 21 per cent of all seats in the Border states. This pattern of results illuminates why Schattschneider's claim that after 1896 "the resulting party line-up was one of the most sharply

TABLE 4.1. *House Seats Won by Republicans in Border States, 1878–1910 (as a Percentage of Total Number of Seats in That Region)*

1878	3
1880	19
1882	14
1884	9
1886	19
1888	27
1890	3
1892	8
1894	65
1896	45
1898	38
1900	41
1902	28
1904	39
1906	44
1908	46
1910	21

Border states comprise Delaware, Kentucky, Maryland, Missouri, and West Virginia.

sectional political divisions in American history" is misleading.[3] In one important respect, post-1896 politics was actually *less* sectional than in the earlier period – the Border states were no longer the weakest members of a Solid South, but behaving more like competitive northern states. It was not until the New Deal that the Democrats were to establish again a higher success rate in sub-presidential contests in the Border states.

The significance of this greater political competitiveness in the Border states for the Democrats' attempts at building a national political majority is examined in Section 6. For the moment, the important point to emphasize is that this shift in the competitiveness of the Border states was not something that actually emanated from the events of 1893–6. To the contrary, increasingly this region had been behaving more like the North. Sectional voting patterns were becoming less distinct as the proportion of the electorate who had had direct experience of the Civil War declined. As is shown in Table 4.2, between the late 1870s and the early 1890s, the median share of the total vote in the Border states that went Republican

---

[3] E. E. Schattschneider, *The Semisovereign People*, p. 77.

TABLE 4.2. *Median Proportion of Popular Vote Won by Republican Presidential Candidates, 1876–1892, in Border States and in the United States (as Percentage of Vote Totals)*

	Border States	United States	Share of Vote in Border States Minus Share of Vote in United States
1876	42.1	48.0	−5.9
1880	39.9	48.3	−7.4
1884	43.2	48.2	−5.0
1888	45.3	47.8	−2.5
1892	43.5	43.0	+0.5
1896	52.2	51.0	+1.2

Border states comprise Delaware, Kentucky, Maryland, Missouri, and West Virginia.

in presidential elections was moving ever closer to the share of the vote the GOP was achieving nationally, and it became larger than the party's national vote share as early as 1892. That is why when the focus is on the number of elections that were won, the contrast between the Democrats' success pre-1893 and post-1893 is misleading; it suggests a sharp break with the past, whereas, in fact, a continuation of the trends already evident up to 1892 would have started to produce a greater number of Republican victories in these states, and by itself that would have made the Democrats' situation more difficult. At best, the events of 1893–6 merely acted as a catalyst to the change.

It is against this background of modest, but perhaps decisive, change in the old balance between the parties that we must assess the capacity of the Democratic Party to build a national majority coalition after the mid-1890s. All was not as it had been, but how difficult was the party's task? To assess this, we employ the framework of analysis introduced in Chapter 2. We begin by examining the nature of the interests that the Democrats now had to aggregate.

1. Had the Interests Within the Democratic Coalition Become Incompatible?

In the years 1880–92, the most Democratic-leaning states in presidential elections had been the 16 southern and Border states. They provided 148 of the 201 Electoral College votes needed for victory (in the 1880s). The remaining 53 votes had to come from northern states – the six most marginal ones (in descending order of their Democratic lean being New Jersey, New York, Connecticut, Indiana, California, and Ohio) could provide 105 between them.[4] As in all coalitions where it is clear who the marginal voter is, that voter should be able to exercise considerable power over the rest of the coalition because it is crucial to victory. Within the Gilded Age Democracy such power rested with the six marginal northern states. It was to these states that the party would tend to look for its presidential nominee – in fact, New York provided four out of the five nominations between 1876 and 1892. Moreover, the marginal voter can also expect to have considerable influence over the party's platform. Until 1896 this had caused few problems, but that year the "old" marginal voter was, in effect, ignored – with the nomination of the Nebraskan William Jennings Bryan and the adoption of a policy of bimetallism. Under the changed conditions of the mid-1890s, it could be contested whether the marginal vote now lay in a different set of interests in the country.

The Old North parties that had been so crucial to Democratic success were themselves coalitions – in most cases, being an alliance between three rather different kinds of political actors. First, there were the small-town and rural Democrats – the kind of people whose predecessors had been attracted to Jacksonianism in the 1830s. Proportionately, there were not nearly as many of them as there were rural and small-town Republicans in the North, but in mainly rural states, such as Indiana, they were important in making the party competitive. The Civil War had hurt the rural Democracy in the North, but they were still a political force in the Gilded Age. Then there were native-stock legal, commercial, and financial men, who were drawn to the Democratic Party because of family ties and who tended to reject at least *some* of the stuffy, moral imperialism associated with the Republican Party. Nevertheless, such men were conservatives in financial matters; they might share with Democrats elsewhere a hostility to the tariff, but they would part quickly with those whose views led them towards policies of "unsound money". Grover Cleveland, governor of New York and three times a presidential candidate (1884, 1888, and 1892), was the best-known exemplar of this kind of politics. The allies of these Democrats were the organization leaders in the cities, popularly called "bosses", who were able to mobilize the vote there, a vote that every year became more Catholic. Increasingly in the Democratic Party, many of these bosses also were themselves Catholics, though their counterparts in

---

[4] Beyond this group the next most Democratic state was Illinois.

the Republican Party continued to include political entrepreneurs/bosses who came from old Yankee Protestant stock.[5]

The alliance was not always an easy one. Notoriously, Grover Cleveland's relations with Tammany Hall in New York City were sufficiently poor that in his re-election bid in 1888, he failed to carry his own state, even though fellow Democrat David B. Hill won the city by a margin large enough to win the governorship. It was alleged that in parts of the city, deals were done between Tammany Hall and the Republicans – deals that were responsible for sinking Cleveland's chances.[6] New York was not typical, though, in that urbanization was relatively much greater there than in other states, and consequently, when its own interests were at stake, Tammany Hall was more able to disrupt modernizers and reformers in the party than could urban "machine" politicians elsewhere. For example, Hill, Cleveland's immediate successor as governor, himself had considerable problems in enacting ballot reform in the state because of the need to placate Tammany, while in most other states, the Australian Ballot was being speedily enacted at the end of the 1880s and the beginning of the 1890s.[7] The interests of the machines lay in a relatively large public sector in the arenas in which they operated, so that they could generate the jobs and contracts that sustained their parties' activities. Since taxes were paid disproportionately by the middle classes, there was a distinct class element to the conflicts between the machines and their opponents. Outside their own bailiwicks, though, machine politicians tended to co-operate with the middle-class interests in their own party, with both tending to support minimal government activity and interference at federal and state levels of government.

Their hostility to an activist state was the result of two quite separate considerations. One factor was that the immigrant voters, whose support they mobilized, feared the kinds of interventions in their lives that moralizing Yankees might attempt, including overt anti-Catholicism and prohibition. The less the state was supposed to do, the easier it would be for them to protect themselves against their enemies. However, urban

[5] For example, "Big Bill" Thompson, who was to become Republican mayor of Chicago in 1915, was such a politician; he mobilized immigrant electorates as well as any Irish or Italian Catholic politician did, but he came from a wealthy Protestant Boston family. Douglas Bukowski, *Big Bill Thompson, Chicago and the Politics of Image,* Urbana and Chicago, University of Illinois Press, 1998, Chapter 1.

[6] L. E. Fredman, *The Australian Ballot: The Story of an American Reform,* East Lansing, Michigan State University Press, 1968, p. 29.

[7] See Alan Ware, *The American Direct Primary,* Chapter 2.

party organization leaders also feared that their own activities might become subject to regulation. Naturally, they accepted regulation and reform when it could be shown to protect those interests, and that was one of the reasons why, for example, in many states, ballot reform was not controversial in the way it was in New York. Yet when it was unclear where their own interests lay, urban leaders tended to prefer the status quo, and for that reason they had a stake in a political ideology that emphasized the virtues of a passive state.

The conservatism of the financial and commercial elements within the Democratic Party thus meshed reasonably well with those of the growing urban party organizations, and, in turn, this commitment to a non-interventionist state served the interests of the largely rural South – both in the southern states themselves and in the southern-oriented parts of the Border states. The Democrats might have had a rather peculiar political alliance, but generally, it was an alliance that had worked. Was its breakdown in the two years leading up to the 1896 election an irrevocable and permanent one? Clearly, the answer to that is "no". As the quotation from VanderMeer about Indiana, cited earlier, illustrates, normal politics could resume after the election itself – because most party politicians wanted it to do so. The frustrations of westerners with an economic system that they saw as biased against them would continue, as the election of Fusion governors in the West in the three years after 1896 demonstrates, but the country would never be divided again on economic issues in quite the way that it had been in 1896. Of course, what had been so striking about that election was not just the superficial regional divide, in terms of which party carried a particular state, but more especially the huge imbalances in the shares of the vote the major parties obtained in different regions. Massive Democratic majorities in the South and parts of the West were more than matched by large GOP ones in most of the rest of the country. (In one key respect, therefore, the 1896 election exaggerated a pattern evident in previous elections: A fairly close result nationally was not paralleled by close results in most of the states.) Yet despite the passion and hatred accompanying that election, what divided the members of the erstwhile Democratic coalition was essentially temporary; in better economic times, the silver issue would become irrelevant, and primary producers in western states would be less likely to believe that their livelihoods were endangered by eastern financiers.

This is what actually happened, although it did not happen immediately at the national level. It took 14 years. Nevertheless, the old coalition between ex–slave states and certain states in the Old North was largely reconstructed, though it was now supplemented by, and indeed had to be supplemented by, some states in the West. The nature of this reassembled Democratic coalition can be illustrated in two ways. The first is to examine the level of state competitiveness in congressional elections in 1910, the year that the Democrats regained control of the House, with that in 1888, one of the last years in which the party's old coalition was evident in a pure form. What is clear is that, with the exception of California, the states where competition had been intense at the presidential level either tended to remain battleground states in 1910 for the control of Congress or even leaned Democratic (see Table 4.3). There was change from 1888, but the overall structure of a Democratic coalition that could win a congressional majority remained broadly the same. Although the Democrats did well in a few states in which they had been relatively weak in the 1880s – Colorado, Maine, Massachusetts, and Nebraska – their victory was mainly the result of electoral strength in Indiana, New Jersey, New York, and Ohio – the very states that had been the most competitive in presidential elections in 1880–92. The same is partly true at the presidential level in the 20 years after 1896. Here, too, much of the alliance between the two wings of the party was eventually re-established, but the impact of the tumult of the mid-1890s did have some important long-term effects that made presidential coalition construction much more complex for the party, even though in many states, earlier voting patterns were still evident as late as the First World War.

A second way of looking at the continuity is to compare the relative strength of state Democratic Parties in presidential elections. For these purposes, we compare the four election years from 1880–92 with a similar number of elections in the period 1908–20. (By 1908 the immediate disruption caused by 1896 had largely passed.) Table 4.4 uses the difference between the Democrats' plurality over Republicans in each state for the four presidential elections between 1908 and 1920 and subtracts the plurality that the Democrats had nationally at that election; the median of those four values is then calculated. The same procedure is then used for similar data for 1880–92. For these purposes, the Democratic Heartland comprises those states where that median is more than 5 per cent of the vote – that is, roughly speaking, it is where, on average, the Democratic plurality was more than 5 per cent of the total vote greater than the party's share of the vote nationally. (Obviously, this does not mean that the Democrats actually won Heartland states; they might well not in years when the party's performance nationally was poor.) Contested Territory is states where the gap between the median plurality in the state

TABLE 4.3. *Competitive and Non-competitive Northern States in 1888 and 1910 Congressional Elections, Measured by Democratic Candidate's Plurality over Republican Candidate in Median District in Each State*

	1888 +10%	1888 +6%	1888 0%	1888 −6%	1888 −10%
1910 +10%		New Jersey			
1910 +6%			Indiana New York Ohio		Colorado Maine
1910 0%			Connecticut Illinois	Massachusetts	Nebraska
1910 −6%			New Hampshire		Kansas Pennsylvania
1910 −10%			California Michigan	Iowa Nevada Wisconsin	Minnesota Oregon Rhode Island Vermont

89

TABLE 4.4. *Classification of States by Size of Democratic Plurality for Both 1880–1892 and 1908–1920*

	Heartland 1908–1920 (17 + 2)	Contested Territory 1908–1920 (5 + 3)	Foreign Parts 1908–1920 (16 + 5)
Heartland 1880–92 (15)	Alabama Arkansas Florida Georgia Kentucky Louisiana Maryland Mississippi Missouri North Carolina South Carolina Tennessee Texas Virginia	Delaware	
Contested Territory 1880–92 (8)		Indiana Ohio West Virginia	California Connecticut Illinois New Jersey New York
Foreign Parts 1880–92 (15)	Colorado Nebraska Nevada	Kansas	Iowa Maine Massachusetts Michigan Minnesota New Hampshire Oregon Pennsylvania Rhode Island Vermont Wisconsin
New States (post 1880) (10)	Arizona Oklahoma	Montana New Mexico Utah	Idaho North Dakota South Dakota Washington Wyoming

and nationally was less than 5 per cent for either the Democrats or the Republicans. Foreign Territory consists of states where the median Republican was more than 5 per cent of the total vote greater at the state level than nationally.

It is clear that much of the older coalition was still present in 1908–20, though the evidence from Tables 4.3 and 4.4 suggests the existence of two slightly different national majorities – one the result of an attempt to aggregate on a specifically national level, and the other an aggregation of district interests. The latter was a continuation of the late 19th century coalition – found at both presidential and congressional levels before the 1890s – and it was largely to disappear between 1910 and 1916. However, in the years immediately before its disappearance it was hugely significant: The congressional Democratic revival in 1910 was driven largely by the party's performance in the East Coast states of Connecticut, New Jersey, and (especially) New York, states that were already becoming more Republican at the presidential level. At that level, several states (notably California, Connecticut, New Jersey, and New York) that had been highly competitive earlier moved into the Foreign Parts category by 1908–20. At the same time, some western states that the party had mobilized over the silver issue in the 1890s (especially Colorado, Nebraska, and Nevada) had become much more favourable territory for the Democrats in presidential contests – a development that is reflected in the structure of the coalition seen in Table 4.4. However, this "trade" of states over time was far from being a good one for the party, if only because of the relative size of the states involved: Small western states were replacing larger eastern ones – a point to be examined in Section 2.

The central point to be made in this section, though, is that the problem facing the Democrats does not seem to have been one of incompatible interests that had been driven apart by the events of the early to middle 1890s; the Democrats faced problems, but not that particular problem. They could, and did, reunite the older elements of their coalition after 1896, though it took them some years to do so. Yet at the same time they were doing so, the longer-term effects of the events of the early 1890s were evident in the party's coalition building at the presidential level. Parts of the West were now places to which the party could look in its attempts to build a national majority. However, if the party did not face a problem of trying to construct a coalition around incompatible elements, we must move on from that issue to the question of whether that coalition was simply too disparate.

2. Was the Democratic Coalition Too Disparate After the Mid-1890s?

All things being equal, a larger coalition is more difficult to form than a smaller one. Even if there are not conflicting interests, the large size of a potential coalition may make it difficult to form. Once again using as data the median difference between the Democratic Party's plurality over the Republicans in each state and the plurality nationally between 1880 and 1892, it is evident that in that period, the Democrats had to win only the most Democratic 19 states (of the then-38 states) to obtain a majority in the Electoral College (see Table 4.5). Correspondingly, the Republicans had to win 20 states – including Connecticut – if they were to win. Similar data for the period 1908–20 show that the Democrats faced a more difficult task in the early decades of the 20th century.

To obtain an Electoral College majority once the number of states increased to 48 in 1912, the Democrats now had to win more states (27) than the Republicans (22). Moreover, it was especially at the margins of their potential coalition that they were faced by a plethora of small states. The 19 most Democratic states yielded 197 out of the 266 Electoral College votes needed, but it would take a further 8 states to generate the extra 69 votes, with only Ohio and Indiana being large or moderately large states in this group. The task in the 1880s had been far simpler; the last 54 votes in the Electoral College coalition could be obtained from only 4 states. Consequently, the Democrats' difficulties were not just the product of there being (after 1912) an additional 10 states in the Union. The configuration of support for the party had changed so that the most marginal states in building a coalition were drawn from among the smallest ones, including some older states as well as new ones. The six most marginal states for the Democrats were New Mexico, Montana, Utah, West Virginia, Kansas, and Delaware, while the four most marginal Republican states were Idaho, New Hampshire, Wyoming, and Oregon. This was a very different political world from one in which six states (New Jersey, New York, Connecticut, Indiana, California, and Ohio) held the key to victory. The number of members needed to form a minimum winning coalition necessarily made party strategy more complex, even while the basic shape of much of the re-assembled coalition was not that dissimilar to the earlier one.

That complexity was magnified by changes to the *kind* of coalition the Democrats now had to try to construct. A minimum winning coalition containing the most Democratic-leaning states would consist at its heart, as before, of the South and the Border states, but that core would now have

TABLE 4.5. *Construction of a Winning Democratic Coalition in the Electoral College, 1880–1892, 1908–1920, and 1920–1932*

1880–1892	1908–1920	1920–1932
South Carolina 9	South Carolina 9	South Carolina 9
Texas 13 (22)	Mississippi 10 (19)	Mississippi 10 (19)
Mississippi 9 (31)	Louisiana 10 (29)	Louisiana 10 (29)
Louisiana 8 (39)	Georgia 14 (43)	Georgia 14 (43)
Georgia 12 (51)	Texas 20 (63)	Texas 20 (63)
Alabama 10 (61)	Alabama 12 (75)	Alabama 12 (75)
Virginia 12 (73)	Florida 6 (81)	Florida 6 (81)
Arkansas 7(80)	Virginia 12 (93)	Arkansas 9 (90)
Florida 4 (84)	Arkansas 9 (102)	North Carolina 12 (102)
Kentucky 13 (97)	North Carolina 12 (114)	Virginia 12 (114)
Tennessee 12 (109)	Arizona 3 (117)	Tennessee 12 (126)
Delaware 3 (112)	Oklahoma 10 (127)	Oklahoma 10 (136)
Maryland 8 (120)	Tennessee 12 (139)	Arizona 3 (139)
Missouri 16 (136)	Missouri 18 (157)	Missouri 18 (157)
North Carolina 11 (147)	Maryland 8 (165)	New Mexico 3 (160)
West Virginia 6 (153)	Nevada 3 (168)	Maryland 8 (168)
New Jersey 9 (162)	Nebraska 8 (176)	Utah 4 (172)
New York 36 (198)	Kentucky 13 (189)	Nevada 3 (175)
Connecticut 6 (204) –	Colorado 6 (195)	West Virginia 8 (183)
winning coalition	Ohio 24 (219)	Indiana 15 (198)
	Indiana 15 (234)	Wisconsin 13 (211)
Indiana 15 (219)	New Mexico 3 (237)	Nebraska 8 (219)
California 8 (223)	Montana 4 (241)	Montana 4 (223)
Ohio 23 (246)	Utah 4 (245)	Oregon 5 (228)
Illinois 22 (258)	West Virginia 8 (253)	Rhode Island 5 (233)
New Hampshire 3 (261)	Kansas 10 (263)	New Hampshire 4 (237)
	Delaware 3 (266) –	Connecticut 7 (244)
	winning coalition	New York 45 (289) –
		winning coalition
	Idaho 4 (270)	
	New Hampshire 4 (274)	North Dakota 5 (294)
	Wyoming 3 (277)	Idaho 4 (298)
	Oregon 5 (282)	Delaware 3 (301)
	New York 45 (327)	Colorado 6 (307)
		Illinois 29 (336)

The states are listed in descending order of their propensity to vote Democratic, as measured by median for 1880–92, 1908–20, and 1920–32 of (Democratic plurality over Republicans in state [as percentage of total vote] minus Democratic plurality over Republicans nationally).

to include eight western states (Arizona, Nevada, Nebraska, Colorado, New Mexico, Montana, Utah, and Kansas) plus two midwestern states that had been heavily contested earlier, Indiana and Ohio. Moreover, if the particular circumstances of an election made it likely that some of the potential coalition members would not turn Democratic, the party might have to cast its net further and attempt, as before, to capture New York. Part of an economically radical West had to be reconciled with a less consistently radical South and a far from radical Indiana, Ohio, and (possibly) New York. This was a broad coalition to attempt to build – certainly not an impossible feat in all circumstances but no doubt a challenging one.

Nevertheless, it did not prove impossible to adapt the old ideology of limited government to new circumstances. In fact, the "New Freedom", the slogan under which Woodrow Wilson campaigned in 1912, can be considered as an adaptation of older ideas, in which states' rights remained prominent, to new conditions in which legal regulation of certain aspects of economic activities was justified because it enhanced freedom. The most important arena of regulation was that of monopoly: "More, perhaps, than any other single theme, antimonopoly rhetoric tied the party of Bryan, Wilson, Smith, Roosevelt, and Truman together in the first half of the twentieth century".[8] After the 1890s, Democrats were far more likely than earlier to envisage a positive role for the state – it was to be used to contain the excesses of private power. In that way, there was an important break with the party's ideas in the 19th century. However, the role of the state was to regulate through law, rather than to do very much itself; in essence, its role was to police and protect freedoms that had been undermined or that might otherwise be undermined. Whatever its limitations, this was a coherent public philosophy. Consequently, even with the increase in the breadth of their electoral coalition after the mid-1890s, victory for the Democrats did not depend simply on opportunism – on winning because of major failure by, or disagreement among, the Republicans. The Democratic Party continued to have a distinctive approach to governing, with less emphasis on the role of the state to promote the interests of commerce and industry than the Republicans were giving. In doing this, the party did not become incoherent or devoid of ideology because of the greater breadth of its coalition. As will be seen later, the limitation of that ideology would likely be a problem once the party attained power, rather than while it was still seeking it.

[8] John Gerring, *Party Ideologies in America, 1828–1996*, p. 199.

To conclude this section, the Democratic Party coalition became more disparate after the mid-1890s, but it was not so disparate that the party would be unable to unite around a common set of ideas at national elections.

3. Did the Democrats Suffer a Decline in Their Resource Base?

In one obvious respect, the Democrats did suffer a decline in their (relative) resources after 1896, although the impact of this on their ability to construct a successful presidential coalition was probably not that great. Between the Civil War and 1896, the typical pattern of election expenditures had been for the party that had lost the previous presidential election to outspend its opponent at the subsequent election. Incumbency had a very different effect then than it was to have in the 20th century; in the late 20th century, political money would usually move in the direction of incumbents because they were the likely winners. In the late 19th century, because in part of the disappointment of many would-be holders of patronage positions, the fragmentation of national coalitions made it more difficult for a president's party to raise money. However, beginning with 1896, an entirely new pattern emerged. Because that contest pitted an agricultural and mining America against a commercial and industrial America, a major imbalance in campaign expenditures developed that year, with the Republicans able to raise more money from their supporters. Their advantage in this regard continued thereafter, and only once (in 1948) were they to be outspent again in presidential elections by the Democrats.[9]

However, the question to be addressed here is whether this undoubted relative disadvantage in campaign money affected the Democratic Party's ability to aggregate the interests in its potential coalition. Of course, the disadvantage did not actually help the party, but to the extent that material resources facilitated co-operation between different interests, it was resources such as contracts and jobs that still did so in the first few decades of the 20th century, and it was a party's access to them at lower levels of politics that really mattered, rather than directly raised money per se. In the decentralized American parties, it was the ability of local parties to help combine different interests and groups of voters that mattered more than centrally directed initiatives. Furthermore, it was that factor that was important in the party's ability to raise sufficient money for national

[9] Herbert E. Alexander, *Financing Politics*, Washington, DC, CQ Press, 1976, p. 20.

campaigns; the local nature of much enterprise, compared with 50 or 70 years later, meant that it was through local and state parties – whether directly or indirectly – that national parties (especially the Democrats) looked for the contacts that would generate campaign funds. So it is the state of the parties at those levels to which attention must be given when considering whether the Democrats had become "under-resourced".

It is necessary to distinguish between long-term and short-term changes in local parties because they were pushing in very different directions. In the longer term, reforms of the funding and administrative arrangements of local governments would weaken the symbiotic relationship between party and government that had characterized the 19th century. In the cities, reform had begun as early as the 1880s, but, in Martin Schiesl's words, by 1920, "politics had not been exorcised from city management. Indeed, four decades of structural reform had intensified rather than depressed partisanship among administrative officials".[10] Moreover, as we have seen, administrative reforms that were designed to weaken the control of parties often made it easier for those parties to control government. While the party machines of the 19th century had often consisted of unstable alliances of local politicos, by the middle to late 1890s, it was becoming easier for party organizations to consolidate their position. Consequently, the following 30 years or so would be the heyday of the urban machine. For the Democrats, this meant that in the cities in which they were the dominant power, their long-term future was generally secured. Nevertheless, they did face three serious difficulties.

The first, which is examined in Section 6, was that consolidation of party power in the cities gave an advantage, though not a large one, to the Republicans in urban America after the mid-1890s.

The second difficulty was that in the Democratic-leaning cities, the disruption prompted by the mid-1890s crisis made more complex the consolidation of that party's advantage – despite the fact that, as noted earlier, in many respects politics was returning to its "normal" state shortly after 1896. Evidence for this comes from data for the share of the vote obtained by the party in congressional elections in districts that fell within the boundaries of non-southern cities containing more than 200,000 people. There were seven such cities in the 1880s; in the core years of party equilibrium (1882–8), three of them leaned Democratic (New York and Brooklyn combined, Boston, and Baltimore) and three leaned Republican

---

[10] Martin J. Schiesl, *The Politics of Efficiency: Municipal Administration and Reform in America, 1880–1920*, Berkeley, University of California Press, 1977, p. 191.

TABLE 4.6. *Democratic Party Share of Vote in Congressional Elections in Large Non-southern Cities, 1882–1938 (as Percentage of Total Vote)*

	New York/ Brooklyn	Philadelphia	Chicago	Boston	St. Louis	Baltimore	Cincinnati
1882	64	44	43	58	49	57	52
1884	59	35	49	49	55	55	47
1886	63	40	19	61	49	71	46
1888	52	48	51	59	45	62	47
1890	54	41	57	63	57	60	42
1892	60	42	62	54	54	58	47
1894	43	27	38	34	47	50	29
1896	45	27	45	29	54	40	40
1898	58	29	50	44	54	48	41
1900	53	26	52	43	54	47	42
1902	57	0	54	49	51	50	29
1904	52	17	29	62	44	50	27
1906	43	16	35	58	39	50	36
1908	49	23	38	51	41	51	45
1910	55	15	51	56	38	51	47
1912	46	34	37	58	40	58	44
1914	50	20	42	59	41	56	46
1916	48	29	43	60	44	53	44
1918	53	25	49	55	45	58	44
1920	38	21	28	46	37	44	43
1922	58	18	48	62	44	48	40
1924	57	14	31	55	38	50	40
1926	64	11	46	62	38	61	39
1928	61	33	49	64	47	53	42
1930	63	21	55	64	14	60	49
1932	68	41	57	62	–	69	47
1934	64	49	63	74	57	62	44
1936	70	59	62	56	61	59	52
1938	59	50	58	64	59	58	41

Congressional districts included in this table are those whose boundaries fell mostly within the city concerned; in 1930 Missouri's House members were chosen on a statewide basis. Brooklyn has been added to New York for all pre-consolidation (1898) years.

(Philadelphia, Chicago, and Cincinnati), while in St. Louis the parties were fairly evenly matched (Table 4.6).[11]

The Democrats' share of the vote in two of the three Republican cities dropped dramatically in the years after 1888 – in Philadelphia from 1894,

[11] Brooklyn was not consolidated into an expanded New York City until 1897, but the two cities are treated as one here for the period before then.

and in Cincinnati (first in 1890, otherwise a year of major gains for the Democratic Party nationally) – and remained low until the 1930s, while none of the Democrat-leaning cities display this pattern. (In Chicago, the Democratic vote share revived on several occasions after 1896 – the Republicans never consolidated as well there.) The Democrats remained the largest party in New York/Brooklyn, but after 1890, it was not until 1926 that they again polled the same share of the vote that had been their median share of the total between 1882 and 1888. The pattern was different again in Boston; the national political crisis had a direct effect, with the Democrats falling well behind the Republicans between 1894 and 1902, but then they regained their dominant position and often came close to matching (or improving on) their 1882–88 performance thereafter. Similarly, in Baltimore the Democrats did badly in 1896 and 1898, and then only just outpolled the Republicans until 1912, when their performance again improved significantly. The marginal city of St. Louis displayed yet another pattern of change. The Democrats actually did better there between 1896 and 1902 than in the 1880s, but then the city swung much more heavily to the Republicans, a situation that was not reversed until the 1930s.

The third difficulty for the Democrats was that urban reform movements in the early 20th century, or pseudo-reform campaigns in the case of those such as William Randolph Hearst's in New York, could harm Democrats in Democratic-dominated cities, just as they hurt Republicans in the cities they dominated.

The key point about this discussion is that in the aftermath of the upheavals of 1893–6, the Democrats did not consolidate as well in those cities, where they might have been expected to take advantage of the opportunities for centralized party control that urban reform offered, as the Republicans did in some of the cities that had leaned towards them earlier. There was no Democratic equivalent of Philadelphia, for instance, and this has contributed to the popular impression that the Democrats were doing much less well in the cities after the mid-1890s than they had done earlier. Undoubtedly, the anti-eastern appearance of the national campaign in 1896 harmed them in some cities in the short and medium term, but there were other factors – such as the role played by William Randolph Hearst in New York – that made major contributions to this failure. During the period under consideration here – that is, up to 1912 – the Democrats' relative inability to consolidate control in "their" large cities meant that they did not acquire consistently all the resources that might be helpful in binding interests together in a party. Quite how much difference this made is difficult to determine; resources do matter, though this was probably one of the less important factors affecting the Democrats' ability to aggregate their potential interests into a national coalition.

4. Were Newly Enfranchised Interests Being Mobilized in Other Parties?

To what extent can the problems of the Democrats in constructing a winning electoral coalition between the mid-1890s and about 1910 be explained by the success of their opponents in mobilizing new interests in their own coalitions? Two claims are sometimes made when compiling evidence that this factor lay at the core of the Democrats' problems. First, the period after 1880 was one of massive immigration into the United States of peoples from southern and eastern Europe, and mostly they settled in larger cities. Secondly, it is claimed that after 1896, it was the Republicans who mobilized a clear majority of urban voters, whereas before then, the Democrats had been dominant in the cities. From this it might be speculated that there was a direct connection between Republican success and the mobilization of new voters. In fact, such a connection is largely spurious.

That there was a major change in the potential electorate between about 1880 and 1920 is undeniable, but it is not true that there was a major Republican advantage that derived from mobilizing this electorate. First, as is well known, the adoption of the Australian Ballot from the late 1880s onwards led to the use of more formal rules of eligibility for voting; previous practices, including the premature naturalization of aliens by partisan judges so that they could vote, were largely eliminated. Immigrants typically waited much longer to acquire the ballot than they had previously, and this reduced the impact that a new electorate might have made. Secondly, as is discussed in more detail later in this chapter and also in Chapter 6, the Republican advantage in the cities has been exaggerated, largely because of the impact that other factors – including weak Democratic presidential candidacies – had on the party's performance. In circumstances in which the Republicans did not enjoy that superiority – as in mid-term election years – their urban advantage was much less pronounced. (Indeed, it largely disappears if Philadelphia, a city in which the Democrats virtually collapsed after the mid-1890s, is excluded from the data.) Thirdly, Republicans could do well in cities, not by mobilizing new voters but by appealing to older immigrants against newer ones. Big

Bill Thompson was still mobilizing older social groups in Chicago at the time of his first election in 1915, and it was only later that he switched to embracing newer groups when he realized that they now afforded the basis of an electoral majority.[12] However, certainly in the years up to 1912, relatively little of the Republican strength in the cities was the result of an imaginative leap by the party in incorporating newer immigrants into their coalition. Fourthly, for all the talk of this being the era of urban America, large cities had to remain a relatively small component of any party coalition overall. Even in 1910, when there were 51 congressional districts that lay primarily within the borders of non-southern cities containing more than 200,000 people, these urban districts constituted no more than 13 per cent of all House districts. (Of course, if these districts had been in the most highly contested states, their significance in presidential elections would have been greater, but less than half of them were in states – like New York and Ohio – that might be marginal for the Democrats in those years when they were capable of constructing a minimum winning coalition.)

Overall, then, there are no compelling arguments to support a claim that Republicans gained an advantage in interest aggregation because they were more successful in mobilizing "new" interests.

5. What Was the Influence of Changes in External Political Structures?

New states had been added to the Union since the Civil War, producing a pronounced Republican bias in the Senate, but the only two additions after the crisis of the early mid-1890s (Utah and Oklahoma) cancelled out any subsequent partisan advantage from that source. (Utah leaned Republican for a time, while Oklahoma was more heavily Democratic.) Nor were there any changes in the *legal* frameworks by which the states could control the selection process of delegates to national conventions. However, there was one institutional reform that did affect interest aggregation by the Democratic party – the passage of anti-fusion laws.

As noted in Chapter 3, one of the techniques of party competition was for a major party to fund third parties that might siphon off some of its opponents' votes. Correspondingly, one of the ways of handling a third party that might do just that was to offer it some kind of fusion arrangement – the sharing of some (or all) candidates on the ticket. On balance, fusion had tended to help the Democrats more, and of course,

---

[12] Douglas Bukowski, *Big Bill Thompson, Chicago and the Politics of Image*, p. 5.

most famously there had been fusion at the head of the ticket in 1896, with Bryan being both the Democrat and the Populist candidate for President. However, it was in helping to construct congressional majorities, and in winning state governorships, that fusion had been most effective. Consider the case of Michigan.

In the 1880, 1884, and 1888 presidential elections, Michigan was won comfortably by the Republicans with pluralities, respectively, of 15.2 per cent, 11.8 per cent, and 4.8 per cent. In straight fights with the Democrats in 1880, the GOP won all nine of the House seats, and in a largely similar situation in 1888, it was to win 9 of the 11 districts. Fusion in 1882 between Democrats and Greenbacks yielded the governorship to the Democrats, and the GOP held only five seats. In 1884, the Republican Party won the gubernatorial election only narrowly and lost an additional House seat. By 1886, the fusion arrangement was collapsing, and the Republicans thereby recovered one of their House seats that year. While fusion was helping the Democrats in Michigan, they were also aided in 1884 and 1886 by the presence of Prohibition candidates on the ballot. Normally, they took votes disproportionately from the Republicans, and in both 1884 and 1886, it is probable that they cost the GOP victory in three House districts. In short, the absence of fusion arrangements between the Republicans and the Prohibitionists harmed their party at the same time as fusion with the Greenbacks had helped the Democrats in a state in which they would normally have been defeated.

In the 1890s, Republicans tended to be more hostile than Democrats to fusion partly because they had found it more difficult than the Democrats to fuse in the previous decade, and partly because the main threat to their maximizing their own vote, the prohibitionists, started to concentrate on interest group tactics and abandoned electoral contestation. After 1896, a number of now-Republican-controlled states introduced anti-fusion laws as a way of gaining political advantage.[13] Consequently, how institutional structures affected the mobilization of interests is of some relevance in explaining the greater problems for the Democrats in aggregating their interests into a winning coalition, but not too much weight should be placed on it. At the presidential level it was the Populists who were destroyed by the 1896 election, and none of the elections up to 1912 featured non-Republican candidates or parties who would have posed a major threat to the unity of the Democrat coalition. Anti-fusion laws

[13] Peter H. Argersinger, "A Place on the Ballot: Fusion Politics and Antifusion Laws", *American Historical Society*, 85 (1980), 287–306.

were probably more important in reducing Democratic strength in House elections – it became more difficult to defeat Republicans by entering into short-term electoral alliances with other political groups.

6. Was There Loss of "Fluidity" in the Electoral Market?

Did some of the Democrats' problem in coalition building after the mid-1890s stem from the fact that Republicans now had a greater hold on sectors of the electorate over whom there had been intense competition earlier? In part, the answer to this is "no", because winning over support from waverers had been a smaller element of electoral strategy since there were relatively few of them. The greater threat to victory came from an "exit" by supporters to third parties that exploited particular grievances or cleavages, rather than insufficient effort in winning over the uncommitted. Consequently, it might be concluded that whatever happened after the mid-1890s did not involve reduced "fluidity" in the electoral market.

What, though, of the popularly accepted argument that the Republicans "captured the urban vote" after the mid-1890s? (Burnham refers to this as "an urban revulsion against the Democrats which lasted into the late 1920s".)[14] Table 4.7 shows the share of the vote obtained by Republicans in congressional elections in districts in non-southern cities with populations of more than 200,000.[15] Several points are striking about it. The Republican share of the vote did increase after 1892, but it was not the major change that is often assumed. In presidential election years, the median increased from 44.2 per cent (in 1884–92) to 52.7 per cent (in 1900–1908). (The median for the entire period 1896–1928 is also 52.7.) However, presidential election years are a poor guide to underlying party strength because of the distorting factor of weak (or strong) presidential candidacies. The mid-term elections are a better, though still imperfect, source. In the mid-term years, the Republican median of 41.3 per cent (in 1882–90) increased to 48.7 per cent (in 1898–1906), while the median for the entire period 1894–1926 is also 48.7. The corresponding figures for the Democrats are 53.7, 46.3, and 46.3. While the clear Democratic edge

---

[14] Walter Dean Burnham and William N. Chambers (eds.), *The American Party Systems,* p. 299.

[15] The congressional districts included were those in which the voting population was primarily resident in cities of more than 200,000. Obviously, some districts were mixed in that they contained residents both from these cities and from those outside city boundaries; these districts have been included if more than half the potential voters were urban dwellers.

TABLE 4.7. *Republican Share of the Vote in Congressional Elections in Non-southern Cities of More Than 200,000 People, 1882–1938 (as Percentage)*

	Presidential Election Years	Mid-term Election Years (Democratic Share of Vote in Parentheses)
1882		41.3 (55.2)
1884	43.6	
1886		39.5 (52.1)
1888	45.1	
1890		43.0 (53.7)
1892	44.2	
1894		52.6 (38.2)
1896	55.6	
1898		50.2 (47.5)
1900	52.7	
1902		48.7 (46.3)
1904	54.8	
1906		48.7 (38.3)
1908	51.5	
1910		45.6 (44.7)
1912	33.7	
1914		42.9 (40.2)
1916	49.2	
1918		47.1 (43.4)
1920	56.8	
1922		47.0 (47.2)
1924	54.9	
1926		50.0 (46.3)
1928	50.0	
1930		50.3 (48.1)
1932	39.8	
1934		37.1 (56.1)
1936	34.9	
1938		41.4 (53.8)

in the cities before the early 1890s disappeared after 1894, the subsequent Republican advantage afterwards was not huge.

However, that is only part of the answer. As was noted in Section 3, changes in urban politics were in the direction of greater party control over municipal government. The instability associated with party machines in the middle to late 19th century was replaced by much more stable control by a single party, and with greater security of tenure for those leaders who happened to be in power in that party. Thus, cities where the Democrats had been in the minority, but had still been capable of mounting an electoral threat between presidential election years, became more firmly Republican – these cases included Cincinnati and Philadelphia. Moreover, in congressional elections, for example, Republicans enjoyed a much larger share of the vote after the early 1900s in previously contested cities like St. Louis and San Francisco than they had had up to the early 1890s. The result was that some highly competitive states, including California, became more difficult for the Democrats to win, while a previous Border state bastion, like Missouri, could be won by Republicans both in some presidential elections and in a few gubernatorial elections as well. While this greater party penetration of urban electorates would have provided a Republican advantage in some cities irrespective of the events of 1893–6, there can be little doubt that being out of office at national and state levels at a time when the opportunity for urban party consolidation was present was significant for the Democrats in some states. Had it been the Republicans who were split by the dispute over silver – because they had won the election of 1892 – then the advantage during a period of urban party consolidation would surely have rested with the Democrats. Consequently, electoral failure in the six or seven years after 1896 probably did have long-term disadvantages in terms of their ability to mobilize urban electorates in presidential elections.

Where electoral "fluidity" really does seem to have hurt the Democrats was in the Border states, and more needs to be said about this. As noted earlier, there is evidence of increasing competitiveness in these states from the beginning of the 1880s, so that by the mid-1890s, the Republican Party would likely have been in a position to win elections there even if there had not been an economic depression in 1893. Contending with Republicans on equal terms in these five states (six after 1907) meant that the Democrats were more likely to lose one of them because of adverse circumstances locally. Of course, to the extent that the interests the party was trying to aggregate were national (or at least regional) in nature, the appeal to voters at a presidential election would not be affected by whether the party presently controlled state government or not. However, local circumstances did (and still do) come into play – a popular governor could help his party in the appeal for votes (although an unpopular incumbent might weaken its chances), local money might be more forthcoming to the party in power, and so on. Most importantly, more resources (including money and visits to the states by the presidential candidate) had to be diverted away from other competitive states to shore up support in the Border states.

However, this new disadvantage must be placed in context. As can be seen from Table 4.4, only one of the Border states changed category with respect to the relative support it gave the Democrats in 1908–20 when this period is compared with 1880–92. (Delaware moved from being Heartland to Contested Territory.) Although the Border states had become more competitive, they were still states that the Democrats would probably have had to win if they were to win presidential elections. These states were still more Democratic leaning than most of the northern states. One consequence was that Democratic defeats in presidential elections were to appear much greater than they did in the pre-1896 era because the Republicans now could well carry many Border states. (Even in close elections, not all the Border states might be won by the Democrats – thus in 1916, Wilson, with a 3.1 per cent national plurality, failed to carry Delaware and West Virginia.)

As in the earlier sections of this chapter, a number of considerations contributing to the Democrats' disadvantage in aggregating interests have been identified, but none has emerged that seems to account satisfactorily for why the Democrats did quite so badly as they did between 1896 and 1912. Not only did they lose four presidential elections in a row, but after 1896 itself, they also did not come that close to winning any of them until their victory of 1912. None of the possible factors examined so far can account for the scale of their failure in these years. We must now turn to the first of three factors relating to the ability of leadership in the party to aggregate interests in support of a winning coalition; the second and third factors are discussed in Sections 8 and 9, respectively.

7. Was There an Absence of Potential Leaders in the Party?

Perhaps the most interesting aspect of the Democrats' performance in the years between 1896 and 1912 is just how few public offices they occupied until 1910. This was most evident at the lower levels of public office. The lower chambers of state legislatures provide a good illustration. In the median northern state between 1877 and 1889, the proportion of seats held by the Democrats ranged from 29.7 per cent of total seats to 40.8 per cent; between 1897 and 1909 (inclusive), the share of seats in the median state was never higher than 25 per cent (in 1898) and fell as low as 16 per cent (in 1904).

However, for the purposes of recruiting a national political leader, in the short-to-medium term it was the absence of incumbents in the higher-level offices that was much more significant. Outside the South, the median number of years served by Democratic governors between 1901 and 1913 was 2 (the mean was 2.6), while the number of Democratic appointments to the U.S. Senate was 27 out of 132, or 20.5 per cent of the total appointments. Now in some respects, these levels of success might be seen as being not that much lower than the modest levels attained by the party in the 1880s. The corresponding figures for a similar 12-year period, 1879–91, were a median of 3 years and a mean of 4.07 for gubernatorial elections, and 27.7 per cent success rate for senatorial appointments. However, this decline was actually catastrophic in several ways.

First, the party was unsuccessful in electing governors in the five states that had been the key to victory in the earlier years. In California, a governor served out his term in 1897–8, but thereafter there was no governor in the state in the years up to 1913; in Indiana, the party did not occupy the governor's mansion until after 1908; in both New Jersey and New York, it took until the end of 1910 to achieve this office; in Ohio, Democrats held the governorship only in 1907 and again after 1908. Of the 60 possible years they could have held those five governorships between 1901 and 1913, the Democrats did so for just 13 years, nearly all towards the end of the period, compared with 38 possible years in a similar period of 12 years between 1879 and 1891. Successful coalition building had depended on selecting as presidential candidates prominent politicians from marginal states – that had been the main basis of party strategy in earlier years – and governors were the most obvious source. Deprived of that source, the Democrats were in trouble.

Secondly, although senators were a less useful set of recruits for a presidential bid than governors, because usually they did not exercise much control inside their state parties, an absence of suitable senators increased the Democrats' woes. (Senators tended to have been wealthy participants in the party, rather than having been directly involved over a long period in the administration of party affairs.) Excluding the South and the Border states, 17 Democrats (out of a possible 112) were appointed between 1900/1901 and 1912/13, but only 6 of them were from states in the Old North, and not a single one of these appointments was made before the end of 1908. (All but one of these 6 – the exception being Maine – were from the five states that had been the most competitive in the earlier period.)

Thirdly, having their politicians in prominent elected offices was a matter of greater importance for parties in the early 20th century than it had been earlier – for several reasons. On the one hand, presidential candidates were expected to play a more prominent role in campaigning than they did in the days when they retreated to their houses and waited for visits by their supporters. Personality now mattered more in politics, and presidential candidates were expected to lead from the front. While James Blaine had been criticized for such an approach in 1884, 20 years later the older practice had been abandoned. On the other hand, the only alternative source of "personalities" to that of major politicians had dried up. For much of the 19th century major military leaders had been attractive candidates for the parties, especially for a party that had few elected officeholders on whom to draw. With the partial exception of the Spanish-American War, there were no major wars that could generate senior officer "heroes" once the Civil War generation had become too old. Thus, Winfield Scott Hancock in 1880 was the last of a long line of such candidacies – with the sole 20th century exception of Dwight Eisenhower – and it was not until late in the 20th century that an alternative source of personalities for the parties (film and sports stars) became acceptable. Electing major public officials mainly in the South, (decreasingly) in the Border states, and only in some parts of the West, the Democrats lacked plausible candidates to oppose the Republicans in presidential campaigns.

Fourthly, in these circumstances, the person who could dominate Democratic presidential nominations in the years after 1896 was William Jennings Bryan. In assessing the significance of this for the party, it is important to distinguish between Bryanism and Bryan himself. The kind of rural radicalism that Bryanism represented was now an essential part of the revised Democratic coalition, and it would remain so. As late as 1932, a Democratic victory would be based, and arguably would have to be based, on a candidate who spoke for that wing of the party, and it was only with the New Deal itself that Bryanism was transformed by Franklin Roosevelt into an urban-based liberalism. In the South, and in parts of the West, the lasting legacy of 1893–6 was that the party now had a constituency that favoured a certain kind of economic interventionism grounded in egalitarian values, but values that could be traced right back to the Jeffersonian era. Interest aggregation by the Democrats had to attend to the demands of that constituency. Their problem was Bryan. There were two reasons why Bryan was an unsuitable candidate after 1896, even though it is arguably the case that he brought the Democrats

much closer to victory in 1896 than anyone else could have done that
year.

One reason was that irrespective of whatever he did, the image of
Bryan, as the leader of rural radicalism at a time of heightened political
conflict, would persist; Bryan would always be anathema to many Old
North voters because of the events of 1896. A far more important reason,
though, was that Bryan's undoubted egalitarianism went hand in glove
with a kind of anti-urban, social conservatism. As an egalitarian, Bryan
could be flexible. For example, in his later political career he was careful
to pay more attention to the interests of industrial workers and of trade
unions than he did in the campaign of 1896. By 1916 Bryan, in some
ways, could be seen as a modern form of left-wing politician, and not
just a leader of agricultural America. However, he never lost his distaste
for urban life, and for the kinds of values and lifestyles evident in the
cities, especially in its immigrant communities. The Bryan who testified
for the prosecution at the 1925 Scopes trial in Tennessee was not an old
man who had wandered away from his original political path. To him,
Darwinism was an anti-egalitarian doctrine that threatened the egalitarian
values and policies for which he stood. Yet in the press reports of his
performance on the witness stand, he came across as someone who was
trying to defend the indefensible and protect the values of a dying rural
and socially conservative America. Bryan's conservatism, and his belief
in the superiority of rural and small-town life, had always been as much
a part of his politics as his egalitarianism, and he was not so cynical as
to refrain from making the kind of comments that made it impossible
for *him* to expand the Democrats' electoral base much beyond its 1896
boundaries.

The Bryan problem for the Democrats was that although he never held
elective office after 1896, he retained a unique position in the party; in the
absence of governors from major states, the party had little alternative but
to turn to Bryan. When they did look elsewhere (in 1904), the result was
even worse; a nonentity of a judge (Alton Parker) was no kind of candidate
to be selected in an era when personality mattered more. The party was
stuck with Bryan until it started to be more successful and had alternative
candidates from whom to choose – and that is what happened after 1910.
Before then, the Democrats were caught in a vicious cycle. Every four
years, presidential elections would pull the party down, whereas in the
pre-1892 era, presidential elections had tended to restore the balance
between the parties – with the advantage lying with the "out" party. Now
the Democrats found themselves suffering major defeats at a variety of

levels of office every four years as the Republican presidential coattails took effect. Starting from such low levels, the recoveries in mid-term years were relatively modest – and insufficient to provide the Democrats with a new pool of leaders. Two years later the cycle would begin again.

In many ways, the post-1896 political world was not that different from the earlier era. But the balance between the parties in the previous era was so precarious that relatively small changes to that equilibrium could then make the party system behave very differently. One of the main differences between the two periods was that disunity in the party holding the presidency – the factor that had been the real engine providing for balance between the parties – became more manageable in the short term. As it became more manageable, the "self-correcting" features of the party system became less strong, and the party that was out of office had to do more to win. However, "doing more" meant having suitable candidates, and that in turn meant winning elections below the level of the presidency; but that was more difficult because of the setbacks that occurred in presidential election years. But why was it becoming easier *in the short run* for the party in the White House to manage the forces that prompted party fragmentation?

The answer is the declining relative importance of patronage. Here it is important to be clear about what is being contended. As Martin Shefter has argued, the Pendleton Act of 1883 did not transform American politics – there were as many patronage positions at the beginning of the 20th century as there were 20 years earlier.[16] In one sense, all the act did was to create new categories of (more technical) jobs that had the protection of civil service rules, while leaving the appointments that mattered most in the hands of the president.[17] However, governments at all levels in what came to be known as the Progressive Era were having to respond to demands for interventionism by numerous interests adversely affected by various aspects of urbanization and industrialization. Patronage had been important for the activists in the party because nothing else was. There was still insufficient patronage, and therefore, there were still the

---

[16] Martin Shefter, *Political Parties and the State: The American Historical Experience*, Princeton, NJ, Princeton University Press, 1994, pp. 74–5.

[17] As G. Calvin Mackenzie notes of the effects of the Pendleton Act, "[I]t was a long time before any substantial number of federal jobs were brought under civil service coverage, and most of those of greatest consequence to the president never were." Mackenzie, "The State of the Presidential Appointment Process", in G. Calvin Mackenzie (ed.), *Innocent Until Nominated: The Breakdown of the Presidential Appointments Process*, Washington, DC, Brookings Institution, 2001, p. 14.

disgruntled who were failing to obtain patronage, but in a more complex world, where politicians were trying to broker deals on substantive matters of public policy, this was less disruptive for the party in power. In part, it became less disruptive because the disputes over public policy brought with them organized groups of all kinds – groups that could sometimes be mobilized in support of political leaders. In a sense, these groups acted as both a stabilizing force and a countervailing force to the necessarily more individualistic politics that patronage had generated within the parties. Patronage would become less central as a source of party unity and disunity, even while the levels of patronage appointment remained high. Thus, the party that had gotten to occupy the White House now not only had its cake but got to eat it as well. Consequently, opposition became more difficult – at least in the short term – because governing parties did not tend to fragment in quite the way that they had. However, in the longer term – that is, by about 1909 – the Republicans would be faced with the problem that intra-party disruption having its origins in disagreements about public policy could be even more serious than squabbles over patronage distribution.

Unlike the Democratic Party, whose coalition-building task became somewhat more complicated after the 1890s, the Republicans faced a task that was still rather similar to the one they had had in the earlier period. For them, constructing a national coalition depended on uniting much of the Old North with parts of the West. "Dumping" much of the West, as they had done successfully in the 1896 election, made sense only so long as the central issue was silver. As that issue lost its centrality, so it became both possible, and desirable, to present the party as being more than just the instrument of eastern capitalism. Yet while that was becoming more possible, so was the nature of politics changing – with the rise of the politics of regulation.

As noted already, during the Progressive Era both major political parties became subjected to demands for new kinds of public policies. The rapid transformation of American society and economy, together with the pressures that placed on a decentralized political system that had been designed originally for a rural country, brought claims for social, economic, and political reform. Many states were to respond to such reforms with legislation on electoral and party procedures, on the regulation of railroad and insurance companies, on the taxation of corporations, and on the legal regulation of employment practices. Although there were instances of conflict within the Democratic Party between their progressive and conservative wings – that between Missouri Governor Joseph Folk and his party in the state legislature being one example – such disputes generally posed fewer problems for the Democrats. There were two main reasons. One was that in a majority of states where party organizations still survived – that is, outside the South – it was the Republicans who controlled state government at the time that the clamour for progressive reforms began. Usually the party controlling a state governorship and legislature faced greater difficulties in keeping the party sufficiently united to prevent subsequent electoral loss. The other reason is that nationally, the interests that were being regulated had greater links to the Republicans than to the Democrats, and in the longer term that was always likely to make party management at that level more controversial for the GOP.

The advantages that the Republicans had enjoyed after 1896, therefore, became offset during the years 1909–12 by the problem of reconciling the two wings of their party. Under those conditions, it became possible for Democrats to get out of the vicious cycle to which they had been confined by the relatively small, but hugely important, shifts in the dynamics of the party system after the mid-1890s. The most significant aspect of that exit from the cycle was through sub-national electoral victories, so that they finally obtained a much larger pool of leaders from whom they could choose a presidential candidate in 1912. The result was that for the first time since 1896, Bryan failed to get a nomination when he really wanted it. By 1910–12, therefore, the Democrats had finally rid themselves of the main long-term problem that the events of 1893–6 had posed for them; they had been able to re-establish a "pool" of political leaders around whom a national coalition might be built at a presidential election.

8. Was the Democratic Party Controlled by Just a Few Interests?

The argument presented in the last section was that it was the absence of any strong alternatives to William Jennings Bryan that lay at the heart of the Democrats' difficulties in producing a presidential candidate who could unite the different interests within the coalition. But was this just a matter of the person (Bryan), or was the problem more fundamental in that the party had become controlled by a faction that wished either to exclude, or to minimize the influence of, other factions?

Many "gold Democrats" of 1896 returned eventually to the party once the silver issue diminished in importance. There were new battles to be fought, and after 1896, Bryan was not so much foisted on the party by one faction as that he placed himself at its heart. While division in the Democratic Party after 1896 was exacerbated by the experiences of 1893–6, it was more a matter of that experience re-shaping division where division had always existed than it was of creating new cleavages and factions.

Or rather, the factions that were to emerge – and that later were to engage
in an intra-party civil war in the 1920s – were not firmly drawn in opposition to each other in the years up to 1912. The later conflicts may have
had their origins in a change in the composition of the Democratic Party
before 1912, but at that time, leaders could still unite the different interests in the party, rather than themselves being mere representatives of a
dominant faction.

An example of this re-shaping of pre-existing division after the mid-
1890s was New York, where the years of turbulence effected a split
between Tammany Hall and its boss, Richard Croker, and the ex-governor
and U.S. Senator David Hill, who had usually been willing to ally with
Tammany in the past. The result was that Hill now led the anti-Tammany
forces. As Richard L. McCormick notes:

> Badly split in 1893 and 1894, the Democrats continued to be paralyzed for the
> rest of the decade. After the loss in 1894, the party's warring factions briefly
> made peace, but William Jennings Bryan's nomination for president in 1896 inter-
> rupted the reunion. While Bryan won the formal, if unenthusiastic, support of
> Tammany Hall in New York City, he got only silence from David B. Hill and
> active opposition from the waning Cleveland Democracy. Under these conditions,
> a new party cleavage replaced the old one. Richard Croker's support for Bryan
> greatly enhanced the Tammany leader's authority in the Democratic party, and
> two years afterward he took control of the state organization. Ironically, Hill now
> became the symbol of unbossed Democracy; demoralized upstate Democrats, as
> well as old Clevelandites, looked to him to lead the battle against Tammany. The
> party's divisions helped to prevent the Democrats from fashioning a unified policy
> program and so lessened interparty conflict on state issues.[18]

Consequently, while the immediate aftermath of 1896 did hurt the
Democrats in some cities and states, where it did so it tended to build
on older intra-party conflicts and to modify them. In general, it did not
directly create new and permanent factions whose disputes would lead to
domination in the party by a single faction and the imposition of particular presidential candidates on it.

9. Changes in the Rules for Selecting Presidential Candidates

There were no significant changes in the way that Democrats nominated their presidential candidates in the years between 1896 and 1912.

---

[18] Richard L. McCormick, *From Realignment to Reform: Political Change in New York
State, 1893–1910*, Ithaca and London, Cornell University Press, 1981, pp. 104–5.

However, in changed circumstances, the old rules did contribute to the Democrats' difficulties. Since the 1830s, and in order to protect southern interests, the party had had a "two-thirds" rule whereby a candidate required the votes of two-thirds of delegates in order to be nominated. The impact of this rule varied depending on the circumstances. Like all super-majoritarian rules, it could favour the "lowest common denominator", making it more likely than with a majoritarian procedure that a candidate who was least offensive to a large number of delegates would be selected. Thus, in some circumstances, unknowns and nonentities were more likely to be chosen. The procedure also ensured that the work of the national convention could be long and arduous, although during this period, only in 1912 were there a large number of ballots (45) for nominating the candidate.

However, when there was just a single well-known and prominent candidate in the party, as was the case with Bryan after 1896, the rules actually advantaged such a person by making it more difficult for moderately well known opponents to stage a breakthrough in the balloting process. The kind of logrolling that might have propelled such a challenger forward under a majoritarian system, because less-committed supporters of Bryan could see that there were alternatives to him, was difficult to mount. The potential waverers would never see sufficient strength in that challenger to warrant breaking with the likely nominee. In other words, Bryan's position in the party was further consolidated by the existing rules for nominating presidential candidates in a way that had not been the case for a candidate before 1892.

10. The Democratic Party in 1912

The central argument presented in this chapter has been that the most important problem facing the Democrats after 1896 concerned the role played by leadership in aggregating the different interests of the party. In particular, exclusion from many major public offices in the North meant that the party did not have a sufficient pool of candidates from whom a plausible presidential challenge might be chosen. With some important modifications, the old coalition consisting of the South and the Border states, on the one side, and some large northern states, on the other side, was still viable. It was exactly that kind of majority that was rebuilt in the mid-term elections of 1910 (see Table 4.3). The party that won a majority in the House that year, and also won several governorships, was essentially a re-assembling of an older party coalition – though with

some important modifications to it.[19] Yet at the presidential level, these
necessary modifications took on a greater significance. It was more complicated to realize the potential coalition there, both because more states
now had to be aggregated into an Electoral College majority and because
the range of interests represented in the most winnable states was more
complex. Nevertheless, if coalition construction for the Democrats was
more difficult, it was still feasible. But how does this argument square
with a traditional argument to the effect that the Democrats returned to
power in Washington in 1912 merely because of the split in the Republican
Party?

Examining the *relative* performance of Democratic Parties in all the
states – assessing what a winning coalition would have to look like, as
we have done in part of this chapter – cannot tell us how likely it was
that the party would actually win a given state. It merely tells us what a
winning coalition would probably look like. Bearing this point in mind, it
might be questioned whether the two occasions on which the Democrats
did win presidential elections between 1896 and 1932 could be said to
constitute their having constructed real national majorities. Of 1912 it
is often said that Woodrow Wilson won merely because the Republican
vote was divided between two "Republican" candidates, while 1916 is
dismissed as a narrow victory obtained by an incumbent president at a
time when America might shortly be entering a major war. What should
be made of such arguments?

Much more will be said in the next chapter about the coalition Wilson
inherited and how he might have consolidated it. For the moment, it is
important to be clear about the nature of the issue raised by this claim.
It cannot be denied that the divisions in the Republican Party that were
evident from 1909 onwards provided an opportunity for the Democrats.
However, as we have seen, the propensity for a majority party to fragment does not indicate that a national party system is not in some sense
competitive; rather, it may be a feature of a particular kind of competitiveness. The crucial question, therefore, is what would have happened had the high-profile split between the conservative and progressive wings of the Republican Party not produced a third-party campaign
in 1912, but merely sniping and bickering between the two wings, and
with incumbent William Howard Taft as the party's only candidate. It

[19] The party also did well at lower levels of office; for example, in the median northern
state in 1910, the Democrats won 42.4 per cent of the seats in the lower chamber of the
state legislature.

TABLE 4.8. *Size of Democratic Majorities in the House of Representatives, 1878–1888 and 1910–1914 (as a Proportion of the Total Number of Seats in the House)*

	% of Total Seats
1878	51.4
1882	61.5
1884	56.2
1886	52.3
1910	58.3
1912	66.7
1914	53.1

is important to focus on Taft, rather than on Theodore Roosevelt, as the Republican candidate because the latter's personal popularity, combined with the fact that he was taking on mainstream Republicanism, inevitably would have put Wilson at a disadvantage in 1912. Roosevelt would probably have won such a contest, but that can tell us little about the underlying balance between the parties. It is by focussing on Taft, in the absence of Roosevelt in the 1912 contest, that we can see the state of the *parties*.

In the absence of poll data, no one can be sure how many of those who actually voted for Theodore Roosevelt would not have voted at all or would have voted for Wilson. However, arguably the most plausible case is that the Democrats would have done sufficiently well outside of the Republicans' northeastern bastions to elect Wilson.

Four arguments can be made in support of the case that Wilson would still have been elected in a straight fight against Taft.

First, the Democrats had already demonstrated their ability to win a majority of votes in congressional elections (in 1910) and were to do so again in 1914; 1912 was not a freak result, therefore, that was dependent on a formal division in the Republican Party. Indeed, the size of the party's majorities in the House in 1912–14 compare favourably with the four majorities they had between 1878 and 1888 (see Table 4.8); in this respect, the party was not evidently in a weaker situation than it had been earlier.

Secondly, the party was doing just as well at lower levels of office between 1910 and 1916, and this suggests that the Democratic revival was deep-rooted. Consider the share of the seats obtained in the lower chamber of legislatures by the Democrats in the median state after each election; their worst situation in the years 1911–17 was when they held 34.2 per cent of the seats, whereas in 1877–89, their worst performance was when the median was only 31.7 per cent. Moreover, the median of these median performances in 1877–89 was only 35.8 per cent – only slightly higher than their worst performance in the years 1911–17. This does not suggest that the Democratic Party had become a long-term minority party that in 1912 was doing no more than benefit from the formal splitting of its opposition.

Thirdly, there was one state (Oklahoma) in which Roosevelt did not appear on the ballot in 1912. In a state that was part of the Democratic Heartland, Bryan had won 4.7 per cent more of the vote than Taft in 1908. In 1912, Wilson's plurality over Taft in Oklahoma was 11.2 per cent. Increased support of that kind in the Border states, Midwest, and West would have been enough for Wilson to have scored a relatively easy victory, irrespective of how well Taft did in the northeast.

Fourthly, the disagreements between the two wings of the Republican Party had reached such an intensity by 1912 that it is difficult to believe that at the very least, there would not have been a considerable number of voter abstentions by Republicans in those parts of the country where insurgent progressivism had been strong; even in the absence of Roosevelt, Taft's task of getting all potential Republican voters to support the party would have been a hard one.

Wilson's victory in 1912 was one for a party that had been able to remove the main impediment to its competitiveness at the national level – the absence of electable leaders. It was a victory that built on the successful partial re-assembling of the constituent components of the late 19th century coalition, though with important modifications to that coalition and to the ideas it propagated. The split in the Republican Party in 1912 distorted the victory in some respects – for example, in giving the Democrats a much larger congressional majority than they could otherwise have expected. However, 1912 was not an aberration – the Democrats did not win by default in an era otherwise dominated by its opponent. The problem for the party was whether it could use its tenure in office to re-shape its electoral coalition, and thereby make it easier for it to win elections in the future.

5

Woodrow Wilson and the Failure to Re-shape the Democratic Coalition, 1912–1920

In 1913, the Democratic Party was in a situation similar to the one in which it would find itself exactly 20 years later. It was possible for the party to win a presidential election and also majorities in Congress with a modified version of its long-standing coalition. Yet on both occasions it faced the same problem: The breadth of the coalition, and the number of states that had to be included in it, made it fragile. It would likely always be vulnerable to a resurgent Republican Party. The Democrats needed to add groups of regular voters in the North to their existing coalition to make themselves more secure against this threat. From 1933 onwards, Franklin Roosevelt succeeded in doing just that, and subsequently, the Democrats could fight elections on at least even terms with the Republicans for the next few decades. This did not happen under Wilson. Indeed, by 1920, not only had his administration created intra-party divisions, but longer-standing differences between different elements of the Democratic coalition were increasingly apparent – conflicts that would last beyond the succeeding decade. This last point might suggest that irrespective of whatever Wilson had done to re-shape the party's coalition earlier in his administration, the Democrats would still have faced difficulties by the beginning of the 1920s. That may be true, but a "re-shaped" party might still have been in a better position than it actually was to recover from the problems it was to face. Thus, it is important to examine the differences between the conditions that Wilson and Roosevelt faced at the beginning of their respective administrations, and how their strategies for improving the position of their party differed. As we shall see, one protected his party's immediate interests, and indeed protected the role of parties in the political system, while the other was able to expand his party's coalition, but at the price of marginalizing the party in the process of governing.

Circumstances favoured Roosevelt more than they favoured Wilson in the efforts to make a fragile party coalition a more secure one. Nevertheless, there was an opportunity for Wilson to add to the "building blocks" that were available to his party at the national level, but he acted inconsistently and that opportunity was lost. How and why that opportunity was lost, and how and why FDR took advantage of the opportunity he had 20 years later, are the focus of this chapter. However, we must begin by examining the changing nature of the relationships between voters and parties, because those relationships constrained what party leaders could do in the early to middle 20th century to make their coalitions more secure.

1. The Linkage of Voters and Parties

As we have seen, from the Jacksonian era onwards, individual voters in America were largely linked to a particular party in one or both of two ways. The first way was essentially "tribal", and there was not necessarily a national pattern to these kinds of links. The second aspect of the voter-party linkage was economic interest. The two main parties tended to appeal to people with rather different stakes in the American economy, and this was reflected in the kind of policies on the role of government in the economy (such as on tariffs) that the parties might support. Partly because of some regional variations in the economic situation of seemingly similar interests, and partly because this economic cleavage could cross-cut the tribal cleavage in a two-party system, the differences in policy between the major parties were often complex. However, by the time Wilson entered the White House, the 19th century links between voters and their parties were already starting to be modified in several ways.

First, the changing scale of American political society meant that voters became more distanced from their politicians; for example, in Massachusetts, between three and four times more people were voting in a typical state assembly district in the late 1880s than 40 years earlier, and this relative gap between politicians and voters continued to grow.[1] More important, perhaps, than the changing ratio of voters to elected politicians was the huge increase in the number of people eligible to vote. With population growth, politicians were increasingly more remote from

---

[1] Alan Ware, *The American Direct Primary*, p. 69.

voters than they had been in a predominantly small-town and rural America. Although urban party organizations were probably better structured and could conduct their business more efficiently than they had done in the middle to late 19th century, necessarily their armies of patronage appointees were less directly involved with most of the potential voters than had been their predecessors. Scale did matter for the efficacy of party activity.

Secondly, from the late 19th century, the more participatory elements of electioneering gave way to forms that involved the voter as spectator rather than as participant.[2] For example, the marching companies in which many participated in the 19th century were generally replaced by grand parades in which a higher proportion of those present were merely spectators. Along with the changing scale of American society, this, too, tended to weaken the links between voters and parties.

Thirdly, the advent of registration laws in the 1890s meant that parties' direct interests in mobilizing new immigrants declined; it was much less possible to round up the willing among the newly disembarked and use a partisan local judiciary to grant them voting rights. Indeed, one of the most important features of the cities in the period from the 1890s to the 1930s was the growth of a politically un-mobilized immigrant population. The greatest foreign immigration into the United States occurred between the 1880s and the 1920s, yet not only were the parties probably ill-placed to mobilize it effectively because of increasing problems of scale, but after the 1890s, they could also less readily exploit registration loopholes to enlist as voters those who had newly arrived in the country.

Fourthly, from the 1890s, parties became the subject of direct criticism by political reformers. Especially in the West, an assault on party power became a strategy for countering economic power. As with earlier reform movements, the reforms actually enacted into law often had as much to do with the perceived self-interest of politicians as with the political strength of reformers themselves. Yet in the early 20th century, popular expressions of anti-party sentiment were much more widely heard than they had been earlier, and this changed the environment in which parties now operated. Although the parties survived, and many voters were still party loyalists in 1912, neither of the major parties could claim the same kind of unquestioning voter loyalty that they could 20 years earlier. Those potential voters who were available to being won over by argument or

---

[2] See Michael E. McGerr, *The Decline of Popular Politics*.

image, rather than their merely responding to party attachments, were greater in number than they had been.

Fifthly, to the potential voter in 1912, the American political world no longer appeared to be such a party-dominated one. Non-partisan interest groups – both in the economic sphere and also lobbying on behalf of issues like prohibition – were far more active than they had been and helped to create an impression of a polity in which parties were only one kind of political actor. Thus, Joel Silbey can speak of

the success of what Daniel T. Rodgers describes as "the explosion of aggressive, politically active pressure groups into the space left by the recession of traditional political loyalties". This nonpartisan occupation had significant long-range effects on the political nation. The emerging organizational society of technicians, bureaucrats, and impersonal decision makers had no faith in or commitment to mass politics, especially as expressed through the parties. As their numbers and reach increased, their outlook became more widespread.[3]

Indirectly this helped to loosen the earlier ties that bound a person to a party. Of course, this development, along with the preceding four, would be that much further advanced in 1933 than it was in 1913.

Clearly, in these circumstances, building long-term support for a party could not be generated by attempts to create or reinforce social identities. Such a strategy might prevent the erosion of support by loyalists, but it could not be the basis of party coalition building. Increasingly, parties had to look to providing reasons for support that lay in their advancement of particular kinds of interest, and in turn that meant, at least in part, placating the various interest groups that were now acting as intermediaries between some of the voters who shared these interests and the parties. Parties had to be able to demonstrate that interests would be harmed if their opponents were allowed to control the national government. Of course, this had always been one element of 19th century politics; the Democrats' ideology of limited government played on the fear of Southerners and Catholic immigrants alike that their enemies would "do something to them" if they were allowed to. By the early 20th century, though, this aspect of coalition construction had become far more important – as the direct effects of tribalism waned in a political universe where party was seen as being less central. Consequently, interest aggregation was now more complex. To a large extent, aggregation had been outside the control of the parties nationally in the previous century; the very localism of party attachments meant that nationally, the parties were dealing with

3 Joel H. Silbey, *The American Political Nation, 1838–1893*, p. 240; Daniel T. Rodgers, "In Search of Progressivism", *Reviews in American History*, 10 (1982), 114.

distributions of support that were fixed by other factors. What remained for the leadership at that time was to devise ideas and symbols in such a way as to bring on board as many non-tribal loyalists as possible, without threatening the tribal base.

Consequently, while they were not programmatic by comparison with European parties, by the second decade of the 20th century, American parties had to discuss certain public issues, and the stance of their politicians on those issues was much more central to electoral politics than it had been. As Gerring puts it:

> Whereas in the nineteenth century, Democratic campaigns were organized for the purpose of celebrating and preserving the past, in the twentieth century the emphasis shifted toward the earnest search for political and social reform. It was no longer sufficient to invoke the ways of the founders or the patented truths of all republics.[4]

The task facing any party that wanted to broaden the base of its support was to find ways of permanently engaging those groups of voters with ideas that they would find valuable (in relation to their interests) in the medium-to-long term, and not just in the immediate future. As we shall see, not only were the underlying circumstances less favourable to Wilson than they were to be for Roosevelt, but the strategies deployed by the latter were also to prove far more effective – even if that meant changing the role of party in relation to government.

2. Un-mobilized "Pools" of Voters

It used to be accepted widely that during the New Deal era, many previously Republican voters switched to voting for the Democratic Party. James Sundquist, for instance, spoke of "millions of voters who switched from the Republican to the Democratic party".[5] On this view, the Democratic Party's strength grew because of dissatisfaction of many Republicans with their party; the Democrats were simply the beneficiaries of that. However, for some time it has been recognized that this model – in which voters acted and parties responded – is a misrepresentation of what happened. In the words of Nie and his colleagues:

> The shift to a Democratic majority occurred largely through the entry of new groups into the active electorate between 1920 and 1936. These new entrants consisted of young voters entering the electorate and older (largely immigrant

---

[4] John Gerring, *Party Ideologies in America, 1828–1996,* p. 192.
[5] James L. Sundquist, *Dynamics of the Party System,* Washington, DC, Brookings Institution, 1973, p. 200.

or second generation) Americans voting for the first time.... [E]ach successive group which came of age in the twenties was different (more Democratic, less Republican) than the populace which it joined. This consistent Democratic bias in the partisanship of the young had the cumulative effect of changing the partisan balance from a relatively even division to a clear Democratic majority.[6]

Roosevelt had a double advantage in terms of the electorate he faced in 1932, compared with the situation of Democrats 20 or more years earlier. First, there was a relatively large number of un-mobilized voters. One of the main sources of this "pool" was the immigrant population; 18.5 million people migrated to the United States between 1900 and 1930 – about 15 per cent of the country's population at the later date. These people and their children constituted a major proportion of the citizens who joined the active electorate in 1932 and 1936. Secondly, even before the onset of the Great Depression, the proportion of Democrats in the population was growing: "[T]he groups which entered the electorate in 1920, 1924 and 1928 – at a time when the Republican party should have been more successful in recruiting young citizens – were ... substantially more Democratic than the population".[7] Whatever the reasons for this growing Democratic advantage before the Great Depression, demographic changes seem to have been working increasingly to the advantage of the Democratic Party from 1920 onwards.

It is quite possible that they were already working to the advantage of the party even before then. Evidence presented in the next chapter suggests that, relatively, the Democratic Party became a more urban-based party in terms of its support around 1918. Indeed, if the long-term future of the Democratic Party was to lie in its developing links with the city-dwelling immigrants and their children, then it must be admitted that much of that resource was already living in the United States by 1912. By far the largest migration to the United States occurred between 1901 and 1910, when nearly 9 million people entered the country. (The decade following might well have yielded even greater numbers – but for the First World War, which stemmed the flow of migrants.) Yet for Wilson in 1912, the pool of "un-mobilized" voters was much smaller than it would be for FDR. For instance, the children of immigrants, for whom English would usually become the first language, were more likely to participate in politics than their parents for whom English might remain, at best,

---

[6] Norman H. Nie, Sidney Verba, and John R. Petrocik, *The Changing American Voter*, pp. 75 and 86–7.
[7] *Ibid.*, p. 86.

a poor second language.[8] That is, there was always likely to be a "lag effect" with respect to the impact that the flow of migrants would have on electoral politics.

Nevertheless, even if the scope for new voter mobilization was much greater in 1933 than in 1913, it may be doubted that it would have happened in either case but for some stimulus from outside the parties. Despite the conventional wisdom that political machines helped to socialize immigrants into politics, it must be admitted that the task facing them became more difficult as the number of migrants rose. Centralization of party organizations probably helped them operate more efficiently than they had in the 1870s and 1880s, but in urban areas they faced much larger potential electorates than earlier. Neither the Democrats nor the Republicans really had the organizational capacity to mobilize effectively these potential new voters and to turn them into loyal partisans. That is probably one of the main reasons for the observed decline in voter turnout. Changed election rules made their task even more difficult. Personal registration laws required a much larger army of party workers to check up on potential voters than the old arrangements (to see if, indeed, they had registered), and the parties simply lacked the jobs and other resources to change the scale of their own operations to perform such tasks. Maximizing the vote, in the way that the parties had come close to doing in the late 19th century, became a receding goal for parties, and voter turnout decline was the result. As McCormick observed of New York City:

Personal registration, which was mandated for all cities in 1890 and for villages with a population of over five thousand in 1895, discouraged participation simply by making voting more difficult. Similarly, the requirement of signature identification for voters in New York City, passed in 1908, undoubtedly helps account for Manhattan's decline in turnout from 80 percent in 1904 to only 70 percent at the next presidential election.[9]

Alongside a lack of capacity for mobilizing many new citizens, frequently there was also a lack of incentive to do so. In the absence of sustained party competition at the local level, neither the Democrats nor the Republicans had much incentive to incorporate new immigrants into the organization. As many urban parties tended to develop more centralized organizations at the very end of the 19th century, so it became more likely

---

[8] Moreover, children born in the United States did not have to acquire citizenship and had an entitlement to register to vote; immigrants had to become citizens, and not all of them chose to do so.

[9] Richard L. McCormick, *From Realignment to Reform*, p. 262.

that one party would "have the edge" in a city, and with that the incentives for voter mobilization would change. The majority party would garner what new votes it could, but often it did not take the steps necessary to vote-maximize – for example, by granting positions in the party organization to members of the newer immigrant groups. Its links with these communities remained weaker than they would have been had it done so, and this affected its ability to turn potential voters into voters. Here, the Republican organization in Philadelphia provides interesting evidence because it was one of the most extreme examples of an organization that was not under electoral pressure in the first three decades of the 20th century. McCaffery analyzed the composition of the party there and also utilized data on the distribution of patronage positions in local government between 1916 and 1938 that had been compiled by John L. Shover. He argues:

[Shover] discovered that county non-civil-service jobs requiring no special skills were overwhelmingly allocated to persons with English, Scottish and German surnames. In 1916 only 5 per cent of these positions were held by persons with Jewish or Italian names. By 1932, according to Shover, Jews and Italians still held only 8 per cent of such jobs. . . . I found that 62 per cent of . . . party committeemen were jobholders [in 1926] and that, like Shover, less than 5 per cent of them had Italian, Jewish or Polish names.[10]

Here we see a classic example of a nested game.[11] It was in the interests of parties nationally to try to vote-maximize (at least within each state), but those who were in a position to put this into effect (the local parties) faced a different incentive – for them, stabilizing the vote when they were the dominant party was important, and that often meant not rewarding newer supporters with jobs that would otherwise go to the more established groups.

The situation in the urban Democratic Parties was little different from that of the Republicans – except insofar as they rarely had the equivalent of the electoral security enjoyed by the Philadelphia Republicans, the incentives to incorporate new voting groups were slightly higher. Yet the Democrats, too, were not quick to reward the newer immigrant groups: Within the Democratic Party, "despite the enormous influx of eastern Europeans, the Irish influence remained stronger than that of the newer groups far into the twentieth century, at least in New York,

---

[10] Peter McCaffery, *When Bosses Ruled Philadelphia*, p. 132; John L. Shover, "Ethnicity and Religion in Philadelphia Politics, 1924–1940", *American Quarterly*, 25 (1973), 499–515.
[11] George Tsebelis, *Nested Games: Rational Choice in Comparative Politics*.

Boston, Chicago and San Francisco".[12] The Irish were an exceptional new-immigrant group in their over-representation among activists. This was partly because their mass migration pre-dated that of other groups; they had arrived in an America in which many urban party organizations had the resources and the incentive to make use of them as voters. (That the Irish spoke English on their arrival in America also set them apart from most of the other new immigrants – they could more easily use a political system for their own advantage.)

To summarize the situation confronting Wilson and Roosevelt, faced with a smaller pool of un-mobilized voters than Roosevelt was to face 20 years later, Wilson, like his successor, lacked the instruments within the party to do much about that potential resource. Mobilization would occur only if it was in the interests of local party organizations to do so and if they had the resources to devote to it; both their capacity and their incentive to mobilize were not always strong, so that it would take other factors to make this matter. There was a difference in the circumstances in which the two presidents had to operate in any attempt to re-shape the Democratic coalition – but it was one that would work to FDR's advantage only when the pool of un-mobilized Democrats had grown sufficiently large, and when some extra-party factors had encouraged an initial mobilization on behalf of the Democrats.

3. The Unelectability of the Republicans

Long-term support for a party cannot be created by promises made, images created, and so on at particular elections. A party needs considerable time in control of an administration so that it can generate reasons why particular categories of voters should start voting for it and continue to do so. Those reasons may include – though they do not necessarily do so – particular policies enacted by an administration that have an impact on the potential voters. M. Stephen Weatherford has argued that potential voters engage in an "experiential search" – a search for knowledge as to what they should think about the new political circumstances, and it is a search that takes time: "Even after the critical election accomplishes the electorate's wish to throw the rascals out, voters do not know all the issue positions that might be relevant to their future choices between the two parties". The victorious party needs time to develop a mode of action

---

[12] David Burner, *The Politics of Provincialism: The Democratic Party in Transition, 1918–1932*, Cambridge, MA, Harvard University Press, 1967, p. 23.

that will actually satisfy key groups in the electorate, and especially those that they need to add to their coalition on a more permanent basis to secure successive re-elections. Voters are not likely to be won over by an immediate "quick fix"; rather, it is a longer-term process by which a party gains adherents following the eviction of the previous, unpopular administration. In Weatherford's words:

> Both the novelty of the crisis and inexperience of the new government make policy experimentation and change inevitable. For a new majority party coming in with much exuberance, many promising but untested ideas, and little experience of governing, the systematic error is likely to be overshooting – going too far in the direction of preferred reforms, and then having to draw back, reformulate, compromise, in order to maintain elite and public support.[13]

For that reason, the "consolidation process is more contingent, open to discretion and strategizing on the part of elites, than the image of realignment in which party positions are set by the initial critical election".[14]

Winning over loyal supporters takes time, therefore. In the case of Franklin Roosevelt it took about four to six years to do this. To be effective, a new administration must retain electoral support both at the succeeding mid-term elections and in the subsequent presidential election. It must win not only majorities in the Congress at these elections but also sufficient majorities to retain freedom of action for implementing the administration's agenda. At those stages, it cannot rely on the voters that it is seeking to attract in the long term to come to its rescue. For that reason, the state of the opposing party is crucial to its prospects for success. An opposing party that has been associated with policy failure, or is badly split, may provide the opening for the new administration to gain the time needed so that it can devise a distinctive policy programme, for as Weatherford argues, "it is the programmatic thrust and not the crisis management activities that guide voter commitments".[15] Consequently, successful re-shaping of the Democratic Party coalition depended on how much the Republicans were identified as "unelectable" in the four years following the change in administration. Here, a much greater advantage clearly lay with Roosevelt than with Wilson.

---

[13] M. Stephen Weatherford, "After the Critical Election: Presidential Leadership, Competition and the Consolidation of the New Deal Realignment", *British Journal of Political Science*, 32 (2002), 229.

[14] Ibid., p. 230.

[15] Ibid., p. 245.

Roosevelt benefited not just from America's worst economic depression taking place during a Republican administration, but more especially from it having begun so soon into the life of that administration. As with "Johnson's War" in Vietnam three decades later, the association of policy failure with a particular president (Herbert Hoover) was made possible because of the length of his term associated with this policy. Economic catastrophe does not necessarily mean immediate collapse of support for the party in power; while the Democrats in 1894 were overwhelmed in the mid-term elections, there was not a similarly large landslide for the Democrats in 1930. Two years more of a still worsening economy, however, did result in blame being attached to the Hoover administration. That was a powerful resource for Roosevelt. He could buy time, as he did, by appearing to be active from March 1933 onwards, and that gave him six years with large majorities in Congress, thereby associating his party with a distinctive policy programme. He could use that association to turn most of the large pool of new voters towards the Democrats, and thus he could change the competitive balance in the North.

It was argued in the last chapter that in the absence of a third-party challenge by Theodore Roosevelt in 1912, Wilson would still probably have defeated Taft that year. Division in the Republican Party contributed to the scale of its defeat, but that did not mean the party was seen subsequently as "unelectable" in the way that it would be 20 years later. Divided parties are not usually attractive to mass electorates, but once the divisions are ended, a party can quickly start to rebuild its links with voters. After 1912, the advantage of Republican weakness would lie with the Democrats only so long as the Republican Party was divided. As is argued in Section 4, this was something the Democrats might have been able to influence, but, in the event, the break-away Progressive Party was much weakened after the 1914 elections, and in 1916 the Republicans (and those who had bolted to the Progressive Party) united behind a presidential candidate previously associated with the progressive wing of their party. Furthermore, far from being linked to a rescue of a national economy ruined by the Republicans, in 1914 it was the Democrats who could (in the short term) be connected to hard times; in the economic depression that year, unemployment rates rose to 7.9 per cent – the second-highest annual rate since 1898. Irrespective of other factors that prevented the Democrats from attempting to re-shape their electoral coalition, they would have been hampered by having insufficient time to try to establish a policy agenda that was developed on their own terms, and with only limited input from the agenda's opponents. Not only were the Republicans not marginalized from the policy dialogue in these years (through appearing to be unelectable), but after 1914, the Democrats also lacked the large majority in Congress that would have made it easier for them to control the implementation of that agenda.

4. Democratic Party Problems in Particular States

One of the features of the late 19th century party system identified in Chapter 3 was that local circumstances could, and did, affect national outcomes. For example, a party could lose congressional seats in a particular state (or even lose the presidential contest in a state) while the party was making gains elsewhere in the same region or in the nation as a whole. The results of national elections were very much the sums of elections in individual states as much as they were national contests. Although in the 20th century the focus of presidential elections shifted increasingly to national campaigning, the significance of party fortunes in particular states was not negligible. Voters' impressions of a party could be affected by problems at the state or local level, and party workers might become disheartened and reduce their effort in such circumstances. Even in the early years of the Roosevelt administration, the Republican Party was able to make some gains – for example, in 1934 the incumbent Democratic governor of Maryland was defeated. Nevertheless, for the most part, reverses in particular states were unusual between 1932 and 1936. By contrast, they were much more important for Wilson, and especially in the case of New York, this hampered the party nationally.

New York, by far the most populous state in the Union, had been a central part of the Democrats' recovery from 1910 onwards. Gains in the House that year had contributed to the congressional majority, the governorship had been won in 1910 and again in 1912, and Wilson's performance in New York in the presidential election was similar to the result he obtained nationally. The party was competitive in the state, and that contributed massively to a national majority coalition. However, the administrations of neither John Dix nor William Sulzer were successful; the Democratic Party became badly split – a split that ended in the impeachment of Sulzer. Underlying much of this was an internal war between Tammany Hall and its opponents. Sulzer's successor as governor, Martin Glynn, could not counteract the damage done in time for the 1914 elections. As Robert Wesser argues:

Measured by the record and performance of his Democratic predecessors Dix and Sulzer, Glynn in the months ahead would achieve solid success in program development and party leadership. Such accomplishments, however, could not overcome the sagging fortunes of the New York Democracy. The heightened and persistent anti-Tammanyism in the wake of the Sulzer impeachment, a combination of rapid Progressive decline and Republican reemergence, and a deepened sectional-cultural cleavage fueled by a resurgent anti-Catholicism foredoomed Glynn and his Democratic colleagues to the worst statewide party disaster in years. In fact, in 1914 the Democracy would fall to it lowest point electorally in New York State during the entire progressive era.[16]

Wilson's fortunes were caught up in this circumstance. A weakened Democracy in New York harmed his re-election prospects. In 1912, Wilson's share of the vote in New York had been the second highest in the 13 Old North states. In 1916, it was to be only the eighth highest, and his increase in the share of the vote between 1912 and 1916 was the lowest in the Old North except for that in his home state of New Jersey. He duly lost New York that year.

This kind of state-level setback in a state that had been crucial to the prospects of Democratic electoral success earlier meant that far from possibly using their tenure in the White House to create a secure national majority, the Democrats would have to fight to maintain the degree of national competitiveness they had re-established in 1910. However, in this fight they were to be helped by neither the strategies the Wilson administration was to deploy nor its policies.

5. Prioritizing the Democratic Party

There is an inevitable tension between the strategies required to broaden a coalition and those required to help keep an existing coalition as a cohesive unit. The pursuit of partisanship aids the latter but not the former. If the Democratic coalition in 1912 had been sufficiently broad as to make the party a majority party in the foreseeable future, then it would have made sense to govern on partisan lines. However, we have seen that although a modified version of the old 19th century coalition could still win, it was a more complex coalition than earlier, and that provided a strong incentive for trying to increase the party's electoral base. But in which direction? One possible direction was back to the 19th century strategy of seeking to be more competitive in the Old North states that had large cities. However, the world in which the likes of Grover Cleveland

---

[16] Robert F. Wesser, *A Response to Progressivism: The Democratic Party and New York Politics, 1902–1918*, New York, New York University Press, 1986, p. 136.

were so important, because they could mobilize the "marginal voter" for a national coalition, was over. Elements of the radical West had to be incorporated now into virtually any winning Democratic coalition, so that a truly conservative Democracy was no longer as viable as it had been. Given that dilemma, the only other direction in which the party could move was into those parts of the West in which it was relatively weak electorally. That is, it could try to increase its vote in those parts of the West that had supported insurgent Republicanism in Congress after 1910 and had given strong backing to Theodore Roosevelt's presidential campaign in 1912.

The aim of such a strategy would have been to "neutralize" major Republican officeholders from these states (especially those in Congress) – by openly supporting policies that they backed – so that they might withhold endorsements from their own party's nominees at subsequent presidential elections, thereby making it easier for the Democrats to carry the state. Indirectly, these officeholders could be used to weaken Republicanism in the state and help to build up the Democracy as the party of progressivism. Should the conservative elements in the Republican Party refuse to re-nominate these incumbents, the Democracy would then be well positioned to assert itself as the only truly progressive party. It was not unreasonable for the Wilson administration to have tried this strategy, particularly given the divisions between the dominant conservative wing of the Republican Party and the progressives (both those who remained Republicans and those who joined the Progressive Party). While it would always have been unlikely that any of these progressive incumbents would actually have changed parties themselves – even George Norris, FDR's most enthusiastic progressive Republican supporter in the 1930s, never became a Democrat – having them support a Democratic presidential candidate was not an unreasonable objective. (For example, a number of western Republicans – Hiram Johnson, Robert La Follette, Jr., and George Norris included – did end up endorsing Roosevelt in 1932.)[17]

In fact, Wilson's entire way of organizing his relations with Congress and the priorities he accorded different policies meant that while he hoped to expand electorally into the West, he did not have the will to effect it. There were two key respects in which the Wilson administration failed to accommodate itself to the western Progressives and Republicans, and in doing so it lost an opportunity to broaden the base of voter support for the Democrats in that region.

[17] Nicol Rae, *The Decline and Fall of Liberal Republicanism from 1952 to the Present*, New York, Oxford University Press, 1989, p. 25.

First, Wilson's ideas of party leadership were very much those of a partisan – the president's task was to mobilize, and work with, his party members in Congress in order to effect a legislative programme. Wilson's own predisposition in this direction was reinforced by changes the Democrats had made earlier in the organization of the House, following both the stripping of powers from Speaker Joseph Cannon and their subsequent majority status in the House after the 1910 elections. In particular, the Democrats had decided then that they would use the party caucus to bind the members to party unity on the floor of the House.[18] This was an ideal complement to the Wilsonian view of party, and in Majority Leader Oscar Underwood, Wilson had the right person to put his policy agenda into effect. As James Fleming puts it:

> The organizational key to Underwood's leadership of the House was his reliance on the party's binding caucus to promote discipline and unity within his party. Underwood used the party caucus in much the same way the leader of a European parliamentary democracy uses the party caucus to achieve unity within the party on matters before a parliament. After a bill had been drafted by the Democratic members of a standing committee (often meeting with Underwood and sometimes President Wilson), it was typically submitted to a closed meeting of the House Democratic caucus.... [O]nce two-thirds of the caucus had made a policy decision, all party members were bound to support it on the floor of the House.[19]

An obvious consequence of this mode of proceeding was that it left the potential non-Democratic supporters of the legislation – mainly western progressive Republicans and Progressives – on the sidelines.[20] Excluding them from consultation, and making them feel powerless because a decision could be pushed through by Democrats, all of whom were bound to vote for it, was not a method likely to endear them to the Democratic Party. And it did not.

Secondly, this determined use of a party majority meant that even before the 1914 elections, when the Democratic majority was reduced, Wilson was engaging in a policy of compromise to retain the support of conservatives within his party. Thus, he weakened the powers of the

---

[18] James S. Fleming, "Oscar W. Underwood: The First Modern House Leader", in Roger H. Davidson, Susan Webb Hammond, and Raymond W. Smock (eds.), *Masters of the House*, Boulder, CO, Westview Press, 1998, p. 97.

[19] Ibid., p. 104.

[20] "In both chambers, Republicans – progressive and otherwise – were barred from participation in the drafting and markup processes [of legislation]". Scott C. James, *Presidents, Parties and the State: A Party System Perspective of Democratic Regulatory Choice, 1884–1936*, Cambridge, Cambridge University Press, 2000, pp. 142–3.

new Federal Trade Commission to mollify business leaders. In doing so, he became vulnerable to the charge from both Progressive members of Congress and progressively oriented Republicans in the chamber that he was not a genuine reformer:

> Ideologically sympathetic Republicans and Progressives were able to save face only by adopting [Theodore] Roosevelt's earlier criticism of Wilson as a sham reformer. They lambasted Wilson for not going much further to push such measures as woman suffrage, abolition of child labor, aid to agriculture and stronger pro-union actions.[21]

He was equally conservative in appointments to both the new and the existing regulatory commissions.[22] The dilution of the policy programme and the partisan way in which Wilson and the Democrats operated precluded the possibility of genuine co-operation with western progressives, and thereby of helping to increase Democratic electoral strength in the West in the longer term.

In effect, the Wilson strategy involved treating the conservative members of his own party, rather than the progressive members of other parties, as the marginal voters in the American polity. Had the Democrats' national coalition been sufficiently large, this might have been a reasonable approach – but it was not. The Democrats needed to add to their national voting coalition, and that meant empowering the non-Democratic progressives, rather than the party's own conservatives. In fact, measures such as the Underwood-Simmons Act (which lowered tariffs significantly), the Federal Reserve Act (which facilitated reform of the banking system), and the Clayton Anti-Trust Act did not play especially well among the latter. As the mid-term elections of 1914 made all too clear, the Democrats' legislation had less appeal in the Northeast, where they lost congressional seats and governorships, but it did play well in the West. The Democratic Party, though, in failing to build on that appeal by not trying to co-opt the non-Democrats from that region via a more radical progressive agenda, ignored the group that it should have treated as the marginal voter.

Twenty years later, Franklin Roosevelt did not make the same mistakes. In the early stages of his first administration, he did not opt for a partisan

[21] John Milton Cooper, Jr., *Pivotal Decades, The United States, 1900–1920*, New York, W. W. Norton, 1990, p. 201.
[22] Elizabeth Sanders, *Roots of Reform: Farmers, Workers, and the American State, 1877–1917*, Chicago, University of Chicago Press, 1999, p. 395.

approach to policy but what Clyde Weed calls "an all-class coalition".[23] Having used that to build up political capital for himself, Roosevelt could then pay close attention to the marginal voter. For him, the marginal voter was now the newly voting, northern city dweller, and much of the thrust of the New Deal after 1935 was directed towards policies that would appeal to those voters; their support would in turn make more competitive a number of states that had otherwise leaned Republican. These Northerners had not been the marginal voter in his 1932 victory. However, they were significant in three ways in the reconfiguration of the Democratic Party. First, these voters had brought into Congress in 1933 a large number of northern, city-based Democratic representatives – a change that was dramatic partly because the 1931–2 reapportionment of districts was the first in 20 years. These Representatives could be mobilized as a new force in Congress. Secondly, the urban electorate that returned these people to Congress was now sufficiently large that it could make states that had otherwise leaned Republican far more competitive. Thirdly, many of the states in which these cities were located themselves had large populations; winning those cities, and then winning the states, made winning the presidency that much easier. In the long term, identifying this new marginal voter, and recognizing its importance, was to change the nature of the Democratic coalition. In the shorter term, it ensured electoral success, so that on three occasions FDR was able to win re-election, whereas Wilson's own single re-election had been a close-run affair. In 1916, the Progressives had largely returned to the Republican Party; however, both big and small "p" progressives continued to operate in Congress as a separate ideological grouping throughout much of the next two decades. Their relations with the rest of the Republican Party were often driven largely by necessity, and Wilson had contributed to that necessity.

Furthermore, there was also a marked difference between Wilson and Roosevelt in their approach to the distribution of federal patronage. Wilson operated in a traditional party way, despite claiming before his inauguration that he would nominate only progressives. Instead, he reverted to the earlier practice of rewarding faithful partisans – irrespective of their views.[24] Moreover, given the popularity of civil-service merit systems among progressive reformers, this resource was in long-term decline, and that increased the pressure to use what there was

---

[23] Clyde P. Weed, *The Nemesis of Reform: The Republican Party During the New Deal*, New York, Columbia University Press, 1994, p. 53.

[24] Sidney M. Milkis, *The President and the Parties: The Transformation of the American Party System Since the New Deal*, New York and Oxford, 1993, p. 54.

to keep the party together. Consequently, in addition to being shut out of congressional decision making by the use of binding decisions in caucus, western progressives outside the Democratic Party gained little by way of material reward to soften their attitude towards the Democrats.

Roosevelt also began his administration by distributing patronage on a largely partisan basis. However, he had far more flexibility in this regard because the number of jobs at his disposal was greater. The various job-creation schemes associated with the New Deal increased the size of the workforce on the federal payroll, and by placing many of them off the so-called classified list, Roosevelt expanded the size of the patronage component so that about 40 per cent of all jobs were in this category. Proportionately, this was the largest federal patronage workforce in 30 years.[25] Patronage on this scale could be deployed to create an organization that went beyond the traditional Democratic Party. As Sidney Milkis argues:

Roosevelt believed that an undue dependence on the regular Democratic party would prevent a fundamental alteration of political alignments in the United States. Accordingly, even during the early days of the administration, his support of regular patronage practices was not complete. Instead, he departed from conventional practices to reward certain Republican Progressives and other reformers outside the Democratic party, thus taking the initial steps to develop a national New Deal organization that operated independently of the regular party apparatus.[26]

This marked the beginning of a long-term shift away from partisan control of government, with positions in both the Cabinet and lower echelons of the administration coming to be occupied by experts of the correct "ideological" perspective, rather than by partisans.[27] However, it also contributed indirectly to the resources needed to shift voter support towards the Democrats.

6. Policies Inconsistent with Successful Coalition Building

After its failure to embrace potential allies in its early years, the Wilson administration later compounded its problem by backing policies that

[25] Ibid., p. 55.
[26] Ibid.
[27] "As the size of the government began to swell in the Depression and World War II, the task of choosing people to its highest levels became more daunting, and the capacity of the patronage system to produce the skilled and experienced people needed to lead the new agencies more wanting". G. Calvin Mackenzie, "The State of the Presidential Appointment Process", p. 15. See also Roger G. Brown, "Party and Bureaucracy: From Kennedy to Reagan", *Political Science Quarterly*, 97 (1982), 279–94.

alienated members of the coalition that was constructed to win the election of 1916. The result was one of the most spectacular collapses of party support in American history. One of the paradoxes of its treatment of the progressives in 1913 and 1914 was that after the 1914 elections, in order for Wilson to be re-elected, the party would clearly have to win in 1916 on the basis of support in the West. As the mid-term elections of 1914 had made all too evident, the Democrats' legislation had less appeal in the Northeast and the "old" Midwest, where they lost congressional seats and governorships, but it could play well in the West. So 20 years after William Jennings Bryan's first western-oriented campaign, the Democrats ended up by contesting – and winning narrowly – a presidential election on the basis of uniting the West and the South. Had the Germans broken through on the Marne in August 1914, or had the French counter-attack there been more successful so that the European war was over by Christmas of that year, the future of the Democrats' election strategy might have been different; they might well have lost in 1916. As it was, the strategy brought them victory in the short term, but the electoral logic of the strategy was not pursued in government. In his re-election bid of 1916, Wilson used the issue of the war as a way of bolstering support for the party. By portraying the Democrats as the party that had kept the country out of the war so far, he was able to consolidate Democratic support throughout most of the isolationist West, and thereby create the basis of his narrow victory over a Republican Party whose strength was concentrated in the East and Midwest. Indeed, the electoral map for 1916 shows patterns of support that, in some ways, are a more extreme version of the 1896 coalition. (Wilson won more Electoral College votes in the West than had Bryan, though his margins of victory in most states in the North were much closer than they had been in 1896.) Ironically, the first election since 1896 in which Bryan was not an important actor at the Democratic National Convention produced a result that, in appearance, was purely Bryanite. This time, though, the Democrats had a 3 per cent plurality nationally, whereas 20 years earlier they had lost by 4 per cent.

Wilson's problem was that with progressive Republicans now firmly (albeit nominally) back in the Republican Party, the "Super West" coalition was likely to hold together only if he continued to keep the United States out of the First World War. Given the path of American diplomacy from 1914 to 1916 and the German response to it, that was not easy, and once America did intervene, western isolationists had little more reason to support the Democrats than they had before 1914. The same was even more true of Germans and Irish in the cities, who similarly had opposed

American intervention in the war. While Wilson's policy played well in the Northeast after 1916 and was acceptable in much of the South, it put the party at risk in an area where there were progressive non-Democrats who had made peace with the Republican Party in 1916. In part, Wilson and much of his party had actually pulled in opposite directions in 1916: Wilson himself had favoured greater emphasis on national unity, and less on pacifist ideals, in the party's platform. But this northeastern-oriented internationalism was at odds with the coalition-building strategy for 1916 that had to emphasize the role of the West as the marginal voter – ever since the 1914 elections had demonstrated that there was little possibility of rebuilding Democratic strength in the Old North.

The Democrats faced other problems after the 1916 election. The Lever Act of 1917 controlled wheat prices, a policy that alienated the many farmers that grew this product since prices were only just over a third of the level they had reached in a free market earlier that year. At the same time, cotton producers from the non-marginal element of the Democratic coalition were not subjected to government control of prices. Distributing social costs in this way – to the disadvantage of the more marginal elements in the coalition – was the very opposite of a strategy driven by the pursuit of electoral victory. Again, civil liberties were eroded during the war, and this produced tension in relations with sections of the labour union movement, as well as with the German American community, among others. Consequently, in November 1918, on the eve of final victory, the president who had taken his country into the war did not receive the kind of electoral support he might have expected. As David Burner said of those mid-term elections,

the net Republican gain over 1916 of twenty-two seats from the Democrats was not especially significant, since the average off-year loss by the party in power in this century has been forty-two seats. It is when the election results of 1918 are measured against Wilson's famous appeal for a vote of confidence that the Republican showing appears to be a crucial triumph in the revival of Republican strength.[28]

In the remaining two years of the administration, Wilson's legacy to his party was such that a likely defeat in 1920 would become a rout. Wilson spent much of 1919 in Europe negotiating the Treaty of Versailles – out of public view, he returned with a foreign policy instrument that many

---

[28] Burner, *The Politics of Provincialism*, p. 35n.

politicians from the West, the region crucial to his victory in 1916, did not want. He was humiliated by its defeat in the Senate, where Republicans knew that politics mattered more than principle and even that party's internationalists did not put up much of a fight for it. Finally, with his presidency ending in serious illness, Wilson made no provision to ease the path of a successor – partly because until quite late, he had entertained the prospect of running for a third term. In the end, the party's warring factions were left to fight out the nomination – a nomination that, in the circumstances, was practically worthless.

The consequences for his party of Wilson's policies were considerable, although as will be argued in the next chapter, the Democratic Party would likely have been in crisis in the 1920s even if he had been more consistent in linking public policy to the demands of coalition formation. The logic of following a "western strategy" in 1916 was that the administration should ensure that the United States did not become a combatant nation, and that it should not give into the campaigning of those eastern progressives (led by Theodore Roosevelt) who demanded an active role for the country in that war. However, Wilson's internationalist views were in conflict with the requirements of party leadership, and it was the former that prevailed. This was to be expected from a president who, for all his known opinions on the need for party leadership, was someone who would always think of putting certain principles above party. Franklin Roosevelt, despite holding elective office for only a few years more than Wilson had had prior to entering the White House, was more steeped in the workings of party politics and was far more aware of the need to maintain electoral coalitions. (Indeed, one of the main criticisms of Roosevelt has been that he was just a political "broker".)[29] Thus, while treating the northern urban dweller as the marginal voter, he recognized the need to placate the white South – especially after 1938. Consequently, his administration kept the issue of civil rights off the national policy agenda – "its record was weak and halting"[30] – even while letting other interests advanced by those members of Congress (from northern urban districts), who were under pressure from African American constituents to take up the issue, become the centre of his administration's policy agenda.

[29] James McGregor Burns, *Roosevelt: The Lion and the Fox, 1882–1940*, New York, Harcourt, Brace and World, 1956, pp. 375–80.

[30] Edward G. Carmines and James A. Stimson, *Issue Evolution: Race and the Transformation of American Politics*, Princeton, NJ, Princeton University Press, 1989, p. 32.

7. Failure to Make Particular Interests Dependent on the Democratic Party

As the role of group identities declined slowly as a factor in generating loyalty to a particular political party, it became more important for that party to make voters believe that their *interests* hinged on its continuation in government. In spite of the popular myth that patronage tied in supporters to their parties, the numbers of people who benefited directly from the patronage system was always relatively small. The size of government was such that the jobs and contracts under the control of a governing party were never more than necessary just to sustain a party organization – few spoils were available to most potential voters. Selective benefits of that sort were of limited direct use in relation to voters. Consequently, for the purposes of coalition growth, it became necessary to construct public policies in such a way that given groups of voters would believe that they had a stake in the continuation of a policy, and that that policy might be threatened by the election of the opposing party. Moreover, because of the role now played by various organized groups that were promoting some of the interests of these voters, it was important to tie in such groups to the party's policy agenda. What was wanted by a party from a group was not their formal co-option but, rather, a desire that particular public policies be maintained; because of that link through policy with the party, indirect or covert forms of support for the party by the group would then be more likely. At the very least, taking such groups out of politics meant that they were no longer resources available to the opposing party in the contest for power; at best, a working relationship between the group and the party might produce money and other resources for election campaigns.

Franklin Roosevelt built up such a basis of support for the Democrats through a system that, 30 years later, Theodore Lowi would call "interest group liberalism" – a system in which "the policy agenda and the public interest [are] defined in terms of the organized interests in society".[31] It solved

a problem for the democratic politician in the modern state where the stakes are so high. This is the problem of enhanced conflict and how to avoid it. . . . It provides a theoretical basis for giving to each according to his claim, the price of which is a reduction of concern for what others are claiming. In other words, it transforms logrolling from necessary evil to greater good.[32]

---

[31] Theodore Lowi, "The Public Philosophy: Interest Group Liberalism", *American Political Science Review*, 61 (1967), 12.
[32] Ibid., p. 14.

But there was also a benefit to Roosevelt and his successors as Democratic presidential candidates because, having been the principal users of this system, they were able to work with the organized groups, including the labour unions, whom the New Deal legislation both empowered and brought into the policy process. This advantage gained by the Democratic president came at a price for his party, though. In Milkis's words:

> Roosevelt aimed at building a more progressive form of government within the presidency, rather than through a more permanent link between the executive and legislature. This required extending the personal and nonpartisan responsibility of the president to the detriment of collective and partisan responsibility. Thus the Democratic party became during the 1930s the party to end all parties. Under Roosevelt's leadership it was dedicated to a program that eventually lessened the importance of the two-party system.[33]

Not all political scientists agree with Milkis that Roosevelt intended to weaken the party. John Coleman, for example, argues that Roosevelt had a desire for "more cohesive parties and for institutional entrenchment of the New Deal, not simply a system of presidential aggrandizement". However, he agrees that irrespective of FDR's intent, "Institutionalizing New Deal reforms in the state would not build a 'party state' but would lead instead to a diminished stature for party over time".[34]

The key point for us is that Roosevelt's construction of the "party to end all parties" can be seen as an appropriate response to the need to expand a party coalition so that the party can win regularly. Whether the cost in terms of party control over the policy agenda was worth paying is an entirely different matter. Moreover, Roosevelt was far from being the only exemplar of the use of this strategy in the mid–20th century. Swedish Social Democratic governments promoted neo-corporatist policy-making styles, a related device that took out of politics potential political opponents, thereby restricting the ability of opposition parties to mobilize against them. Four decades of continuous government in Sweden was one consequence of that approach.

While the organized groups were being neutralized by New Deal policies, such as the establishment of the National Labor Relations Board, the loyalty of individual voters was being developed through policies like the Social Security Act, which gave them a stake in the continuation of these programmes. The dependence of some voters on these programmes

---

[33] Milkis, *The President and the Parties*, p. 5
[34] John J. Coleman, *Party Decline in America: Policy, Politics and the Fiscal State*, Princeton, NJ, Princeton University Press, 1996, p. 59.

meant that claiming to be their protectors was always a possible campaign tactic for Democrats, something that Republicans could neutralize only by embracing the programmes as their own. Thus, when campaigning in 1938, former New Jersey Senator Warren Barbour said that he had voted for both the Wagner Act and the Social Security Act and noted, "I am proud of the part I took in bringing these things to pass".[35]

For all its legislative achievements – and, if some of them were compromises, the achievements were considerable nonetheless – the first two years of the Wilson administration did not produce a policy programme that would create lasting links between important groups of voters and the Democratic Party. This is a crucial difference in the performance of the two administrations. The continuing benefits of Social Security were all too evident to a large number of people; the effects of bills such as the Clayton Antitrust Act were not. Irrespective of the effect it actually had, the latter was not something of which many voters had direct, everyday experience. That was the weakness of the Wilson programme – in relation to coalition building; its successes would easily pass from view, as public attention moved to other issues. Once the popular enthusiasm for reform began to wane, the Democrats would be left trying to find a new issue with which to keep their coalition together. By the end of 1914 it was clear that that time had come. As Theodore Roosevelt noted in the light of the election results and the concomitant economic depression that year: "The fundamental trouble was that the country was sick and tired of reform. . . . [People] were suffering from hard times. They wanted prosperity and compared with this they did not give a rap for social justice or industrial justice or clean politics or decency in public life."[36]

That Wilson did not invent the solution to coalition building used by Franklin Roosevelt two decades later cannot be held as a criticism of him. Times were different, and what was acceptable as an expansion of the role of government in the wake of a major depression was simply not acceptable earlier. Progressivism stood for a very different set of values from those that were to be embodied in the New Deal. That FDR's strategy could not have been deployed successfully 20 years earlier can be illustrated by the history of the relationship between Roosevelt and the aging, western Republican progressives in his own time. At first supportive of his election, they became increasingly alienated from the administration – especially after the failed Supreme Court–packing plan

[35] Weed, *The Nemesis of Reform*, p. 196.
[36] Cooper, *Pivotal Decades*, p. 213.

in 1937. Their fear of government power and of centralization in the economy would have been sufficient to have provoked a split with the Democratic president, even if matters were not being made worse by their commitment to isolationism while the administration was moving in the direction of internationalism in light of the growing crisis in Europe.[37] That the options open to Wilson were arguably more restricted than they were to be for FDR made it even more imperative that his policies be consistent with the logic of coalition formation. That is why the failure to court the western non-Democratic progressives in 1913 and 1914, and the later failure in relation to war policy, was to prove so costly. After 1916, the administration was decreasingly providing reasons for people to continue to vote for it.

8. The Democratic Party and the North After 1912

The year 1912 can be understood as a cross-roads in relation to long-term change in the Democratic Party. As with the congressional elections of 1910, there are clear elements of 19th century coalition politics evident here. For example, if we consider the share of the vote in the states in descending order of how Democratic they were in 1912, it was New York that was pivotal. It was the 25th most Democratic state, and its Electoral College votes were the ones that ensured a Democratic victory (see Table 5.1). Of the other marginal states from the earlier era, Indiana (19th) was won by the Democrats in 1912, while California and New Jersey were, respectively, the 24th and 26th most Democratic states.[38] Ohio was the 28th most Democratic, and only Connecticut had moved away from its earlier position of being one of the highly competitive and marginal states. However, the presence of western states in the 18th, 20th, 22nd, and 23rd positions in this table illustrates the point made in Chapter 4 that after the mid-1890s, this was a modified version of the older, 19th century Democratic coalition.

After 1912, the party moved even further away from that earlier coalition. States in the Old North that had been of importance for coalition building by the Democrats became relatively less important.

---

[37] Ronald L. Feinman, *Twilight of Progressivism: The Western Republican Senators and the New Deal*, Baltimore and London, Johns Hopkins University Press, 1981, p. 101.
[38] Because of the strength of Theodore Roosevelt in California, he actually won the state narrowly, although two Electoral College votes went for Wilson.

TABLE 5.1. *Rank Ordering of States by Share of Votes Obtained by Democratic Candidate in Presidential Elections of 1912, 1916, and 1932*

	1912	1916	1932	(2000)
South Carolina	1	1	1	(38)
Mississippi	2	2	2	(39)
Louisiana	3	3	3	(29)
Georgia	4	4	4	(33)
Texas	5	5	5	(40)
Alabama	6	6	7	(35)
Florida	7	7	8	(16)
Virginia	8	8	13	(31)
North Carolina	9	12	10	(32)
Arkansas	10	9	6	(27)
Tennessee	11	14	15	(21)
Maryland	12	19	21	(4)
Kentucky	13	21	23	(36)
Missouri	14	24	16	(22)
Oklahoma	15	23	9	(41)
Delaware	16	28	42	(8)
Nebraska	17	16	19	(45)
Arizona	18	13	14	(30)
Indiana	19	36	34	(37)
Colorado	20	10	33	(34)
West Virginia	21	27	35	(28)
South Dakota	22	40	17	(42)
New Mexico	23	25	20	(19)
California	24	34	26	(10)
New York	25	41	36	(2)
New Jersey	26	44	41	(5)
Wisconsin	27	45	18	(20)
Ohio	28	22	40	(25)
Nevada	29	18	12	(26)
New Hampshire	30	30	42	(24)
Maine	31	32	46	(15)
Kansas	32	26	37	(43)
Connecticut	33	33	44	(6)
Iowa	34	46	28	(17)
Wyoming	35	17	31	(47)
Massachusetts	36	35	38	(3)
Illinois	37	43	31	(9)
Montana	38	15	24	(44)
Oregon	39	39	27	(23)
North Dakota	40	29	11	(46)
Utah	41	11	47	(50)
Pennsylvania	42	47	45	(13)
Rhode Island	43	38	22	(1)
Idaho	44	20	25	(49)
Minnesota	45	37	22	(18)
Michigan	46	42	39	(11)
Washington	47	31	29	(14)
Vermont	48	48	48	(12)

Similar data for 2000 are included in parentheses in this table to show the extent to which support for the Democratic Party has shifted since this earlier era; Alaska and Hawaii were included in the calculation of that data but omitted from the table.

TABLE 5.2. *Rank Ordering of States by Share of Votes Obtained by Democratic Candidate in Presidential Elections of 1912 and 1916: States That Changed More Than 10 Places in the Ranking, by Region*

	States Rising by More Than 10 Places in the Rank Ordering Between 1912 and 1916	States Declining by More Than 10 Places in the Rank Ordering Between 1912 and 1916
South		
Border States		Delaware
Old North		Indiana
		New Jersey
		New York
West	Idaho	Iowa
	Montana	South Dakota
	Nevada	Wisconsin
	North Dakota	
	Utah	
	Washington	
	Wyoming	

Correspondingly, states in the West became relatively more important. Despite Wilson's failure to woo non-Democratic western members of Congress, and thereby aid his party's fortunes in that region, the party moved decisively towards a western orientation between 1914 and 1916. As noted earlier, Wilson's re-election bid hinged on his creation of a "Super-West" coalition. One (admittedly rather crude) way of illustrating the importance of the West is to consider change in the relative electoral strength of the Democratic Party in the states between 1912 and 1916 (see Table 5.1). Table 5.2 lists the states that moved by more than 10 places in the rankings, shown in Table 5.1, between 1912 and 1916. All 7 of the states that were at least 11 places higher in the rankings in 1916 were in the West; of the 7 states that were lower by that degree in the rankings, 3 were in the Old North and 3 in the West, with one being a Border state. Significantly, 3 of the states that became relatively less Democratic were among the ones that had been most marginal in the late 19th century – Indiana, New Jersey, and New York. Within the West, it was essentially states in the less-populated Rocky Mountains region that were becoming more Democratic. "Swapping" states the size of New York could make sense in relation to expanding the Democrats' coalition, but at a cost; the small size of the states they "gained" complicated decisions about party strategy even more. It exposed the consequences of having engaged

TABLE 5.3. *Rank Ordering of States by Share of Votes Obtained by Democratic Candidate in Presidential Elections of 1916 and 1932: States That Changed More Than 10 Places in the Ranking, by Region*

	States Rising by More Than 10 Places in the Rank Ordering Between 1916 and 1932	States Declining by More Than 10 Places in the Rank Ordering Between 1916 and 1932
South		
Border States	Oklahoma	Delaware
Old North	Illinois	Connecticut
	Rhode Island	Maine
		New Hampshire
		Ohio
West	Iowa	Colorado
	Minnesota	Kansas
	North Dakota	Utah
	Oregon	Wyoming
	South Dakota	
	Wisconsin	

only half-heartedly with western progressives in other parties in 1913 and 1914.

Given what has been said about Wilson's re-election strategy, we would have expected to find this trend towards the West in the data. What is less obvious, perhaps, is that the shift westwards would reappear later, in 1932. Table 5.3 compares 1916 with 1932. The pattern here is less clear-cut than the shift between 1912 and 1916, but generally it was a few states in the West that became relatively more Democratic in these years, while on balance, the shift in the Old North was away from the party. Finally, Table 5.4 shows the longer-term shift in the relative strength of the Democrats between 1912 and 1932, which exposes the pronounced westward drift over a 20-year period – in spite of Wilson's ambivalence.

Overall, the two shifts just described in these 20 years seemingly provide evidence of the increasing importance of the West for the Democratic Party by 1932 and a decreasing significance for the party of the Old North. In particular, by 1932 the four medium-size and large states that had been highly competitive in the late 19th century (Indiana, New Jersey, New York, and Ohio) ranked, respectively, as the 34th, 41st, 36th, and 40th most Democratic states. It is not surprising, therefore, that Roosevelt's strategy in 1932 should have been described as "essentially agrarian, an appeal to rural elements", because in terms of the northern states that

TABLE 5.4. *Rank Ordering of States by Share of Votes Obtained by Democratic Candidate in Presidential Elections of 1912 and 1932: States That Changed More Than 10 Places in the Ranking, by Region*

	States Rising by More Than 10 Places in the Rank Ordering Between 1912 and 1932	States Declining by More Than 10 Places in the Rank Ordering Between 1912 and 1932
South		
Border States		Delaware
		West Virginia
Old North	Rhode Island	Connecticut
		Indiana
		Maine
		New Hampshire
		New Jersey
		New York
		Ohio
West	Idaho	Colorado
	Minnesota	
	Montana	
	Nevada	
	North Dakota	
	Oregon	
	Washington	

were most Democratic, those were the interests that were predominating in his coalition.[39] By 1932, the party seemed to have shifted to being even more dependent on many elements of rural America than it had been in 1912. That there was the potential for Roosevelt to reverse that change to the party's advantage – to make the Democrats a more urban-oriented party – is an issue to be examined further in the next chapter. One paradox to be explored there is that just as it was becoming even more of a rural-oriented, southern and western party, so at the same time was the Democratic Party increasing its relative electoral strength in the large cities. Consequently, while Roosevelt changed the direction of coalition formation in his party, he actually did it on the back of subtle changes in party support that were already occurring.

---

[39] "As Raymond Moley observed, Roosevelt's 1932 strategy "might be called essentially agrarian, an appeal to rural elements – farmers and residents of small towns and cities". Kenneth Finegold and Theda Skocpol, *State and Party in America's New Deal*, p. 72.

6

How Could a Winning Democratic Coalition Be Constructed, 1920–1932?

One of the temptations in historical analysis is to assume that what would later appear to be a successful solution to a problem should have been obvious to most actors at the time. If the western progressives were alienated from the Republican party in 1912, as a Democratic leader, why not court them? If a Super West coalition could win in 1916, why not persist with it? To understand why such a coalition did not appear to be *the* obvious strategy in the years from 1916 to 1932, we must return to the issue of how the potential for building a majority Democratic coalition changed after the early to middle 1890s.

In the post–Civil War era, it was quite clear what the Democrats had to do to win a national majority – carry enough of the small number of marginal Old North states to add to their strongholds in the ex-slave states. After 1892–5, the optimal strategy became more complex. The Border states were no longer as reliable as they had been, and the Democrats now had hopes of winning in some of the western states, as well as continuing to do so in part of the Old North. The earlier strategy could still be the basis for some successes, as it was in the congressional elections of 1910, but to the extent that there were divergent interests between East and West, the Democrats were now faced with a dilemma. Should they try to shore up support in the Old North by supporting the kind of conservative, small-statist ideas that had brought victory in the 19th century? The risk was that they would lose the ground they had made in the West and alienate the more radical parts of the South. Or should they continue as a radical, neo-populist party and thereby give up their chances of winning states in the Old North, where there were more

Electoral College votes at stake, and also run the risk of alienating the more conservative areas of the South?

This dilemma was more than one to be debated quietly in the proverbial smoke-filled rooms. It reflected growing tensions in the Democratic Party between two sub-cultures that, increasingly, were becoming estranged from each other. The debate about whether to pursue an eastern or a western strategy following Wilson's re-election in 1916 was not just about what was a winning strategy for the Democrats but a fight for control of the party. In fact, after 1916 it was not until 1932 that the party again deployed an essentially western strategy. That is why the structure of the Democratic coalition looks rather different if we consider the elections of 1920–32 (as shown in Table 4.5) than if we just compare 1916 with 1932 (Table 5.1). To get from 1916 to 1932, the Democrats had to resolve what amounted to a civil war; only then could they regain power on the basis of an alliance with the West, and only then would FDR be able to use that alliance to transform the nature of the Democratic coalition. In the meantime, the legacy of Wilson's collapsing administration, followed by the civil war, was to bring electoral disaster for the party. Using the framework outlined in Chapter 2, the main part of this chapter analyzes the coalition-building problems facing the Democrats after the end of the Wilson administration. First, though, we assess the scale of the Democrats' electoral difficulties in building a national coalition in the 1920s.

1. The Electoral Disasters of the 1920s

In the 1920s, the Democrats recorded the three worst sequential performances by a major party in presidential election history. In 1920, 1924, and 1928, the party's share of the vote was 34.1 per cent, 28.8 per cent, and 40.8 per cent. Outside of the 11 southern states, the only states it carried in these years were Kentucky (in 1920), Oklahoma (in 1924), and Massachusetts and Rhode Island (in 1928). One widely accepted interpretation of these years is that the Democrats had simply returned to the minority status they had occupied before the split in the Republican Party in 1912, and that it took a cataclysm, in the form of the Great Depression, to change that status. The argument presented in this book disagrees with that interpretation in two crucial respects, although it accepts one of the main assumptions of that interpretation. First, as was argued in Chapter 4, the Democrats did not become a minority party after 1896; between 1896 and 1912, their revamped coalition – but one that drew substantially on its late 19th century basis – remained a viable vehicle for winning presidential elections, and indeed, their victory in 1912 was largely the result of re-assembling, with some modifications, that coalition. The main reason they failed to do so before then lay in the absence of suitable candidates to unite that coalition, and in turn, that can be linked to the failure to win major public offices, particularly in large, competitive states. The party lacked leaders around whom the coalition could be reconstructed. Secondly, it is argued later in this chapter that despite their problems, it was quite possible for the Democrats to have been able to unite the two warring wings of their party in the early 1930s, and win the 1932 presidential election, even if the economic depression had been much less severe than it was.

However, the account presented here is not wholly revisionist. It accepts an assumption made by other scholars that, increasingly, the 19th century foundations of the Democratic coalition were becoming much less viable than the Republican coalition as a vehicle for *holding on to power*. The real significance of the Great Depression in American electoral history was that it provided an opportunity for Franklin Roosevelt to transform the Democrats' coalition, thereby enabling the party to overcome the serious long-term problems that it was facing. While it is quite possible to argue that he might well have won the 1932 election even with a much less severe economic downturn, it is not clear that in those circumstances, he could then have introduced public policies that would have enabled the Democrats to aggregate successfully a slightly different set of social interests than those of their old coalition. The year 1932 was thus important in a way that 1896 was not: It enabled a majority party to use public policy to change the basis of party competition at the national level.

So, by the 1920s, what did the Democratic coalition embrace? As in the 1880s, constructing a minimum winning majority in the Electoral College involved carrying all the southern and Border states. However, by 1920 they accounted for only 66.1 per cent of the 266 votes needed for victory, whereas in the 1880s, those same states had accounted for 76.1 per cent of the required votes. To win, not only did the Democratic Party have to do better outside the South than was necessary in the 19th century, but the remaining votes now had to come from a wider variety of states as well. However, even outside the South, the early 20th century Democratic coalition was slanted towards rural interests. Only a minority of the northern and Border states that contained cities with populations of more than 200,000 were in the group needed by the Democrats for a minimum winning coalition between 1908 and 1920.

Only Colorado (Denver), Indiana (Indianapolis), Kentucky (Louisville), Missouri (St. Louis and Kansas City), Maryland (Baltimore), and Ohio (Cleveland and Cincinnati) fell into this category. Even if New York (New York City, Rochester, and Buffalo) and Oregon (Portland) are added to the list as places where the Democrats might have had electoral hopes, this still left many large cities in states in which the party stood little chance: Chicago (Illinois), Philadelphia and Pittsburgh (Pennsylvania), Boston (Massachusetts), San Francisco and Los Angeles (California), Detroit (Michigan), Newark and Jersey City (New Jersey), Minneapolis and St. Paul (Minnesota), Milwaukee (Wisconsin), Seattle (Washington), and Providence (Rhode Island).

Paradoxically, of course, between 1896 and 1932, the Democrats were doing much better overall in the cities vis-à-vis the Republicans, than is usually acknowledged (see Table 4.7). Nevertheless, in the years up to 1920, the big-city vote was likely to make only a relatively small contribution to the winning of the first 266 Electoral College votes by the Democrats. The party's "presidential wing" had a largely rural and small-city profile by comparison both with the Republican Party and with its own "congressional wing" (at least until 1914). This appears to change somewhat in the 1920s.

In part, the appearance of change is the result of the Democratic presidential nominees in the years 1920–8 being politicians who saw the key to victory as lying – as it did in the late 19th century – in certain medium-size and large states of the Old North. The consequences of their approach to coalition building can be seen in Table 4.5; even including the western-strategy year of 1932, the winning of a bare majority in the Electoral College in the 1920s would likely have required the Democrats to carry states containing the following cities: New York City, Buffalo, St. Louis, Baltimore, and Milwaukee. The party would also have had to pay some attention to another state with a major city, Illinois, which was on the fringes of the party's "hit list". This strategy, one that gave such prominence to states containing large cities, many of which were in the Old North, was not necessarily "whistling in the dark". As is seen shortly, the relative contribution of the urban vote to the Democratic Party in congressional elections was much greater after 1918 than it had been earlier, and this could be thought to provide evidence that the future of the party might well lie in the cities.

Irrespective of the optimal strategy for building their national coalition in the 1920s, there was one respect in which the party was clearly better placed than it had been between 1896 and 1910. Despite the fact that the scale of their presidential defeats was greater in the 1920s than in the immediate post-1896 period, the Democratic Party's base in northern state politics was considerably more secure than it had been then. Consider, first, governorships. It is true that between 1920 and 1932, the median number of years in which the Democrats occupied these offices was 2 – the same as in the comparable 12-year period 1900–1912. (The median is low in both cases because there were a large number of non-southern states in which the party hardly ever won any governorships.) In the years 1900–1912, though, the party's success outside the South and the Border states had been slight; the only states in which they held the governorship for at least 4 years were Montana (12), Nevada (8), North Dakota and Oregon (both 6), Ohio (5), and Colorado, Idaho, Indiana, and Minnesota (4 each). By contrast, between 1920 and 1932, the party held governorships in the following: Oklahoma (12 years), New York (10), Colorado, Montana, New Jersey, and Utah (8 each), Arizona (7), Nevada, New Mexico, Ohio, and South Dakota (6 each), and Kansas, Oregon, and Wyoming (4 each). Not only was the extent of the success greater in the later period, but the states in which they were winning were much more varied. At the state level, Democrats were competitive in places like New Jersey and New York, whereas during the earlier period, it was not until 1910 that they had been competitive there. Moreover, in the selection of senators (now directly elected), the party did as well in the non-South as it had done in the years 1878–90, and better than in 1900–1912. Of all non-southern Senate nominations, 27.7 per cent were Democrats – exactly the same as in 1878–90. The "spread" of these nominations is also interesting. In 1878–90, most non-southern nominations were from the Border states, with only 12.5 per cent of non-border (and non-southern) nominations going to Democrats; in 1920–32, 25 per cent of all such nominations went to Democrats.

Two preliminary conclusions can be drawn from this brief discussion, ones which inform the subsequent analysis of 1920–32. The first is that the travails of the Democratic Party at the presidential level appeared to affect them much less at lower levels of politics than in the post-1896 era, at least with respect to officeholding. The second conclusion is that the party system had become much less sectional than it had been earlier. After 1910, and continuing into the 1920s, the Democrats started doing *relatively* well outside their traditional, ex-slave heartland. Overall, the party was still lagging far behind the Republicans in much of the non-South, but the strictly sectional lines of division in the nation were far less pronounced in the 1920s than they were 40 years earlier. If this created problems for the party in terms of the diversity of the coalition it had to put together in presidential politics, it also created opportunities for it.

We must now turn, therefore, to the various factors that might, conceivably, have made building a national coalition difficult for the Democratic Party. We begin with the most significant factor: In the 1920s, the Democratic Party nationally became a party engaged in a civil war. To a large extent, the difference between its performance in presidential elections and sub-national elections in the 1920s is to be explained by the incompatibility of the interests that the party was trying to aggregate. Here it is important to distinguish "incompatibility" from the "range" of the various interests to be embraced; the next section is concerned primarily with the former, while the following section deals with the latter. We are concerned first, then, with "why the war occurred" and later (in Section 3) with whether, even in the absence of overt hostilities, there was now sufficient in common between the two wings of the party for them to form a viable basis for a party in the long term.

2. The Incompatibility of Interests in the Democratic Coalition

Why did the party have warring factions? In explaining this, we need to examine the underlying structural factors in the party with which the particular circumstances of the Wilson administration interacted. As noted earlier, the Democratic coalition in the 19th century had been one in which three-quarters of the Electoral College votes required by the party came from the less-competitive ex-slave states, while a few competitive northern states supplied the rest. The party had generally followed the rational strategy of selecting candidates from these northern states as a way of building a winning coalition. Normally, relations between northern urban party bosses and other Democrats had been guided by self-interest, though for many southern and western Democrats, dealing with people like the leaders of Tammany Hall was seen as a price that had to be paid for victory.

However, for most of the 19th century, those sorts of "unspeakable" urban leaders had been kept at a distance by others in the party – in three respects. First, overall, urban America could never be more than a relatively minor component of the Democratic coalition – albeit a key one – simply because only a fairly small proportion of all Americans lived in large cities at that time. Secondly, dealing with "ethnic" urban leaders was usually something that was mediated by other politicians in their states. It might be a Grover Cleveland, who had poor relations with Tammany, or it might be a David Hill who co-operated with them more closely, at least until the mid-1890s. Generally, though, machine politicians lacked the votes to control their state parties actively, so that the extent of direct negotiations between party elites and the ethnics had been limited. The riffraff were being kept in their place. Thirdly, although it is usually argued that the cities were mainly Democratic before the 1890s, the contribution of the cities to Democratic victories in presidential elections was more limited than this view usually posits.

Consider David Burner's evidence showing that the Democrats typically won about 65 per cent of the vote in the 10 largest cities in presidential elections between 1876 and 1892.[1] In fact, with the notable exception of the cities in New York State throughout the period, and arguably those in Maryland in 1888 and in Illinois in 1892, the large cities did not help the Democrats to win states in presidential elections. Although, overall, Democrats had a plurality of big-city voters, only in New York was this a key factor in the compilation of Electoral College votes. Philadelphia, for example, was a Republican-leaning city in a Republican state, and the Democrats never won Massachusetts or Ohio in the period 1876–92, so that the contributions of Democratic voters in Boston, Cincinnati (which leaned Republican anyway), and Cleveland were not decisive. Nor were the St. Louis Democrats pivotal – the state would have gone Democratic in 1884, 1888, and 1892 even if St. Louis had been disenfranchised.

This point becomes apparent if we look at the year of the party's greatest presidential triumph since 1856, 1892; even that year the Democrats still lost three of the eight states that contained cities with more than 200,000 people (Massachusetts, Ohio, and Pennsylvania). Furthermore, they would have won in Maryland and Missouri irrespective of the big-city vote. Only in California, Illinois, and New York did the urban vote make a difference to the party. Since 1892 was the only occasion on which the Democrats won Illinois between 1876 and 1892, it could be said that Chicago contributed to the Democratic coalition nationally when it was least needed. While the value of San Francisco in enabling the Democrats to win California (which they did in 1880 and 1892) should not be underestimated, it is difficult to escape the conclusion that the big-city vote was really crucial for the party only in New York. This point is important because there is a danger of misunderstanding the significance of change in national electoral coalition building after the mid-1890s. Part of that significance is that increasingly, cities became a larger component

---

[1] David Burner, *The Politics of Provincialism*, p. 20.

of the national coalitions of *both* parties, as the populations of major cities increased rapidly.

For intra-party relations among Democrats, the rise of the cities raised the prospect both that city politicians would now have to be dealt with more directly – as in New York in 1898 when Tammany took control of the state party – and that they would expect more from other elements in the party. They would expect respect and they would want a share of power so that their interests could be protected. Both were problematic. Many rural and small-town Americans, and many politicians from such places, regarded the non-Protestant peoples who were fuelling the growth of the cities as having lifestyles that were inferior to those of real Americans, and following the Jeffersonian ideal, they believed real Americans did not live in cities. In Burner's words:

> The aim of the rural faction [of the Democratic party] became larger than the economic and political; it sought not less than the rescue of traditional American virtue, and that virtue it identified with the countryside, which must now resist the moral corruption of the cities. . . . [I]n *The Commoner* [Bryan] wrote that the [1916] election was a victory for "the West and South without the aid or consent of the East. The sceptre has passed from New York, and this is sufficient glory for one year".[2]

Toleration of city life by rural Democrats had been less of an issue in the 1880s because of the smaller role played in national politics by city parties then. As the cities grew and their politicians sought more from the Democratic Party, so the issue of how the two kinds of America would relate to each other in the party became more contentious. City politicians demanded the kind of respect, and the political influence, that the size of their electorates increasingly warranted.

Moreover, alongside a general distrust of "alien" cultures, there were now political issues to divide rural from urban Democrats that were far more contentious than even free silver had been. In particular, there was prohibition. Prohibition was to split the Democratic party along broadly rural/urban lines, but in asserting this, it is important to be clear about two aspects of the context in which prohibition came to play such a devastating role within the party. First, it was not a partisan matter. Prohibitionists had abandoned the strategy of running candidates under their own banner, or alternatively infiltrating the Republican Party, during the 1890s. After that, they operated as a pressure group using a deliberately bi-partisan strategy. Consequently, the impact on the Democratic Party

---

[2] Ibid., p. 11.

was, in a sense, indirect, rather than direct. Secondly, while prohibition intensified the rural/urban cleavage ("the politics of respect") in the party, it was not always a rural/urban issue; there were predominantly "wet"-inclined rural counties just as there were "dry" residents of the cities. But disproportionately, the latter group tended to be Republicans, so that overall the typical urban Democrat was more inclined to be wet. Prohibition thus exacerbated a tension within the party that was grounded initially in different identities, and turned it into something that, in the short term at least, made it difficult to reconcile the two wings of the party that had so willingly come together in 1912 to nominate Wilson.

Prohibition is a curious policy. Since its repeal, most people have found it difficult to comprehend. The enormously adverse consequences it generated have tended to obscure why it would ever have seemed attractive as a policy at all. For future generations, only the foolish or those with the most anti-liberal of religious sentiments could ever be imagined as favouring it. Yet had the passage of the 18th Amendment depended solely on support by fools or moral authoritarians, it would never have come close to being enacted. Prohibition eventually became law because of support from two additional quarters. To begin with, after early 1917, alcohol and its production could be presented as interfering with the war effort – it diverted economic activity elsewhere and its consumption interfered with the efficient operation of a war economy. That many brewers were of German origin further enhanced the argument from a position of patriotism. However, even this cannot account for the passage of a constitutional amendment on an issue that had been highly controversial.

More significant than the factors discussed so far, and certainly for the purposes of the arguments in this book, is that prohibition was, in many ways, an obvious extension of the radical arguments that underpinned the Bryanite economic agenda. On this view, just as monopolies hurt the working person through the selfish actions of privileged economic interests, so too did alcohol; it was a product promoted by powerful businesses that provided no benefit for those who consumed it, and which actually harmed them. Monopolies had to be constrained to prevent harm from being imposed on third parties, and so too, it was argued, did the distillers. Consequently, prohibition was really an extension of the progressivist policy agenda, rather than a perverse mutation of it. At least some of those who took this progressive line wanted to prohibit only the sale of distilled alcohol and did not believe that, in voting for the 18th Amendment, they would also be banning the consumption of wine and beer when the subsequent Volstead Act was passed. Thus, the form that prohibition took under the Volstead Act was more rigorous than at least some progressives wanted, although the momentum for the reform by 1918 meant that this produced little controversy in its enactment. However, that did not mean that many urban residents were just resigned to accepting a policy that impinged seriously on the lifestyles they had brought from non-Protestant Europe. Rather, it remained a source of resentment and controversy, and one that acerbated the clash of the two cultures – the urban and the rural – in the Democratic Party.

The battleground for that clash of the two cultures was the presidential nomination, so that far from recovering from the chaos at the end of the Wilson presidency, the Democrats lurched from one disastrous presidential campaign (in 1920) to another. In 1924, it took nine days and 101 ballots to produce a supposed compromise candidate, John W. Davis, who satisfied neither wing of the party. In 1928, it was clear that the Catholic New York governor, Al Smith, could not really be denied the nomination, partly because the leading progressive candidate, William Gibbs McAdoo, declined to run for fear of splitting the party. Nevertheless, this concession did not produce a united party. Many southern Democrats refused to support (or to support actively) a politician whose Catholicism, speech, and lifestyle epitomized for them the New York City immigrant – however well that immigrant might have done for himself. Consequently, the Republicans actually won five southern states that year (Florida, North Carolina, Tennessee, Texas, and Virginia).

That the battles took place primarily in the national party – and especially at the national conventions themselves – is significant because in the 1920s, there was also a major split in the Republican Party, but for them it was Congress that formed the arena in which disunity was apparent. There were several reasons for this difference. The Democrats' two-thirds rule made nominations more problematic for their party than it did for the Republicans. (The impact of the rule is discussed again in Section 10.) Furthermore, ever since the split in the party in 1912, eastern Republican politicians made certain that they retained a firm grip over the party machinery both in the states where they were dominant and at the national level. In addition, not only were their opponents (western progressives) highly individualistic, but the radical nature of their policy agenda also varied, so that co-operation between them was difficult to effect. Finally, Congress was not a place in which urban Democrats could exercise the clout that corresponded to the size of the electorates that they represented because of the absence of electoral reapportionment in the 1920s, the result being a major under-representation of the urban electorate. By

TABLE 6.1. *The Difference Between the Democrats' Performance in Congressional Elections in Non-southern Large Cities and Their Performance Nationally in Congressional Elections, 1896–1938 (as Percentage of Total Vote)*

(Democratic Share of Vote in Large Cities Minus Republican Share of Vote) Minus (Democratic Share of Vote Nationally Minus Republican Share of Vote)	
1896	−10.8
1898	−3.7
1900	−0.5
1902	+0.2
1904	−4.0
1906	−3.9
1908	−5.7
1910	−1.8
1912	−5.4
1914	−3.2
1916	−5.5
1918	+12.8
1920	−0.5
1922	+7.2
1924	−0.8
1926	+13.1
1928	+10.7
1930	+7.6
1932	+3.1
1934	+7.1
1936	+8.7

contrast, western progressives in the Republican Party were not so under-represented, and Congress (especially the Senate) was the most appropriate forum, therefore, in which to confront the policy agenda of the Republican administrations and of the eastern wing of the congressional party.

Nevertheless, it is important to recognize that the long-term change in the Democratic Party that had produced conflict was not the only change relevant to the party's future. It was not just a question of urban Democrats having a much larger constituency in the party than they used to have two or three decades earlier – because the cities were larger. There was also a remarkable, and little remarked on, transformation in the propensity of urban and non-urban voters to vote Democrat during the Wilson years. The hinge year was 1918 (see Table 6.1). The data cited in Table 6.1 are for congressional elections in non-southern cities;

the difference between the Democratic Party's plurality over Republicans nationally is subtracted from their plurality in all congressional districts that lay primarily within the boundaries of cities containing more than 200,000 people. Up to and including 1916, the Democrats got a smaller share of the vote in the large cities than they did nationally; the party really was a rural-leaning one. Between 1896, and 1916 only in one year (1902) was there a (small) bias in favour of the urban Democrats. The median difference between the two pluralities was −3.9 per cent of the vote. By contrast, in 1918 the difference was +12.8 per cent. Only in two years after that (1920 and 1924) did the party vote return to being relatively more rural and small city, and in both those years, differences in the relative shares of the vote were small by comparison with those evident in the pre-1916 period. The median for the years 1918–30 is +7.6 per cent. Of course, this shift in the relative contributions of the two groups might be the result of either a greater "big city" vote for the Democrats or a smaller contribution from non-urban America; either way, the balance in the party was shifting, and that is evident even in 1932 when the party won with a pronounced "western" strategy.

In spite of Wilson's taking the party in the direction of a western strategy in 1916, and in spite of the loss of votes from (primarily urban) Irish and German voters in 1918, following American participation in the war, the Democratic Party was becoming a different kind of party by the end of the Wilson years. In one sense, therefore, the great Bryanite project can be seen as reaching its zenith in 1916, and that its long-term potential was in decline thereafter – in spite of the fact that it was through the use of a western strategy that Franklin Roosevelt was to construct his coalition in 1932. It is difficult to explain what caused this shift in the balance of voter support within the party. Arguably, it was the result of changes within state parties between about 1916 and the mid-1920s – and probably, in the case of rural decline, in states that lay to the east of the Rocky Mountain region. For example, after decades of close competition in largely rural Indiana, the Democrats started to become markedly less competitive in the 1920s. Moreover, there are instances in the 1920s of urban parties starting to increase the range of social groups that they mobilized as a way of building power – for example, in Kansas City the Democrats started to mobilize black voters in the mid-1920s. (Republican policy towards African Americans also contributed to the ability of the Democrats to attract their votes; in Indianapolis, for example, there was a marked shift away from the GOP in 1924 because of the party's overtures to the Ku Klux Klan.[3]) One conclusion that can be drawn from the congressional electoral data is that the later urban basis of the Democratic Party should not be seen as dating from the New Deal or even, as some commentators maintain, from Al Smith's campaign in 1928, but from about 1918.[4] However, this leads us to the question of whether a new kind of Democratic coalition, one in which urban America was to be allied with other elements in the party, would be viable. Was the Democratic Party trying to aggregate too wide a range of interests to be a successful national party?

3. Had the Democratic Party Become Too Disparate by the 1920s?

There are two answers to this question. One is that in the short term, it was possible for the Democrats to win presidential elections – and probably they would have done so even without an economic depression that was as severe as the Great Depression. The other answer is that even with such a victory, the party would still have been left with a problem of how to devise a set of ideas (and a few policies) that in the future could unite all the groups that were now backing them. We should begin examining these two answers by recognizing that, not surprisingly, during the 1920s two quite distinct strategies emerged for revitalizing the party and constructing a winning coalition in the Electoral College, each reflecting the core division within the party.

Under the party chairmanship of John Raskob, a New York financier who had been appointed by his close ally Al Smith, the "eastern strategy" was pressed; it involved abandoning the economic interventionism of the Bryan-Wilson years in favour of a more restricted role for government acceptable to business interests in the East. At the same time, the party was to move towards a much "wetter" position on prohibition as a means of bolstering the immigrant vote in the large cities. In essence, this meant accepting the erosion of the party's western wing, but its proponents argued that competitiveness in the larger eastern states, and in the midwestern cities, would more than make up for this loss.

---

[3] See William W. Giffin, "The Political Realignment of Black Voters in Indianapolis, 1924", *Indiana Magazine of History*, 79 (1983), 133–66.

[4] Samuel Lubell was one of the original proponents of the view that Al Smith kick-started the New Deal realignment in 1928, but other authors, including James Sundquist, have taken up the theme. Lubell, *The Future of American Politics*, p. 12 (this book was first published in 1951); James L. Sundquist, *Dynamics of the Party System*, Chapter 9. See also Kristi Andersen, *The Creation of a Democratic Majority, 1928–1936*, Chicago, University of Chicago Press, 1979.

After 1928, critics of this approach could point to the decisive defeat of Al Smith when he lost even New York by more than 18 per cent of the vote at the same time that Franklin Roosevelt was winning the state governorship, albeit narrowly. Yet by 1930 there was some merit to the strategy. In particular, it recognized that a distinct advantage would accrue to the Democrats from distancing their party from the more prohibitionist Republican Party. This was because by about 1926 or so, the disrepute into which bootlegging and gangsterism had brought the law seemed to have prompted a major shift in public opinion away from prohibition.[5] A policy of partial, or especially complete, repeal that might have played into the hands of the Republicans earlier in the decade was now an optimal position to hold on the issue in future elections.

Furthermore, although there was a wet wing in the Republican Party, its members were in no position to shift the party nationally in their direction. (Crudely, that wing can be characterized as the "Wall Street" side of the "Main Street versus Wall Street" divide in the party; Wall Street was Episcopalian, or secular and wet, while Main Street was Methodist and dry.) The party had always been attractive to dry voters, which meant that by comparison with the Democrats, it was going to be more difficult to take on a wholly wet platform. In addition, after 1928 the president was Herbert Hoover, and he was both firmly committed to the prohibition cause and largely beyond the influence of congressional Republicans – even if the latter had favoured repeal.[6] In other words, there was a good opportunity for the Democrats in 1932 to compete with the Republicans on an issue that placed the latter at a disadvantage. However, Raskob and his allies linked this wet policy to a rejection of the kind of economic intervention advocated by the Bryanite wing of the party. But here interpretations of his economic philosophy, and that of his close ally Al Smith, differ.

For some historians, Raskob was little more than a traditional Democratic conservative on economic matters; thus, Douglas Craig argues:

Raskob's views of the proper role of government bore strong resemblance to the "sum of good government" as described in Thomas Jefferson's first inaugural.... Raskob believed that both federal and state governments should limit themselves to the provision of defense and law, the protection of the individual's

---

[5] David E. Kyvig, *Repealing National Prohibition*, Chicago and London, University of Chicago Press, 1979, pp. 67–8 and 116–17.

[6] In Jordan A. Schwarz's words, "Hoover belonged to the GOP in name only and this never ceased to rankle many congressional Republicans. He was almost a party unto himself". Schwarz, *The Interregnum of Despair: Hoover, Congress and the Depression*, Urbana, University of Illinois Press, 1970, p. 45.

life and property, the fostering of trade, and the provision of nonprofit social infrastructure such as schools, roads and sanitation. Government should not interfere with the normal functioning of the free market.[7]

Others have claimed that Raskob was a moderate in relation to economic interventionism, and not the pure Jeffersonian depicted by Craig; David Kyvig had earlier said of him that "for a businessman in the twenties, Raskob held quite progressive views. He remained adamantly conservative only on the need for action to come through state government to protect against distant, excessive federal power".[8]

Nevertheless, whichever interpretation of Raskob is taken, the crucial point is that the kinds of economic policies favoured by Al Smith, Raskob, and their allies were much less interventionist than those favoured by the inheritors of the Bryan and Wilson mantle in the party.

This brings us to the second strategy. This was to revive the coalition that had sustained Wilson in power, relying on certain kinds of interventionist policies that would attract support from farmers and others in the West. In the early 1920s, the leader of this wing of the party had been Wilson's son-in-law, William Gibbs McAdoo. Although he was "not so conspicuously country-bred as Bryan", he shared the latter's attitude towards urban America and "his utterances were replete with condemnations of the city [New York] as the home of Wall Street and with praise for the country as the hope of America".[9] His failure to secure the party's nomination in 1924, when he seemingly embraced the Ku Klux Klan, reduced the likelihood of his ever being the party's candidate, but the kind of party strategy he advocated persisted as a strong element in the party. On this view, the Democratic Party was to remain primarily a party of the South, the Midwest, and the West, and the party was to win national elections by differentiating itself from the Republicans on economic policy. Partly for instrumental reasons, because it would help prevent fragmentation in the southern and western alliance, and partly because of a continuing progressive belief in the argument that alcohol was one of the means by which workingmen could be exploited, the strategy was usually linked to continuing support for prohibition.

The attraction of this second strategy lay in the fact that it drew on existing areas of Democratic voting strength. Its weakness lay in the fact

---

[7] Douglas B. Craig, *After Wilson: The Struggle for the Democratic Party, 1920–1934*, Chapel Hill and London, University of North Carolina Press, 1992, pp. 148–9.

[8] Kyvig, *Repealing National Prohibition*, p. 146.

[9] Burner, *The Politics of Provincialism*, p. 12.

that that relatively narrow base was being eroded already – with states like Indiana and Colorado moving away from the Democratic Party in the 1920s. Although, in theory, it was still possible to construct a Wilsonian-type alliance, that feat was arguably more difficult in the 1920s than it had been. This is the basis of the conventional wisdom that Roosevelt could win in 1932 only because of the severely depressed state of the American economy, for which blame was heaped on an incumbent Republican president. On that view, without the greatest economic depression ever, the Democrats did not have a winning strategy; neither the eastern nor the western strategy could have produced an electoral majority. Years of minority status would have faced the Democrats.

Yet it can be argued that the Democrats did have a potential winning strategy in 1932, even if, to employ modern parlance, there had been a "much softer landing" for the economy after the boom of the mid-1920s. In fact, that strategy was the one that was actually adopted by the Democrats in 1932; it involved combining "wetness" with economic interventionism. That is, it meant de-coupling the prohibition element from Raskob's eastern strategy, and using that to attract votes in the industrial cities of the East and Midwest, while appealing to western voters, partly on interventionist policies designed to help farmers, and partly by selecting a candidate whose personal style would not alienate them. Al Smith was not going to secure the needed votes in the South and West however many times he ran, and that would have been the case even if he had experienced a Pauline conversion on economics. Like Bryan, it was as much what he was as what he advocated that was his liability. An urban Catholic who flaunted his culture in the way Smith did would always divide the party. (The concern about a Catholic candidate was to haunt the Democrats until 1960.) That was why Franklin Roosevelt was the ideal candidate. He was an Easterner but with the values and the kind of support that would appeal in the South and West. Moreover, he had the necessary flexibility on the prohibition issue that would make it possible for the Democrats to be both economic interventionists and wet. FDR was nothing if not the consummate politician, and on an issue on which public opinion was shifting, but where the strength and directions of those shifts were usually not clear, he himself shifted his position frequently – much to the annoyance of his opponents. As Kyvig says of his period as governor:

Initially, he ordered state law-enforcement officials to arrest Volstead Act violators and turn them over to federal courts, since New York had no prohibition law. Then at the 1929 Governors' Conference, he urged that states be delegated full responsibility for prohibition enforcement. The New York Democratic convention in 1930 included in its platform a call for prohibition repeal.... Finally, on September 9 [1930], with the political tide in New York running strongly against prohibition, Roosevelt announced that he favoured repeal of the Eighteenth Amendment and its replacement with an amendment giving states the right to sell liquor through state agencies, or to ban it, as the people wished."[10]

This was not the end of the matter. When running for the presidency, FDR bolstered his support in the South and West by favouring prohibition. He did so right up to the point at which the national convention voted for outright repeal of the 18th Amendment, by the massive majority of 934¾ to 213¾, at which point he became an enthusiastic supporter of repeal. To fuse the western strategy with the prohibition element of the eastern strategy required a politician like Roosevelt to make it work. Once it was effected, though, the new strategy had the potential for doing what the Democrats needed: keeping its core vote in the South and West loyal, while providing sufficient votes in the cities of the East and Midwest to make it possible for the Democrats to win enough of the states in those regions to provide for victory overall.

But would this mixing of the strategies have been possible had the economy soft-landed in 1929–30, rather than crash-landed? There are two possible lines of objection to the argument I have proposed. One is that the Great Depression provided economic arguments in favour of repeal of prohibition that could be used in support of other arguments for it; after 1930, the case was made frequently that repeal would create jobs. Given this, it might be argued that with only a modest recession, the shift in public opinion on the issue might have moved more slowly, and hence outright repeal might have been far more divisive at the 1932 convention than it actually was. This is probably true, but even if it is, it does not mean that the 1932 Democratic convention would have become split on the matter. What might well have happened is that a "wet" plank that fell short of outright repeal would have been adopted then, but it would still have been sufficiently different from the Republican policy as to give the Democrats a major electoral advantage in urban areas.

The other objection is that part of the momentum that FDR attained in seeking the Democratic nomination was made possible by the severity of the depression. He was not without major opponents, in any case. Al Smith from the party's eastern wing, John Garner trying to "run down

---

[10] Kyvig, *Repealing National Prohibition*, p. 147.

the middle" as a southern moderate, and William Gibbs McAdoo seeking to reclaim leadership of the Bryanite wing, all sought the nomination. Given that before 1936 the nomination depended on a two-thirds majority in the convention, Roosevelt's nomination was not ensured until deals were made there. While in hindsight it is apparent that he was the type of candidate needed to unite the party around the new strategy, that might well not have been evident at the time, and in different circumstances. Consequently, the argument could be made that Smith might well have run a stronger campaign in 1932 had the economy undergone only a moderate recession, and that might have made Roosevelt's nomination less likely. Obviously, there is something to this argument, though how likely it is that Roosevelt would have failed to obtain the nomination in the circumstances outlined is impossible to tell. The two-thirds rule had made the nomination of a candidate especially divisive in 1920 and 1924, and might have done so again. On the other hand, Democrats were all too aware of the damage done to the party by those two conventions, and it is at least arguable that in 1932 a new strategy, and a candidate capable of promoting that strategy effectively, would have emerged in spite of the decision-making procedures. Past failures would likely have intensified the desire to win and that might have made compromise easier.

The central point of my argument is that the Democrats' ability to construct a coalition that was capable of defeating Hoover in 1932 may well not have depended on the severity of the downturn in the economy following the years of boom. The Republicans were potentially vulnerable to the construction of a particular type of coalition by their opponents. Nevertheless, even if they had won that year, the Democrats arguably would have had the same difficulty that Wilson had faced – how to change the existing coalition into one that was sustainable in the long term. Perhaps a lengthy and convoluted route to the eventual repeal of prohibition might have helped them in this attempt, but the Democrats would still have faced the task of keeping together a rather unwieldy, and possibly thin, majority. There is also the issue of choosing the "big ideas" or "themes" around which partisans could rally. The party had moved some way from its pure (19th century) minimal government ideology, which really had served to link the various components of the party. However, while specific policies might be devised to fit with that overall "small government" stance – as with the "New Freedom" – the problem was that the particularistic nature of those policies had meant that there was little holding the party together once they had been enacted or become irrelevant. That

had been the problem facing Wilson arguably by 1914 and certainly by
1916 – where to take the party now?

The real significance of the Great Depression for the Democrats, therefore, was not so much that it made a presidential victory possible as that
the context in which victory was achieved meant that the policy agenda of
the party could be transformed. Because of the circumstances in which he
entered office, Roosevelt could provide a radically different approach to
public policy from that of other Democrats. This was a form of economic
intervention that looked to empower capitalist enterprises as well as elements of the Democratic voting base. The greatest impact was to be felt
in the cities where urban leaders could now perceive the value to them
of "bigger government", something that they had resisted in the past.
FDR, the representative of rural radicalism, sustained a constituency for
urban radicalism from 1933 onwards, thereby transforming the nature
of Democratic Parties in states that contained large cities. Subsequently,
the Democrats became more competitive in states in the East and in the
Midwest that had leaned to the Republicans – in many cases since the
Civil War. The Democratic coalition was thereby re-created by Franklin
Roosevelt, and that is why, in relation to the nature of the party system,
the New Deal era does mark a much sharper break with what preceded
it than had been the case with the upheavals of 1893–6.

An important aspect of this reconfiguration of the Democratic Party in
the 1930s was that it helped provide for a long-term shift in the party's
ideology. John Gerring has argued that in the 1890s, the Democratic Party
switched from a Jeffersonian ideology to one of Populism:

> At the heart of the Populist drama lay the poignant struggle between honest
> commonfolk and politicoeconomic elites.... Whereas Jacksonian Democrats
> spoke of "the people" at large, Democrats from Bryan to Truman were more
> likely to speak for the "common people", "ordinary Americans", or the "strug-
> gling masses". The clear implication . . . was that Americans were *not* all the same;
> some were unjustly privileged over others. Populist Democracy was thus distin-
> guished from the previous century of Democratic rhetoric by "its implicit class
> orientation."[11]

As an ideology for *retaining* political power at the national level in
America, there were four main limitations of this post-1890s Populist
ideology.

First, by itself, railing against "the powerful" may be an effective device
for gaining public office in the first place, but after a certain period in office

[11] John Gerring, *Party Ideologies in America, 1828–1996*, p. 196. Italics in original.

it becomes much less effective. Essentially, it is a strategy used by political "outs" to get in; it is not a strategy for long-term government by a party. Being in government often weakens the plausibility of a party's claim that it is necessary, or even useful, for controlling "the powerful".

Secondly, in the United States, there was no history of parties developing specific policy programmes on which they contested an election, and which would then be re-shaped once they were in office. Commitment to specific policies was more sporadic. Thus, once the Democrats had gotten elected, and once they had passed certain legislation in a first term, what was there for them to do? As was argued in Chapter 5, this was the difficulty that Wilson had faced. Reinvigorating populist rhetoric when in office requires such rhetoric to be linked to specific policies – new programmes to tackle social problems. But if all that was supposed to be needed was certain kinds of regulation to control the powerful, and if that legislation was enacted, as in 1913 and 1914, what remained to be done in government by populist politicians? In a sense, they would legislate themselves into irrelevance.

Thirdly, given the particular role played by class in American society, class politics could be practised only in a covert way. No major party could come out and identify itself as being the party of particular classes; it had to be its opponents who were the ones who stood for class. However, that meant that it was easy for the Republicans to produce their own version of populist rhetoric, and if the Democrats invented the "ordinary" American, after the 1920s the Republicans responded with the "diminutive" American, and this period saw

the adoption of a whole cast of characters who had never before appeared in Republican scripts, including the "average man", the "small man", the "little fellow", the "small farmer", the "little taxpayer", and of course the "small business man". The hallmark of virtue within the Republican liberal mindset was to be little and diminutive status was bestowed upon all manner of political groupings.[12]

If the opponents could, in a sense, parody an electoral appeal based on "us against them", because the boundaries of the "us" were both imprecise and largely not discussed by politicians, populist rhetoric had obvious limitations as the cornerstone of a winning strategy.

Fourthly, many of those eastern businessmen who had returned to active support of the party after 1896 (and their successors) had little sympathy with populist rhetoric and covert class appeals. That was one of the reasons they had continued to be suspicious of Bryan. Populism may

---

[12] Ibid., p. 144.

have embraced many of the leading Democrats in the decades after 1896, but it did not embrace what had been an important component of the Democratic coalition. Unlike Jeffersonian ideas of limited government, which really could unite disparate components of the Democratic coalition in the 19th century, populism could not – at least in the long term. It was simply not an ideology suited to bringing together the different elements of the party, as it was then constituted.

The Great Depression gave the Democratic Party breathing space. Both the length of the depression and the discrediting of the Republicans enabled Democrats to continue using populist rhetoric, even while a new kind of rhetoric could emerge, one that could be utilized by a party that aimed at keeping itself in power and not just attaining it intermittently. The broadening of the party's egalitarian agenda that was to become prominent after the Second World War was a means of returning to something that Jeffersonianism had provided – an ideology that really linked the different interests in the party – although the content was very different, of course. It provided the party with a set of ideas and symbols that had the potential to unite the different kinds of interests that the party hoped to aggregate.

4. Was There a Declining Resource Base in the Democratic Party?

The resource bases of both parties were declining in the long term, and in urban areas many of the reforms separating the party from the administration of local government were already in place by the early 1920s. However, if anything, the 1920s represented high tide for the power of local party organizations in the United States. As we have seen earlier, many urban parties consolidated power successfully two decades earlier, so that much of the Democratic Party's traditional resource base remained intact in the short term. Of course, the decentralization of the American parties meant that at the national level, these local resources remained available only indirectly, but there was nothing special about this in the 1920s. The party's difficulties in the 1920s did not stem, therefore, from the absence of means with which leaders could aggregate the various interests – the problem really lay in the interests themselves.

5. Were the Republicans Mobilizing New Interests in the Electorate?

Emigration, especially before 1922, had continued to fuel the growth of the cities and hence of potential new voters. Whereas the census of 1900 had produced a reapportionment of House districts such that 13 per cent of all districts lay primarily in the borders of cities with more than 200,000 people, the 1930 census would produce a House in which more than 20 per cent of districts were of this kind. Nationally, neither party had secured a firm hold over the new voters, and the coalitions they constructed still owed much to local circumstances. As in the period before 1912, the Democrats had no particular claim to be the party of newer immigrants *in general*. As noted in Chapter 4, presidential election results provide a poor guide to the underlying strength of the parties because the Democratic vote was often reduced considerably by the weakness of the party's presidential candidates or by its internal divisions. The results of mid-term elections provide a somewhat better guide, and what they show is a relatively even split of the urban vote between the parties (Table 4.7), though with a slight edge to the Republicans. In relation to the two-party vote only, the median mid-term plurality of the Republicans over the Democrats in districts in cities containing more than 200,000 people was 2.7 per cent between 1898 and 1926. Moreover, this rather even division of the vote is evident throughout the period. Only once (in 1906) is the Republican lead as much as 12.0 per cent, and only once (1918) is the Democrat plurality as high as 4 per cent of the vote; for all other mid-term elections, the best Republican performance gave them a mere 3.8 per cent lead in the cities (1926), while the best Democratic performance (1922) produced a 0.2 per cent lead for them.

The relevant point here is that neither party established a consistent advantage in the large cities at any time during these years. In urban America, the overall balance between the parties that was established with party consolidation in the 1890s persisted right through till the New Deal; there was even a Republican plurality in the two-party vote of 2.2 per cent at the beginning of the Great Depression in 1930. Indeed, what is most significant is how few of the potential voters in the cities were mobilized by either party before the 1930s. As we have seen, it was that under-mobilized electoral resource that Roosevelt used in changing the party balance after 1932. The Republican advantage in presidential elections in the 1920s was not the result of the GOP's stealing an edge in the main arena where potentially there were new voters to mobilize – the large cities.

6. What Was the Influence of Change in External Political Structures?

The short answer is none. There were no changes in the political frameworks within which votes were aggregated in presidential elections that could have generated problems in coalition building. No new states joined the union, nor were there any constitutional reforms that affected the process of interest aggregation.

7. Loss of "Fluidity" in a Previously Competitive Electoral Market

In a direct way, this, too, was not a relevant factor, but there is a sense in which there was a problem of "fluidity" facing the Democratic Party. The ability of the Republican Party to mobilize its voters did not depend on Republican-leaning voters identifying more closely with that party. As we have seen, in both parties urban organization remained strong in spite of the long-term transformation that was occurring in the interpenetration of party and government. However, the distribution of voters among the states did advantage Republicans in building a winning coalition, in that potentially there were more safe Republican states than safe Democratic states, so that fewer states had to be added to the core to create a minimum winning coalition.

If we assume that a party that does well in a particular state in gubernatorial elections has a building block that might be used in constructing a winning national coalition, how did the two parties compare? To answer this question, we can examine the performance of the Democrats in gubernatorial elections between 1920 and 1929, and in particular, the mean difference in the share of the vote obtained by the two major parties in those elections in that period. These might be classified into five categories: safe Democratic states, where the mean plurality for the Democrats was at least 10 per cent of the total vote; Democratic-leaning states, where the mean Democratic plurality was between 5 per cent and 10 per cent; competitive states where the mean plurality of one party over the other was less than 5 per cent of the total vote; Republican-leaning states, with pluralities of between 5 per cent and 10 per cent; and safe Republican states, with pluralities over 10 per cent of the vote (Table 6.2). For the most part, there is a correspondence between the party's performance in these gubernatorial elections in the 1920s and its relative performance in presidential elections in the same era (see Table 4.5).

What would be the task facing the two parties in building on their performance at the state level and constructing a national coalition? The first point to note is that if they carried all the states that were safely Democratic, leaned Democratic, and were competitive, the Democrats would win the Electoral College by 297–234. In other words, the Democrats did not have to hope for miracles occurring in Republican states. This is important because it helps to demonstrate that the Democratic Party's

TABLE 6.2. *Median Democratic Plurality of Democrats over Republicans in Gubernatorial Elections, 1920–1929*

Safe Democratic States (144 Electoral College votes)	1st Georgia (n/a) 2nd Louisiana (n/a) 3rd Mississippi (n/a) 4th South Carolina (n/a)	5th Alabama (+59.4) 6th Arkansas (+52.8) 7th Texas (+52.7) 8th Florida (+49.2)	9th Virginia (+34.7) 10th North Carolina (+16.1) 11th Tennessee (+14.3) 12th Maryland (+14.2)	13th Oklahoma (+10.2)
Democratic Leaning States (4 Electoral College votes)	14th Montana (+5.6)			
Competitive States (149 Electoral College votes)	15th Colorado (+3.5) 16th New York (+2.2) 17th Kentucky (+1.7) 18th Oregon (+1.6)	19th Utah (+1.2) 20th Nevada (+0.9) 21st Wyoming (−0.4) 22nd Arizona (−0.5)	23rd Ohio (−0.9) 24th New Mexico (−1.4) 25th New Jersey (−1.7) 26th Nebraska (−2.2)	27th Missouri (−4.9)
Republican Leaning States (23 Electoral College votes)	28th Indiana (−7.7) 29th West Virginia (−8.7)			
Safe Republican States (211 Electoral College votes)	30th New Hampshire (−11.1) 31st Rhode Island (−11.5) 32nd South Dakota (−14.6) 33rd Massachusetts (−17.6) 34th Illinois (−17.6)	35th Delaware (18.1) 36th Kansas (−19.4) 37th Idaho (−20.8) 38th Connecticut (−21.5) 39th Maine (−22.4)	40th North Dakota (−22.5) 41st Washington (−24.6) 42nd Pennsylvania (−31.9) 43rd Wisconsin (−32.2) 44th Michigan (−33.6)	45th Iowa (−35.0) 46th California (−35.1) 47th Minnesota (−44.3) 48th Vermont (−46)

problems lay in aspects of coalition building, rather than in any supposed lack of bases in the states from which a winning coalition could be constructed. The Democratic Party in the 1920s was not a minority party.

However, the Democrats' task was a more difficult one than the Republicans' in two important respects. They had a much smaller "core" support than the GOP: safe Democratic and Democratic-leaning states controlled only 148 votes; Safe Republican and Republican-leaning states controlled 234. The Republicans needed to obtain only 32 Electoral College votes from among the "competitive" states (at the gubernatorial level) to win a presidential election. Secondly, based on their performance in gubernatorial elections, to win a presidential election the Democrats had to put together a coalition that included at least one northeastern state (New York) and at least one western state, as well as the Border states. Moreover, if they lost Ohio, they had to carry both New York and New Jersey, as well as Kentucky and Missouri and quite a few of the competitive western states. In other words, they required a more complex coalition than they had needed even in the Wilson years, and it was more complex than that needed by the Republicans. In theory, of course, it was possible for a winning coalition to be constructed without having to win in states that leaned Republican, but whether such a broad coalition could be built easily was an entirely different matter.

The conclusion reached earlier in the chapter was that combining a "wet plank" with economic intervention might well have been a winning strategy for a single election for the Democrats after 1928. However, the real problem they faced was not that they might be excluded from the presidency altogether, but how they might string together a run of presidential successes. The Republicans' task was easier in that regard, in that they had more alternatives open to them in adding to their "core" support, simply because they needed so few extra votes to make their coalition a minimum winning one.

8. The Absence of a Pool of Suitable Leaders in the Democratic Party

As has been noted earlier in this chapter, the Democrats held more northern governorships and northern Senate seats in the years 1920–32 than they did in the similar 12-year period of 1900–1912. There were also more governors of the larger northern states than there had been in 1900–1912. The absence of a pool of leaders was less pressing than it had been at a time when there were no public officials who had the clout to mount a serious challenge to William Jennings Bryan. Yet by comparison with, for example, the situation that was to face the Republicans in the 1940s, the Democratic Party still had relatively few senior public officials to whom to turn. This was especially evident in 1924 when the convention was deadlocked between the leader of the rural, progressive wing of the party, William Gibbs McAdoo, and the Catholic urbanite Al Smith. The eventual compromise was the relatively unknown John W. Davis. Davis had served only a single term in the House, and that had been more than a decade earlier. He had neither a public image with which to appeal to Democratic voters nor a core following in the party such that, as the compromise candidate, he could be seen by both sides as representing a "positive" outcome in the process of interest aggregation. Davis was very much the "lowest common denominator" in that he did not actually prompt open rebellion at the convention itself, but he did little more than that for his party.

Moreover, the South remained a continuing problem for the party as a potential source of leaders. Although the memory of southern "rebellion" was far less salient among some segments of voters than it had been even two decades earlier, and that had made southern candidacies difficult to sell in the North, there was a relative lack of suitable southern leaders. As V. O. Key observed at the end of the 1940s, not all southern politicians were "clowns or knaves", but demagoguery was a common style in the party-less world of the South: "the South as a whole has developed no system or practice of political organization and leadership".[13] Thus, even in an era before the issue of race would make many white Southerners a potential liability among northern urban voters, the South's contribution to national leadership could be limited. Consequently, the pool of politicians available to the Democratic Party as potential presidential candidates was smaller than it was for the Republicans, and this did contribute to the party's difficulties.

9. Was the Democratic Party Controlled by Just a Few Interests?

In the 1880s, Democrats in the ex-slave states, the major source of their electoral strength, recognized the strategic position of the Democratic Parties in a few key northern states and, for example, nominated candidates drawn from those states. In doing so, the powerful interests in the party acknowledged the role played by the party's marginal voters. In the 1920s, there was a problem of rivalry between large blocs in the

[13] V. O. Key, Jr., *Southern Politics*, pp. 3–4.

party, with disagreement about the basis for accommodation between them. Consequently, this was not an era when a few interests were trying to create a party in their own image, thereby paying little attention to the role of the marginal voter in the party; rather, it was one of an overt struggle between factions. The party's problems, therefore, did not lie so much in a failure by leadership to aggregate interests in an optimal way as in the absence of conditions in which leaders might attempt such aggregation. At least, that was the situation until 1932. In 1932 itself, Roosevelt's recognition of the need to abandon some of his rural backers over the issue of prohibition represented the return to a political world in which the business of interest aggregation could actually be undertaken.

10. Changed Rules of Leadership Selection

The Democrats did not change their rules for selecting a presidential candidate until 1936, when the two-thirds provision was abolished. Until then, the old "super-majoritarian" system was still in use, but with the clash of two cultures in the party in the 1920s, its impact was rather different than in the pre-1912 period. Then, the party's main difficulty had been that the rules made it difficult for Bryan to be dislodged. In the 1920s, the more likely problem was that nominating a candidate would become the equivalent of trench warfare: time consuming and debilitating for the party. Bandwagons that might have rolled were more easily stopped, given the two-thirds rule, and with neither side willing to concede and a lack of many alternative compromise candidates, the process could just drag on. And in 1920 and 1924 it did.

11. The Democratic Party in 1932

In the 1920s, both parties had major lines of division within them. In the case of the Republicans, these cleavages were mainly manifested in Congress, and at the presidential level the party had little difficulty in uniting around its candidate. Even when Robert La Follette bolted to run as a Progressive in 1924, much of the 16.6 per cent of the total vote he attracted appears to have come from Democrats, and hardly any of the other Republican progressives supported his campaign actively. For the Democrats, division centred on the presidential nomination and the presidential election campaign, and the party's performance in three successive elections was weak. Furthermore, there is little to sustain the argument that Smith's campaign in 1928 actually helped to construct the New Deal coalition. Certainly, there is a strong association between having been foreign born (or having at least one foreign-born parent) and a vote for Smith.[14] Smith also polled especially well in places where there were high concentrations of his fellow Irish Americans, and thus the party attained a high poll in Massachusetts and Rhode Island. Yet the overall performance of the Democratic Party in large cities that year was no better, relatively, than it had been in the immediately preceding years. Two aspects are worth emphasizing. First, the role played by the foreign-born element in the Smith vote meant that some of the greatest improvements in his party's share of the vote between 1924 and 1928 were in unlikely states – including North Dakota. Secondly, whether because other groups in the cities simply did not join the foreign born in voting for Smith or because some of them were counter-mobilized by the Republicans against Smith, the shift in foreign-born voting behaviour did not trigger a generally enhanced Democratic performance in the cities that year.

Nor did the mid-term elections of 1930 transform the party. Its overall share of the vote in the congressional elections increased, as would be expected given the economic conditions, but the Democratic Party going into the 1932 elections was very much the party that had been racked by division for over a decade. What had changed was the real prospect of winning, and the availability of at least one candidate who would not be vetoed by either of the main factions in the party, even though he was identified with one wing – the party's rural, progressive wing. The party also benefited from changes in public attitudes on prohibition since about 1926, so that the urban wing of the party could obtain a wet plank in the party platform to offset its failure to get Smith nominated again. In later years, Smith would break with FDR over the New Deal, exposing just how great were the fissures in the party over economic policy, as well as over "culture". But by then, Roosevelt had been able to construct a new urban constituency for economic intervention, one grounded in the very organizations that had once supported the kind of views espoused by Smith, by using the federal government in a way that benefited urban electorates. Smith's brand of urban Democracy largely collapsed, and it was mainly in the South that a type of economic conservatism would survive in the Democratic Party after 1938. This was the transformative

[14] Ruth C. Silva found this variable to be stronger than any of the other variables she tested for the 1928 election – Catholicism, Liquor, Residence in a Big City, or Population Density of Place of Residence; see Silva, *Rum, Religion and Votes: 1928 Re-examined*, University Park, Pennsylvania State University Press, 1962.

aspect of Roosevelt's leadership of the party. However, it was brought about by President Roosevelt and not Governor Roosevelt. The election of 1932 represented a victory for an older Democratic coalition, one that had been expanded and made more complex after the 1890s. That coalition had a restricted future as a potential party of government, though.

Of course, what Roosevelt did after 1932 was not just to change the structure of the Democratic Party but to change the nature of party politics in America. In doing that, he made it possible for the party to become programmatic, and to develop ideas about governing, that in the longer term could replace the "out" party style of populist rhetoric that had been characteristic of its national campaigning since the 1890s. Moreover, perhaps, as Sidney Milkis explains, the key change was to make a national party system that was more than the sum of local parties:

Roosevelt's massive partisan effort – this departure from many conventional partisan practices – began a process whereby the party system was eventually transformed from local to national and programmatic party organizations. This change did not occur overnight, but significant developments took place during the 1930s that signalled a shift in the locus of party politics from the state and local level to the nation's capital.[15]

In the shorter term, the effect of Roosevelt's transformative efforts was to advantage his party by making them competitive again in the largest states, and that was one of the factors making it easier to construct a winning coalition for the party in the next 20 years.

[15] Sidney W. Milkis, *The President and the Parties*, p. 62.

7

Democratic Party Dominance or Restored Party Equilibrium, 1938–1952?

No one has ever doubted that the Democratic Party scored a remarkable series of electoral successes between 1932 and 1936. Furthermore, there is also widespread agreement now that having used the Democrats' control of government to change public policy in America, FDR provided a reason for first-time voters to vote disproportionately for his party. What is much less clear is where this left the balance between the parties thereafter. The popular version of the account is that he created a majority coalition of voters for his party – the New Deal coalition. As Everett Ladd notes, "In the 1930s, a new majority party coalition, the Democratic, took shape".[1] This overly large coalition embraced white Southerners, farmers, Catholics, urban dwellers, those on lower incomes, union members, Jews, and, where they were not disenfranchised, African Americans.

There are three related problems with this characterization of the consequences of Roosevelt's actions. First, the idea that Roosevelt constructed a near-grand coalition is arguably correct in relation to his "all class" strategy in the early stages of the New Deal. However, by the mid-1930s, neither his policies nor the patterns of opposition to the Democrats that were emerging provide evidence that that had been anything other than a short-term strategy. Secondly, after the early years of the Roosevelt administration, when the members of these groups in the New Deal coalition voted, generally they did not give their votes overwhelmingly to the

[1] Everett Carll Ladd, Jr., *American Political Parties: Social Change and Political Response*, New York, W. W. Norton, 1970, p. 229.

Democrats. African Americans were to be the notable exception.[2] For the rest, the older pattern persisted – local circumstances mattered in voter choice as did cross-cutting group memberships, so that nationally, at least a third of the members of a New Deal coalition group, and often as many as 40 per cent or more, might vote Republican. Thirdly, even if the list of groups within the New Deal coalition cited here is in some sense accurate, the fact is that many individual members of these groups were voting Democratic before 1932. What Roosevelt did was to affect votes at the margin – admittedly a rather large margin – but nonetheless a margin. In that sense, the New Deal coalition can be seen as an augmented version of the preceding coalition. The main difference in the two coalitions lay in urban America; it was there that many of the shifts in relative voting power occurred, and they were enough to change not just the balance between the parties but also the fulcrum of power within the Democratic Party.

Where did this leave the Republicans after FDR had made urban America more Democratic than it had been? By focussing solely on the number of national elections won, the conventional and popular view of the New Deal coalition tends to overstate the underlying strength of the Democratic Party nationally. By 1938, the Republicans were coming close to matching the Democrats in voting strength, and this pattern continued for nearly 15 years. The Democrats had a slight edge, and that edge was usually decisive, but they did not enjoy the kind of advantage that popular versions of the history of that period usually suggest. In this chapter, the focus is on the position facing the Republicans because it is only by understanding that that we can possibly evaluate what Roosevelt had been able to achieve for his party. How "northern" a party it could become was dependent partly on the Republican response to the New Deal.

1. Evidence of the Republican Revival After the Early Years of the New Deal

At first glance, the Republicans' election record after 1932 appears weak. Excluding the period of the Civil War, only one major party in the United States has lost five consecutive presidential elections, and that party was the Republicans between 1932 and 1948. Moreover, in the 20 years after 1932, the Republican Party controlled Congress for just two years,

---

[2] A point made, for example, in Robert Axelrod, "Where the Vote Comes From: An Analysis of Electoral Coalitions, 1952–1972", in Jeff Fishel (ed.), *Parties and Elections in an Anti-Party Age*, Bloomington and London, Indiana University Press, 1978, 86–99.

1947–9. Again, at all levels of public office, the defeats sustained between 1932 and 1936 were among the heaviest in American electoral history. For example, in some respects, the Republican share of the national vote in three consecutive congressional elections was the worst sequence of any three elections in American history.

However, the scale of even these defeats should not be exaggerated; the median share of the congressional vote for the Republicans in 1932–6 was 41.4 per cent, while the median for the Democrats in 1924–8, when Democratic identifiers already outnumbered Republican identifiers in the electorate, was only 40.5 per cent. Moreover, if the first two terms (and certainly the first six years) of the Roosevelt presidency are excluded, the performance of the Republicans compares well with that of the Democrats both between 1896 and 1912 and between 1920 and 1932. For example, the median proportion of the total vote obtained by the Republican Party in the three presidential elections of 1940, 1944, and 1948 was 45.1 per cent; the median for the Democrats in the three elections from 1900–1908 had been just 43 per cent, while for 1920–8 it was only 34.1 per cent. Moreover, at other levels of election there is evidence that the underlying Republican strength post–New Deal was even greater than this.

In gubernatorial elections the Republicans did especially well. On 47.2 per cent of all possible occasions between 1940 and 1952 state governorships were occupied by Republicans. (If the first two years of this period, when there were still Democrats elected in 1938 in office, are excluded, the proportion of governors who were Republicans increases to 48.5 per cent of the total.) By contrast, in the two previous 12-year periods that had culminated in eventual victory in a presidential election for the "out" party, the outs (in these cases the Democrats) had not done as well. In 1900–1912 they had controlled governorships on 41.3 per cent of possible occasions, while the corresponding figure for 1920–32 is 44.3 per cent. Nor is this high level of success for the post–New Deal Republicans an illusion caused by the presence of a number of small, but highly Republican, states. In fact, between 1940 and 1952, the Republicans did especially well in the larger states. If, for each state, the number of Electoral College voters is weighted by the proportion of the 12-year period in which the Republicans controlled the governorship of that state, it is the Republicans who appear to be (just) the majority party in the nation; 50.1 per cent of the Electoral College vote, calculated on that basis, would have been Republican.

Part of the significance of this finding is that it exposes just how persistent a factor the separation of sub-national electoral politics from presidential politics has been in the United States. Of course, the rise of candidate-centred politics from the 1960s onwards was enormously important in increasing that separation, but it is a mistake to attribute long-term change solely to that period. From the 1890s to the 1960s, there was a steady, but major, shift in how much state politics depended on the fate of national politics. In the 19th century, the "balance" in the state party systems had been provided, in part, by the "pendulum effect", in which (primarily) majority Republican coalitions fragmented, enabling Democrats to win gubernatorial and state legislature elections that they could not otherwise have won. That effect declined in the 20th century, but in its place emerged a different kind of separation of national from state-level party politics – one mainly centred on political issues. Defeated parties in presidential elections could now win at the state level because the issues that drove state politics were somewhat different from those that drove national politics. All this was happening long before the 1960s.

One respect in which this Republican success in gubernatorial elections in the 1940s is important is the light it sheds on accounts of party-system behaviour that rely heavily on electoral realignment. There is little doubt that of all the periods in American electoral history, the New Deal era is one in which there was a shift in voting behaviour – in particular, those who had recently joined the electorate displayed different voting patterns from previous voters.[3] However, if party identification was as important as it is supposed to be in determining electoral behaviour, and hence in affecting the opportunities facing parties that have incurred a serious presidential defeat, we would expect party to be even more significant in contests for lesser offices. After all, it is at the presidential level that we would expect voters to have most information about the personality of the candidate or, possibly, about public issues. Yet, as we have just seen, a Democratic realignment in the early to middle 1930s actually produced a slight advantage to the Republicans in the holding of "weighted" governorships between 1940 and 1952. Indeed, the Republican performance is even better than the data cited so far suggest. None of the electoral realignment occurred in the South, where the Republicans did not hold any governorships in this period. Outside the South, the median number of years the Republicans held a governorship was 8, the mean was 7.0,

---

[3] David R. Mayhew, discussing Clubb et al.'s calculations on the long-term electoral impact of 1932, says that that year is "a bull's eye for the realignments perspective"; "Electoral Realignments", p. 458. Jerome M. Clubb, William H. Flanigan, and Nancy H. Zingale, *Partisan Realignment: Voters, Parties and Government in American History*, Beverly Hills, CA, Sage, 1980.

TABLE 7.1. *Difference Between Republican and Democratic Parties' Shares of Votes in House Elections and Differences Between the Two Parties' Share of House Seats, 1940–1952*

	Republican Party Plurality over Democrats in Vote for House Elections (as Percentage of Total Vote)	Republican Party Plurality over Democrats in Seats in House (as Percentage of Total Number of Seats)
1940	−5.7	−24.2
1942	4.5	−3.0
1944	−3.4	−12.2
1946	9.3	13.4
1948	−6.4	−21.2
1950	0	−8.1
1952	−0.4	1.8

and the "weighted" share of Electoral College votes in northern states was 65.8 per cent.

Now, it might be claimed that victories by Republicans in non-presidential election years are not really relevant. They might just reflect a similar sort of pendulum effect to that evident in the 19th century – though that would leave unexplained why the Democrats in 1900–1912 and 1920–32 had not done as well in mid-term elections as the Republicans did in 1940–52. The problem with this claim is that although there is clear evidence that a coattails effect did help Democratic gubernatorial candidates in the 1940s in presidential years, the level of Republican success in 1940, 1944, and 1948 was still remarkably high in such contests. Twenty-six non-southern states held gubernatorial elections at the same time as presidential elections, and the Republicans won 57 per cent of them.[4] Nor are these results purely a function of Republican-leaning states biasing the data because, as always, they elected Republican governors. If states that went Republican in the presidential election are excluded, the success rate of Republicans in 1940, 1944, and 1948 is still 42.8 per cent of the total (21 out of 49 instances where Roosevelt or Truman won the state produced a Republican governor at the same time).

A similar pattern of near-parity with the Democrats was also evident in House elections at this time (see Table 7.1). The median plurality in the total vote for the Democrats between 1940 and 1952 was a mere 0.4 per cent. However, of three occasions when the Republican share of the vote

---

[4] Idaho alone among these states did not hold a gubernatorial election in each of the three presidential election years; it did not do so after 1944.

was the same as that of the Democrats, or exceeded it, they had more seats on only one occasion (1946). (Nevertheless, the opposite result occurred in 1952 when the Republicans won a majority of seats despite obtaining slightly fewer votes.) On balance, the slight advantage the Democrats had in overall votes in these years tended to pay off for them in terms of House majorities: Only 2 of 7 elections produced a Republican-controlled House of Representatives.

It is less easy to compare party balance in Senate elections because only a third of the seats are contested in each election year. Because of the electoral disasters between 1932 and 1936, the Republicans held less than one-quarter of Senate seats – even after the 1938 mid-term elections. Yet they made steady gains – a median of 5 seats (and a mean of 3.5 seats) at each election. Not only did the party control the Senate after 1946, but the near parity in seats after the 1950 election provides further evidence that from about the mid-1940s onwards, the two parties were evenly matched in Senate contests overall. Nevertheless, as in the House, the Republicans were not doing quite as well as the Democrats – again they controlled the chamber after only 2 of the 7 elections between 1940 and 1952. In terms of years as a congressional majority party, the slight Democratic electoral majority overall did matter.

It is impossible to escape the following conclusions: (1) The Democrats' New Deal coalition had not destroyed the Republican Party at the sub-national level in the 1930s; to the contrary, in the subsequent decade or so, the GOP enjoyed a degree of electoral success that was almost on a par with that of the Democrats; (2) the Democrats' position, nonetheless, had been improved by comparison with the pre–New Deal era – whatever divisions there were in the party were not now hampering its ability to be competitive with the Republicans; and (3) in spite of the Republican recovery in terms of their vote share, the Democrats got the spoils when it really mattered; they won the presidential elections of 1940, 1944, and 1948 and held Congress after 5 of the 7 elections between 1940 and 1952. So we need to consider two questions: How was it that the Republicans became competitive again so quickly after 1936, and why did that increased competitiveness still not result in greater success in controlling the national government before 1952?

2. The Rise of Moderate Republicanism

There are two very different aspects involved in answering the first question. The first has to do with change in relatively small, but significant, elements in the Republican Party that made it possible for a new form of Republicanism to become powerful; this new, moderate Republicanism could provide an effective challenge to the New Deal agenda of the Democratic Party. The second aspect has to do with the limited scope of what Franklin Roosevelt could have hoped to achieve for his party; in effect, he could make the party competitive in states in which it had been less competitive, but he could not have hoped to make it the dominant party in those states. We consider each of these aspects in turn.

Our starting point is with the disappearance of the major source of earlier division within the Republican Party. We have noted in previous chapters that the party had been split in the 1920s, especially in Congress, but by the early 1940s that conflict became far less important. From the time of its reunification (in 1916) until about 1940, the Republican Party had had two distinct congressional wings. The larger wing, centred on the eastern seaboard, was conservative in economic matters and represented continued support for a traditional component of the Republican coalition – financial and manufacturing interests. The smaller wing was centred in the West and pursued, in a modified form, progressive social and economic policies of a kind that had been associated partly with Theodore Roosevelt in the two decades before 1916. In practice, during the 1920s the main split between the two wings of the congressional party occurred over agricultural policy, and it was only on such matters that the progressives ever came close to maximizing their potential voting strength in Congress. Following the rejection of the Treaty of Versailles in 1919, and with economic prosperity in the decade after the war, neither isolationism nor the tariff generated a high level of conflict within the party. The party never experienced the equivalent of the Democrats' "culture war". Nevertheless, the quite distinct interests represented by the two wings of the Republican party meant that in some respects, it is correct to say that there were two Republican Parties in Congress. In general, the eastern wing prevailed, but not without a fight. In presidential politics, though, the Westerners were virtually powerless. Before 1936 when a former progressive (Alf Landon) was nominated, they had not come close to nominating one of their own kind as a presidential candidate. Furthermore, neither the party platforms nor the public utterances of the presidential nominees made many concessions to the interests of the Westerners. It was the larger of the two wings in Congress whose allies controlled the presidential party.

Although it survived quite well until about 1937, during the later 1930s the progressive wing went into terminal decline, for which there were several causes.[5] First, after 1932, the Democrats became more competitive in some western states where they had been less competitive earlier, and New Deal Democrats now proved attractive alternatives to progressive Republicans.

Secondly, although some well-known western Republican progressives in the House and Senate were able to keep their seats in the 1930s by supporting many (and, in some cases, all) aspects of the New Deal, gradually they left their chambers through retirement or death. (Senator George Norris of Nebraska, an Independent after 1936, had been the most loyal of the New Dealers, and his defeat in 1942 symbolized the end of this style of politics.)

Thirdly, more numerous than those progressives who continued to side with the New Deal were those who abandoned it when it became clear that FDR's approach, particularly in relation to monopolistic practices, was far more accommodating to them than the progressives had been. Consequently, veteran politicians like California Senator Hiram Johnson ended up by opposing much of the later New Deal – in effect, some elements of traditional progressivism became associated with conservatism in the post–New Deal era. New Dealism may have grown out of progressivism, but in practice, it was in conflict with some of the core beliefs of the earlier "ism", and that contributed to the sidelining of mainstream progressivism.

Fourthly, over about a 20-year period there was a shift in the political values of part of the Rocky Mountain areas of the West, such that by the early 1950s there was growing electoral support for conservative ideas in that region. In part, this was the result of migration from outside the region, and in part, too, it reflected a change in the socio-economic bases of these states, as levels of urbanization and suburbanization increased. Not only did this affect states where the Republicans had always done well by transforming Republicanism, but this new conservatism also started to win elections for them in a state like Arizona, one that before the late 1940s had been a Democratic bastion. Consequently, parts of the West became more conservative and, in doing so, it was the Republican

---

[5] On the western progressives in the Senate in the 1930s, see Ronald L. Feinman, *Twilight of Progressivism*, and Ronald A. Mulder, *The Insurgent Progressives in the United States Senate and the New Deal*, New York, Garland, 1979. In the early 1930s, defeat of orthodox Republicans bolstered the *relative* position of the progressives within the Senate. After the 1934 elections, 10 of the remaining 25 Republican senators were western progressives; Nicol Rae, *The Decline and Fall of the Liberal Republicans: From 1952 to the Present*, p. 25.

Party that became the party of conservatism in the region – pushing non-conservatives towards the Democratic Party. Naturally, given the time span over which these changes were occurring, there were some states in the West where Republicanism in the 1940s still displayed a progressive face: Minnesota was one such case. But for the most part, it is true to say that the older, non-conservative wing of the Republican Party was in terminal decline by the mid-1940s and had virtually disappeared by the end of that decade.

To conclude, at worst the main impact of the party's progressive-conservative division during the 1930s was that some senior progressives in 1932 (and some again in 1936) either refused to support their party's national ticket or actually endorsed Franklin Roosevelt. But until 1938, the overall situation of their party was so bad that the significance of these defections in weakening the party should not be exaggerated. By 1940, as the western progressives became an impotent element in the party, few of them could be a source of instability in the party's efforts at coalition building, and this was an enabling factor in the revival of the Republican Party.

At the same time as the conservative-progressive cleavage in the party was weakening, the beginnings of a new kind of factionalism among the Republicans were to be found. The division that resulted was not harmful electorally to the party in the period under consideration here, 1938–52; to the contrary, the new faction, "moderate Republicanism", was to provide the basis for the party's revival in presidential contests. The new form of non-conservative Republicanism was centred in the states of the East Coast and, to some extent, in those of the West Coast as well. There were two components to this moderate doctrine that served to differentiate it from orthodox Republicanism, whose heartland was increasingly concentrated in the "old" Midwest. It was internationalist, and also it did not reject every New Deal–type extension of the power of the federal government in domestic affairs in the way that mainstream Republicanism did. Neither element of moderate Republicanism was prominent in electoral politics at the time of the 1938 elections, and it was internationalism that first became apparent with the nomination of the internationalist Wendell Willkie, a Wall Street lawyer, as the presidential candidate in 1940. There had long been internationalists in the Republican Party – Republican international financiers had been strong supporters of the League of Nations and had been prominent in the establishment of the Council on Foreign Relations in 1921, for example – but the Great Depression, the New Deal, and the rise of Hitler all served to reinvigorate this East Coast–centred brand of Republican belief by the end of 1939.

Internationalism conceived American interests as being linked to those of other regions in the world, rather than defining its interests exclusively with respect to the North American continent. It rejected explicitly the "America First" conception of the country's role, by which America should be concerned only with the defence of the homeland and its interventions in affairs outside the United States confined to matters that bore directly on that defence. In the 19th century, this anti-internationalist view had prompted a focus on matters only within "the Americas" and, later, it had involved an outright rejection of American intervention in European affairs. The outbreak of the European war in 1939 enabled those who saw American interests as being adversely affected by a German victory to consolidate their position in the party, and it was in this context that someone like the businessman Wendell Willkie could be nominated by the Republican Party. Although Thomas Dewey was the front-runner for the 1940 nomination, his internationalism at that stage was not robust enough for its adherents. They preferred to have someone who was strong on that issue:

As leading isolationists turned to Vandenberg or Taft . . . internationalists were equally determined to block them. Neither of the party's 1936 nominees, Landon or Knox, wanted an isolationist. Internationalists (including Landon) preferred Dewey to Hoover, Taft, Vandenberg, Nye or MacNider, but there were those who hoped to do better. The result was the well-financed and skillfully organized drive to nominate the former Democrat Wendell Willkie of Indiana and New York City.[6]

On the domestic policy side, as noted, moderate Republicanism involved a much greater willingness to accommodate New Deal interventionism than was accepted by orthodox Republicans. It must be stressed, though, that not all of the latter were political Luddites – they could understand the election returns, and by 1936 many had recognized that outright condemnation of *all* interventionism did not play well with most voters. Consequently, initially at least, they had been careful when campaigning in 1936 to indicate *how* they opposed the Democrats' agenda; only in the later stages of the campaign did Landon's utterances lay them open to the charge that they would simply "turn back the clock". The electoral damage that this had appeared to cause was not lost on orthodox Republicans in the aftermath of the landslide.

---

[6] Wayne S. Cole, *Roosevelt and the Isolationists, 1932–45*, Lincoln and London, University of Nebraska Press, 1981, p. 391.

However, the moderates went much further than their orthodox colleagues in embracing aspects of state interventionism. Thus, in 1945, when urging his state legislature to enact compulsory health insurance in California, Governor Earl Warren argued: "Such things as workmen's compensation, unemployment insurance, social security benefits were 'startling' in contemplation but now are accepted and conceded to be essential to our system – not merely human but actually essential".[7] Yet with a few exceptions (such as Jacob Javits), most of whom did not become key political actors until the 1950s, these moderate Republicans were not full-blown supporters of the entire New Deal agenda.[8] They were most comfortable with two kinds of governmental interventionism: compulsory insurance–type policies, especially ones originating in the states rather than with the federal government, and those direct governmental expenditures that represented a form of investment in the socio-economic infra-structure that private enterprise was unlikely to undertake. Thus, expansion of state universities or highway construction would often be defended by moderate Republicans. (There are some obvious parallels between this sort of policy agenda and the economic nationalism that 19th century Whigs and Republicans had propounded.) Moderate Republicans also tended to be much less supportive of the empowerment (through law) of previously disadvantaged groups and, in particular, of organized labour. Thus, those moderate Republicans who did not depend directly on unions for electoral resources could often ally with fellow Republicans in support of legislation restricting union rights (or in defending court decisions that did so). Although most of Wisconsin Senator Joseph McCarthy's later opponents in the GOP were moderates, some of them had been willing to go along with McCarthyism in its early stages and with the other anti-communist crusades preceding it. Alliances with the Right were feasible for moderate Republicanism, therefore, even though there were clear differences between moderate and orthodox Republicanism.

Many of the leading Republican politicians of the 1940s and 1950s – Willkie, Warren, Thomas Dewey, Henry Cabot Lodge, and (later) Eisenhower – were very much part of this new, moderate wing of the party.

---

[7] Ed Cray, *Chief Justice: A Biography of Earl Warren*, New York, Simon and Schuster, 1997, p. 162.

[8] An obvious possible exception is Fiorella LaGuardia, a Republican member of Congress before he became mayor of New York City. But by the time he became mayor he was very much a Republican "of convenience", distrusted by many Republicans outside the city because of his alliances with liberals and labour unions. By the time of the New Deal, LaGuardia was a Republican only because of the entrenchment of Tammany Hall within the city's Democratic Party.

However, one of the most interesting features of that wing is that it was clearly a minority in the party, and far from being that large a minority. As will be seen shortly, the coastal states that were at the heart of the moderate wing did not command anything like a majority at Republican national conventions. Moreover, even within their own states, the leading moderates were often "out ahead" of the mainstream of their parties on particular issues. Thus, for example, Warren failed to get the Republican majority in the California State Assembly to back his health insurance programme, but then, of course, it might be argued that California is an uninteresting case in this regard because of the weakness of party organizations there since the Progressive Era.

A more pertinent example, perhaps, is New York. As Judith Stein has shown, the transformation of that party was not the result of a direct assault on the "old guard". Indeed, the attempt by the state party chairman (and ex-Progressive), William Kingsland Macy, to do just that in 1933 and 1934 failed. Rather, it was change from within the old guard that occurred, prompted by the emergence of younger party leaders around 1936, though these politicians "had risen to power with the blessing of the Old Guard".[9] Moreover, what the change really amounted to at the state level – though not in New York City – was just a change in campaign strategy, in not attacking the New Deal directly. By the late 1930s, there were differences between urban Republicans (especially those in New York City) and upstate Republicans, with the latter far less committed to interventionist programmes that might attract potential urban Democratic voters to the party. Consequently, the cooperation in New York City between Republicans and both anti-Tammany Democrats and labour unions was the subject of much hostility upstate. What saved the New York party from a possible civil war, and turned it instead into a party of government, was finding a candidate, Thomas Dewey, who could win votes throughout the state. Dewey's narrow defeat for the governorship in 1938, and his subsequent victory in 1942, made him the leader of the state party, and until the mid-1950s and because of his electoral success, he could "impose a settlement" on the party. That settlement involved not challenging the New Deal, as well as expanding the scope of state government activity on a pragmatic basis. It is far from clear that had there been a civil war in the party pre-Dewey, the urban Republicans would have won. Instead, they won because an electorally successful, pragmatic politician,

---

[9] Judith Stein, "The Birth of Liberal Republicanism in New York State, 1932–1938", PhD dissertation, Yale University, 1968, p. 231.

whose previous political record was merely that of a crime-busting district attorney (and not a party reformer), chose to align himself with the emerging quasi-moderate wing of the party that was based in the largest cities. Dewey was the classic example of the electoral entrepreneur who knew where he had to position his party on key issues in order to win office statewide.

Politicians like Dewey, who combined internationalism with acceptance of much of the New Deal programme, could exercise the power that they did within their states because the Republicans had to do well enough in elections in the large cities to carry those states. Ignoring urban voters entailed electoral defeat, and they could be courted only if the Republicans accepted the more popular elements of the Democratic agenda. The urban voter was now the marginal voter, and it was Dewey's recognition of the kind of policies that that voter wanted that made him powerful in New York. In part, the same argument can be made in relation to the party nationally. Moderate Republicanism could be successful within the party because, although a relatively small proportion of elected politicians were moderates, that was the stance that would maximize the chance of winning a national majority. Consequently, a clear division became evident in the 1940s between the presidential wing of the party, where the moderates prevailed, and the congressional wing (and other arenas), where most Republicans held orthodox views.

In fact, the argument developed in this book is that during the period from about 1940 to 1952, moderate Republicanism enjoyed two kinds of strategic advantage over its opponents in presidential nominations – advantages that enabled it to overcome the disadvantage of being a minority nationally within the party. Because of these advantages, a very different kind of presidential party could develop from the party operating in Congress – the latter being much more grounded in the "grass roots" of the party. First, during the New Deal era, the coastal states that were the home of moderate Republicanism had two linked resources within the party: They were a sizeable presence in the Republican voting coalition, and they became its marginal voter in presidential elections. That latter position facilitated leverage for the moderate faction in the party (a faction that used internationalism and limited forms of government interventionism as policies for attracting, especially, urban voters) in selecting presidential candidates. Secondly, the governorships of the coastal states were normally held by Republicans between 1939 and 1952; indeed, the party was far more successful in those gubernatorial elections than in gubernatorial contests in other states. This had a major impact on the internal dynamics of the party. Moderate governors from the coastal states could usually exercise tight control over their own delegations to the national convention, while orthodox Republicans from the interior states were disadvantaged because the centralizing power provided by state governors in the delegate-selection process was less available to them.[10] The significance of each of these strategic advantages can now be explained in more detail, beginning with the marginal voter argument.

To the extent that (relative) voting support for the two main parties is fairly stable, it is possible to provide for any given period a step-by-step guide as to how a party would construct a winning coalition in the Electoral College. (The first step would be winning that state in which the party had done best in preceding elections, the second step would be winning its second most supportive state in previous elections, and so on.) Table 7.2 provides such a sequential guide for the earlier period, 1920–32. The basic data are how much the Republican plurality over the Democrats deviated from the average plurality in all non-southern states at each election of the four contested in these years. The median deviation for each state is calculated, and the states are listed in descending order of their "Republican-ness".[11]

It is evident that on this basis, New York was the most marginal state in 1920–32, making the difference between Republican victory and defeat. Obviously, New York's position as the marginal state in this sense was the result of the strategies actually pursued by the Democratic and Republican Parties in the 1920s. Consequently, had the Democrats pursued a more western strategy in the three elections of the 1920s, New York would surely have ranked higher in Republican-ness. Moreover, given the variability from one election to another as far as a party's performance in a particular state was concerned, a political strategist calculating whence to place campaign resources would also have had to take into account states like Rhode Island or Oregon, which the Republicans might well have needed to win in a particularly close election, should they have failed to win states that were seemingly more Republican on the basis of earlier elections.

---

[10] Of course, there were some states with weak parties where the governor was not in a position to control the delegation – this was often true in California, for example.

[11] Thus, Vermont, the most Republican-leaning state, would provide 4 Electoral College votes and be the first step towards the 266 votes required for the nomination. (Southern states have been excluded from all the ensuing calculations for the period before 1952, but not thereafter, because they were overwhelmingly non-Republican in most elections and their inclusion might distort the relative strength of the parties in the various non-southern states.)

TABLE 7.2. *Construction of Winning Republican Coalition in Electoral College, 1920–1932, in Descending Order of "Safeness" (Number of Electoral College Votes Provided by Each State Indicated in Parentheses)*

266 Electoral College Votes Required to Win Presidential Election

Heartland States (1st–89th Electoral College Votes)

*VT (4)	*CA (13)
MI (15)	MN (12)
*ME (6)	*MA (1)
*PA (38)	

Intermediate States (90th–178th Electoral College Votes)

*MA (17)	*NJ (14)
OH (24)	KS (10)
IA (13)	SD (4)
*WA (7)	

Marginal States (179th–266th Electoral College Votes)

SD (1)	*DE (3)	*NY (30)
WY (3)	ID (4)	
IL (29)	ND (5)	
CO (6)	*CT (7)	

Democratic Marginal States (267th–311th Electoral College Votes)

*NY (15)	MT (4)
*NH (4)	NE (8)
*RI (5)	WI (4)
*OR (5)	

States are ranked in "Safeness" by calculating the median value for the 1920, 1924, 1928, and 1932 elections of (Republican plurality over Democrats in given state) minus (Republican plurality over Democrats in all non-southern states).

States shown in italics have Electoral College votes in more than one category in this table.

* = coastal states (those on East or West Coast)

For that reason, rather than engaging in a "small" step-by-step approach to coalition building, it is more useful to conceive of the problem of presidential coalition building as involving primarily four categories of Electoral College votes ("larger steps"), as far as early to middle 20th century Republicans were concerned:

(a) **Heartland;** this consisted of the first one-third of Electoral College votes needed to win the presidency, and of course, these votes came from the most Republican states.

(b) **Intermediate;** in this category were the second one-third of the most-winnable Electoral College votes for the Republican Party.

(c) **Marginal;** this category contained the last one-third of the most winnable Electoral College votes. Winning all the Electoral College votes in the Heartland, Intermediate, and Marginal categories would provide a Republican victory.

(d) **Democratic Marginal**; these were the one-sixth next-most-winnable Electoral College votes for the Republicans – votes from states that would be unnecessary for victory if all the preceding votes had actually been obtained.

How large to make the Democratic Marginal category is (to some extent) arbitrary – it depends on how much variation in the Republican vote share there is in each state between the four elections. For the purpose of illustrating the argument here, 45 Electoral College votes (half the number in the other categories in the period 1920–32) was chosen as the size of this category.

Of the 531 Electoral College votes in the 1920s, 126 were in the South and 405 in the non-South. Of those 405 votes less than half (177) were in coastal states, while 228 were in the interior states.[12] However, of the 312 most Republican-leaning Electoral College votes, just over half (169) were in the coastal states (see Table 7.2). Thus, one condition for the exercise of power within the Republican coalition by the coastal states was present in the 1920s – they were members of that coalition in considerable numbers. But the distribution of these votes between the four categories identified here – Heartland, Intermediate, Marginal, and Democratic Marginal – shows only a slight edge for the coastal states vis-à-vis the interior states in those categories possessing the greater leverage (see Table 7.3). Although there were rather more coastal state votes in the combined Marginal and Democratic Marginal categories than there were votes from interior states (73–61), that advantage was not great. Thus, given this distribution of Electoral College votes, it is far from evident that either the coastal or the interior states could have gained the upper hand in relation to each other, had there been a conflict of interest. Both were present in substantial numbers in the coalition, but neither had a greater claim to being the marginal voter, and hence neither of them would have had an opportunity to exploit that position.

One of the consequences of the New Deal was to transform the distribution of Electoral College votes among the four categories of states. In the elections between 1936 and 1948, the coastal states continued to contribute more than half of the most winnable 312 Electoral College

---

[12] Both Pennsylvania, which has no seacoast, and the landlocked state of Vermont are treated as "coastal" states in this analysis.

TABLE 7.3. *Distribution of Electoral College Votes by Type of State, 1920–1932*

Heartland States (1ˢᵗ–89ᵗʰ Electoral College Votes)
Coastal 62
Interior 27

Intermediate States (90ᵗʰ–178ᵗʰ Electoral College Votes)
Coastal 38
Interior 51

Marginal States (179ᵗʰ–266ᵗʰ Electoral College Votes)
Coastal 40
Interior 48

Democratic Marginal States (267ᵗʰ–311ᵗʰ Electoral College Votes)
Coastal 29
Interior 16

States are ranked in "Safeness" by calculating the median value for the 1920, 1924, 1928, and 1932 elections of (Republican plurality over Democrats in given state) minus (Republican plurality over Democrats in all non-southern states).

votes to the Republican Party, but their distribution among the four categories of states was now much better suited to the exercise of power by one party faction. The Republican Heartland became dominated by the interior states, where they enjoyed an advantage of more than 7 to 1 (see Tables 7.4 and 7.5), but this was the position of least leverage in the coalition. In the Intermediate category, there was an almost even division between the interior and coastal states. Most importantly, in the Marginal category, the coastal states became dominant (66–22), as they were in the Democratic Marginal category (30–15). This was the basis of the coastal states' power during the period in which their agenda and their candidates – moderate Republicanism – came to the forefront of Republican presidential politics. The Electoral College votes in the coastal states were clearly the marginal votes now; it was these states, far more than any others, that could tip the balance between victory and defeat in the Electoral College. As the centre of Republican voter loyalty switched to the Midwest (from the Northeast), so that region was able to exercise relatively less power over the direction taken in presidential politics. The politician usually known as "Mr. Republican", Ohio Senator Robert A. Taft, failed to get the presidential nomination on all four occasions between his coming to national prominence in 1938 and his death in 1953. Irrespective of whether Taft's public persona was ill-suited to national electoral politics, there is the crucial point that the basis of his support was in those

TABLE 7.4. *Construction of Winning Republican Coalition in Electoral College, 1936–1948, in Descending Order of "Safeness" (Number of Electoral College Votes Provided by Each State Indicated in Parentheses)*

266 Electoral College Votes Required to Win Presidential Election

Heartland States (1ˢᵗ–89ᵗʰ Electoral College Votes)

*VT (3)	*ME (5)	*NH (4)
KS (8)	ND (4)	OH (25)
NE (6)	IA (10)	CO (6)
SD (4)	IN (13)	*MI (1)*

Intermediate States (90ᵗʰ–178ᵗʰ Electoral College Votes)
MI (18)
*PA (35)
IL (28)
NJ (8)

Marginal States (179ᵗʰ–266ᵗʰ Electoral College Votes)

NJ (8)	*DE (3)
*NY (47)	*MO (10)*
*CT (8)	
WI (12)	

Democratic Marginal States (267ᵗʰ–311ᵗʰ Electoral College Votes)

MO (5)	*MD (8)
WY (3)	*MA (16)
ID (4)	MN (3)
*OR (6)	

States are ranked in "Safeness" by calculating the median value for the 1936, 1940, 1944, and 1948 elections of (Republican plurality over Democrats in given state) minus (Republican plurality over Democrats in all non-southern states).

States shown in italics have Electoral College votes in more than one category in this table.

* = coastal states (those on East or West Coast)

areas of the country that (relatively) were the safest for his party. If his party had been motivated by a desire to win a national majority, his ability to exercise leverage within the party would have been much reduced.

Nevertheless, this advantage of the coastal states in securing victory for their candidates and their agenda at the presidential level within the party was reinforced by a second advantage. Despite the fact that at the presidential level many of the coastal states had now become marginal states, or even leaned to the Democrats slightly, at the state level of politics the Republicans actually did better there between 1938 and 1952 than they did in the interior states (see Table 7.6). Republican control of governorships was more extensive: In these 14 years, the median period for which they controlled the governorships of interior states was 8 years, whereas the party did so for 10 years in the case of coastal states.

TABLE 7.5. *Distribution of Electoral College Votes by Type of State, 1936–1948*

Heartland States (1st–89th Electoral College Votes)
Coastal 12
Interior 77

Intermediate States (90th–178th Electoral College Votes)
Coastal 43
Interior 46

Marginal States (179th–266th Electoral College Votes)
Coastal 63
Interior 22
(Coastal) Border 3

Democratic Marginal States (267th–311th Electoral College Votes)
Coastal 22
Interior 15
(Coastal) Border 8

States are ranked in "Safeness" by calculating the median value for the 1936, 1940, 1944, and 1948 elections of (Republican plurality over Democrats in given state) minus (Republican plurality over Democrats in all non-southern states).

TABLE 7.6. *Number of Years, 1939–1953, in Which Republicans Controlled State Governorships, by Type of State*

Interior States (Median = 8)			
AZ (2)	KY (4)	NM (2)	WV (0)
CO (10)	MI (8)	ND (8)	WI (14)
ID (10)	MN (14)	OH (8)	WY (8)
IL (8)	MO (4)	OK (0)	
IN (4)	MT (8)	SD (14)	
IA (14)	NE (12)	UT (4)	
KS (14)	NV (2)		
Coastal States (Median = 10)			
CA (10)	NJ (8)		
CT (10)	NY (10)		
DE (8)	OR (14)		
ME (8)	PA (14)		
MD (2)	RI (2)		
MA (8)	VT (14)		
NH (14)	WA (10)		

Occupying the gubernatorial mansions provided a number of benefits, of which the most obvious one related to the ease with which a national coalition could be constructed within the party. Although there were exceptions, such as California, usually state governors could expect to control their party's delegations to a national convention. They could be influential in the delegate-selection process in their states, and then they could personally be active at the convention itself. This meant that such delegations were less likely to fragment, so that their votes at the convention were not split between more than one candidate and the votes could be used to maximum strategic advantage. The solidity of the delegates' votes from their states compensated for the main disadvantage facing the coastal states – namely, that throughout the period, there were more Electoral College votes at stake in the interior states than in their own region (and hence they had fewer votes at the convention). Consequently, in general, and with the exception of 1940 itself, coastal governors had an advantage over their opponents, for the latter's delegations had the greater potential to fragment. Although in 1940 the coastal Republicans had started at a slight disadvantage in this respect (see Table 7.7), their position relative to interior Republicans improved consistently over the next 12 years, so that by 1952 they enjoyed a considerable superiority. In short, their potential voting strength, while smaller, was likely to be more solid. It proved to be so throughout this period.

The cohesion of the coastal states, and the ability of their governors to exercise power at crucial stages of the nomination process, is well illustrated by three ballots – at the 1940, 1944, and 1952 National Conventions.[13] As can be seen in Table 7.8, the coastal states voted overwhelmingly for Willkie, Dewey, and Eisenhower, respectively. They were far more cohesive than their opponents were within their "home" region, and control of the governorships of these states at the times of the conventions increased their cohesion (see Table 7.9).

The net result of the moderates' (growing) strategic advantages was a sequence of presidential elections in which the Republicans either nominated party moderates or nominated candidates who had to take account of the moderates. As we have noted, at the same time, the Republican Party in Congress continued to be dominated by conservatives, although

---

[13] These votes were the 5th ballot in 1940 involving a straight fight between Willkie and Taft, the 1st Ballot in 1948 in which Dewey was competing against Taft and Harold Stassen, and the pro-Eisenhower report on the Georgia delegation in 1952, in which Taft would have benefited from the report's rejection.

TABLE 7.7. *Number of Electoral College Votes Controlled by States Having Republican Governors at the Time of 1940, 1944, 1948, and 1952 National Party Conventions, by Type of State*

1940

Coastal States (Maximum possible = 186)		Interior States (Maximum possible = 221)		
CT (8)	OR (5)	CO (6)	MI (19)	WI (12)
ME (5)	PA (36)	ID (4)	MN (11)	WY (3)
MA (17)	RI (4)	IA (11)	OH (26)	
NH (4)	VT (3)	KS (9)	SD (4)	
TOTAL (82; 44% of maximum)		TOTAL (105; 48% of maximum)		

1944

Coastal States (maximum possible = 188)		Interior States (maximum possible = 212)		
CA (25)	NY (47)	CO (6)	MI (19)	SD (4)
CT (8)	OR (6)	ID (4)	MN (11)	WI (12)
DE (3)	PA (35)	IL (28)	MO (15)	
ME (5)	VT (3)	IA (10)	MT (4)	
MA (16)	WA (8)	KS (8)	NE (6)	
NH (4)		KY (11)	OH (25)	
TOTAL (160; 85% of maximum)		TOTAL (163; 77% of maximum)		

1948

Coastal States (maximum possible = 188)		Interior States (maximum possible = 212)		
CA (25)	NJ (16)	ID (4)	MN (11)	WI (12)
CT (8)	NY (47)	IL (28)	MT (4)	
DE (3)	OR (6)	IN (13)	NE (6)	
ME (5)	PA (35)	IA (10)	ND (4)	
MA (16)	VT (3)	KS (8)	OH (25)	
NH (4)		MI (19)	SD (4)	
TOTAL (168; 89% of maximum)		TOTAL (148; 70 % of maximum)		

1952

Coastal States (maximum possible = 192)		Interior States (maximum possible = 206)		
CA (32)	NY (45)	AZ (4)	NE (6)	WI (12)
CT (8)	OR (6)	CO (6)	NV (3)	WY (3)
ME (5)	PA (32)	ID (4)	NM (4)	
MD (9)	VT (3)	IA (10)	ND (4)	
NH (4)	WA (9)	KS (8)	SD (4)	
NJ (16)		MN (11)	UT (4)	
TOTAL (169; 88% of total)		TOTAL (83; 40% of total)		

TABLE 7.8. *Number of Votes Cast on Behalf of "Moderate" Candidates by State Delegations in Crucial (and Close) Ballots at 1940, 1948, and 1952 Republican National Conventions, by Type of States*

	Coastal, Non-southern, States	Interior, Non-southern, States	Southern States
1940 5th Nominating Ballot (Willkie v. Taft, won by Willkie, 429–377)	221/268 (82.5%)	142/357 (39.8%)	53/160 (33.1%)
1948 1st Nominating Ballot (Dewey v. two other candidates – Taft and Stassen; won by Dewey, 434–381)	212/269 (78.8%)	145/357 (40.6%)	70/162 (43.2%)
1952 Pro-Eisenhower Ballot on report on the seating of the Georgia delegation at the convention (won 607–531)	395/462 (85.5%)	176/530 (33.2%)	31/125 (24.8%)

TABLE 7.9. *Share of Vote in Support of "Moderate" Candidates in 1940, 1948, and 1952 Republican Conventions Cast by Delegations from Coastal States with Serving Republican Governors and by Delegations from Coastal States with Democratic Governors (as Percentage)*

	Coastal States with Republican Governors	Coastal States with Democratic Governors
1940 5th Nominating Ballot (Willkie v. Taft)	94.4%	76.4%
1948 1st Nominating Ballot (Dewey v. two other candidates – Taft and Stassen)	84.3%	55.6%
1952 Pro-Eisenhower Ballot on report on the seating of the Georgia delegation at the convention	86.1%	81.0%

the form that conservatism took did change between 1938 and 1952, becoming less obstructionist.[14] However, the evident gap in the politics of the presidential and congressional arenas could not have been clearer. The sequence began with Wendell Willkie's nomination in 1940. Although

[14] See, for example, John W. Mansberger, *From Obstruction to Moderation: The Transformation of Senate Conservatism, 1938–1952*, London, Associated University Presses, 2000.

Willkie was an internationalist, he was an outspoken opponent of a number of aspects of the New Deal, so that in some ways he can be regarded as a transitional figure in the move to domination by the moderates. It was with the selection of Thomas Dewey in 1944 that that process was completed. Dewey was nominated again in 1948, and this was followed by the Eisenhower nomination in 1952. After the period under consideration in this chapter, the sequence continued with Eisenhower's renomination in 1956 and then that of Vice President Richard Nixon, who was the clear front-runner for the nomination in advance of the national convention. While some observers may balk at characterizing Nixon as a moderate because of his use of the anti-communism issue in the 1940s, particularly in his defeat of Representative Jerry Voorhis in California in 1946, he was not an orthodox, conservative Republican. As his entire political career would demonstrate, he was a man of virtually no political beliefs or values – he was the ultimate pragmatist who would say and do whatever was necessary to secure political benefit for himself. In this context it is significant, therefore, that in order to shore up his own nomination bid in 1960, Nixon reached a pre-convention agreement with the new emerging force among the moderates, Nelson Rockefeller. (This concordat (the "Compact of Fifth Avenue") was to alarm orthodox Republicans, who once again saw themselves as being sidelined.)

Thus, throughout the 1940s and 1950s the Republican Party continued to nominate presidential candidates whose views were rather different from those of the vast majority of Republican members of Congress. However, this domination of the presidential selection process was not always easy. In particular, after the failure of the moderates' "dream ticket" in 1948 (Dewey and Warren), there was always going to be fierce resistance to a similar nomination in 1952. Even with a popular war hero (and Kansan) available to head the moderates' cause, the outcome was by no means certain at the beginning of the convention. It took close votes involving the non-recognition of Taft delegates from several of the party's "rotten boroughs" in the South (Georgia, Louisiana, and Texas) to ensure Dwight Eisenhower's eventual nomination. For years, many supporters of Robert Taft continued to believe that he had been cheated of the nomination, and it is a mark of how well organized and co-ordinated the Eisenhower backers were (of whom Dewey was the most prominent perhaps) that they could swing even that nomination.[15] However,

---

[15] It was not just at the national convention itself that this organizational capability was apparent. In the preceding primaries, the moderates had been able to create the impression of widespread public support for Eisenhower. Thus, crucially, in Minnesota on March

underlying their position was a strategic advantage that arose directly from the changed nature of party competition in the country after the New Deal.

At the heart of that change was the Democrats' greater ability after 1932 to mobilize voters in large cities, and the significance of that factor on the future of the Republican Party was huge. Because the Democrats had greatly improved their share of the vote in the cities of many coastal states, a new type of Republican leader emerged there to compete against them, and because those states were often the most marginal ones in building a minimum winning coalition, those leaders could exert enormous power in the Republican Party. However, and this point is crucial, the impact on the Republicans of new Democratic strength in eastern cities was on their optimal strategy for winning a presidential majority – it did not prevent the Republican Party from actually winning such a majority. A winning Republican coalition was thus viable at the national level in the 1940s, in spite of FDR's success in transforming the basis of American party politics. Mobilizing voters in the cities in the way that he did had not marginalized the Republicans nationally. To the contrary, its main effect was to prompt a Republican response that provided for a period of close political competition nationally. Had the pattern of gubernatorial election successes by the Republicans been slightly different – had they been slightly less successful in the coastal states and rather more successful in the interior – the Democrats might have benefited more than they actually did from FDR's policies. As it was, moderate control of key states often provided the margin of victory for the moderates over the conservatives at Republican national conventions, thereby ensuring that the Democrats had to face the strongest possible opponents at the ensuing presidential elections.

3. The Limits of the New Deal Revolution

Thus far we have explored one reason why the Republicans became competitive again so quickly after 1936 – the balance of power within that party changed. There is now a second reason to be explored – the limited scope of what FDR could have hoped to achieve for his party in the long

---

18th a write-in campaign for Eisenhower produced over 37 per cent of the vote for him, leaving him trailing the state's former governor, Harold Stassen, who was on the ballot, by less than 7 per cent of the total vote. By contrast, the write-in votes for Robert Taft in Minnesota accounted for only slightly more than 8 per cent of the total vote.

term as a result of the New Deal policy agenda. We must begin, however, by acknowledging just what Roosevelt did achieve for his party.

The New Deal turned a slight pro-Republican bias among voters in large cities into a larger Democratic bias. For example, even in 1938, the year of the Republican resurgence, the Republican Party received only 43.5 per cent of the two-party vote in congressional elections in non-southern cities of more than 200,000; in 1930, they had received 51.1 per cent of the vote and in 1926, 51.9 per cent. As we have seen, voting studies have shown that in part, this transformation involved the Democrats mobilizing previous non-voters and turning them (mainly) into Democratic voters.[16] Casualties of this electoral surge included Republican urban machines; an obvious example is the one in Chicago, headed by Big Bill Thompson until 1931, which was replaced soon after his defeat by a Democratic machine that was then to control the city for decades. Not surprisingly, the entrenched organization in Philadelphia fared better; it continued to control the city until as late as 1951, when hundreds of local leaders started to defect to the Democrats, a process that continued through 1955.[17] By the end of the 1930s, however, many urban machines were in decline, and to the extent that they had survived that decade, they were now Democratic machines. (Most machines were to be overtaken by a new style of urban politics in the late 1930s and 1940s that was hostile to spoils.) Nevertheless, the importance of that shift in urban voting behaviour is often misunderstood because two points are conflated.

The first is that in House elections, the rise of "big city" Democrats helped to make it much easier for their party to gain a majority in that chamber. It really did become the majority party there; even when it had a slender lead in total votes nationally, usually the party could win control of the House (1952 was to be an exception). Previously, the Democrats' great advantage since Reconstruction in its attempts to control the House had been the huge share of southern seats that they commanded. The South provided about half the seats required for a majority, and the Democrats' problem had been building on that percentage. Had there been congressional redistricting in the 1920s, though, the Democrats' share of the seats would undoubtedly have been larger than it was because they came

[16] As Clyde P. Weed says of the 1930s, "A massive number of urban voters, concentrated primarily in the industrial centers of the Northeast and Midwest, surged into the American electorate through the Democratic party". *The Nemesis of Reform*, p. 3

[17] David R. Mayhew, *Placing Parties in American Politics*, Princeton, NJ, Princeton University Press, 1986, p. 58.

close to obtaining half the vote in the large cities, whereas they received nothing like that in those parts of the North that would have lost seats under redistricting. Redistricting in 1932, combined with a major, and permanent, shift to the Democrats in most cities following the New Deal, meant that the party had to pick up only about 80 of the 289 seats in the North (less than a quarter of those seats) in order to control the chamber. Before 1932–6, that task had been more difficult, and what Roosevelt did in office made it easier. This is a clear sense in which it can be said that the Democrats built a national majority based on the cities. Furthermore, it was the policy agenda of those urban *congressional* Democrats that was to form the cornerstone of the policy of Democratic administrations in that period. As Finegold and Skocpol note of the 1932 elections, "many newly elected Democrats were especially anxious to consolidate their electoral majorities by enacting popular programs to alleviate unemployment."[18] The support of these Democrats made it possible for Democratic administrations to push policy well beyond the agenda for which a national majority might have voted, had presidential campaigns focussed on specific policy proposals. A previously conservative sector of the political system now provided the engine for the transformation of government – because the representatives from those districts wanted to consolidate their preciously won victories.

The second point is that their increased share of the vote in the big cities helped to make the Democrats competitive in the states in which those cities were located. But, and this point cannot be overemphasized, it did no more than make them competitive at the state level. It did not turn those states into a Democratic heartland; rather, several of them were to be ranked among the most highly contested states during the years from 1936 to 1948 – (see Table 7.10).[19] The states containing cities of 200,000 inhabitants that were in this category included California (Los Angeles, Oakland, and San Francisco), Kentucky (Louisville), Maryland (Baltimore), Massachusetts (Boston), Minnesota (Minneapolis and St. Paul), Missouri (St. Louis and Kansas City), New York (New York City, Buffalo, and Rochester), Oregon (Portland), and Wisconsin (Milwaukee). This point about the contestability of states that contained large cities can be made in the following way: Of the

---

[18] Kenneth Finegold and Theda Skocpol, *State and Party in America's New Deal*, p. 72.

[19] In this context, I take the most contested states to be those containing the one-third most marginal Electoral College votes, i.e., those states possessing the 177 Electoral College votes in which the median margins of victory of one party over the other were the lowest in the period 1936–48.

TABLE 7.10. *Construction of a Winning Republican Coalition in the Electoral College, in Descending Order of Republican Strength, 1936–1948*

Vermont 3
Kansas 8 (11)
Nebraska 6 (17)
South Dakota 4 (21)
Maine 5 (26)
North Dakota 4 (30)
Iowa 10 (40)
Indiana 13 (53)
New Hampshire 4 (57)
Ohio 25 (82)
Colorado 6 (88)
Michigan 19 (107)
Pennsylvania 35 (142)
Illinois 28 (170)

New Jersey 16 (186) – (177 is one-third of Electoral College votes)
New York 47 (233)
Connecticut 8 (241)
Wisconsin 12 (253)
Delaware 3 (256)

Missouri 15 (271) – (266 votes needed for Electoral College win)
Wyoming 3 (274)
Idaho 4 (278)
Oregon 6 (284)
Maryland 8 (292)
Massachusetts 16 (308)
Minnesota 11 (319)
New Mexico 4 (323)
West Virginia 8 (331)
Kentucky 11 (342)
Montana 4 (346)
California 25 (371) – (354 is two-thirds of Electoral College votes)

10 largest cities in the United States in the 1940s, 5 were in states that were won by the Republicans in the closely contested election of 1948 (New York, Philadelphia, Detroit, Baltimore, and Pittsburgh) and 5 in states won by the Democrats (Chicago, Los Angeles, Cleveland, St. Louis, and Boston). The 4 states that went Republican had 109 Electoral College votes – exactly the same number as the 5 that went Democratic. Thus,

the cities were important for the Democrats in *presidential* elections – but only because they were now more competitive in the states containing them. Indeed, one of the main characteristics of electoral competition in the New Deal era is that so much hinged on these states, and that was one of the two reasons why moderate Republicans could be the force in their party that they were.

An electoral strategy of moderate Republicanism provided the means by which the party could revive in a number of these states after 1936, but underlying that factor was the pre-existing strength of the Republican Party organizations there. Heavy defeats had not destroyed the party infra-structure, except in the case of a number of urban machines. Elsewhere, and at other levels, the party could re-group after 1932–6 – it still had many resources in the form of activists, access to political money, and so on that were essential to electoral competition. What FDR had done was, in some sense, limited in relation to underlying Republican organizational strength – but it did tip the balance decisively in terms of enabling his party to control the national polity for most of the next two decades.

4. The Problems in Sustaining a Republican Resurgence at the National Level

If the incursion into the Republican North by the Democrats in the later 1930s was relatively modest, this raises the question, posed at the end of Section 1, of why subsequently the Republicans were not even more effective than they were in reclaiming power at the national level. The conventional answer to this, to which undoubtedly some weight must be attached, is that the proportion of Republican identifiers in the electorate declined steadily from 1920 onwards while the proportion of Democrats increased a little in the 1920s and then remained fairly stable during the 1930s and 1940s. In 1932, 39 per cent of voters had claimed a Republican identification, whereas only 28 per cent did so in 1952.[20] Moreover, the voters who voted for the first time in the 1930s, and who were more likely to vote Democrat than their predecessors, were only slightly less likely to vote at all than their predecessors. Because the rate of turnout by the New Deal generation was almost as high as the preceding generations, the Democratic advantage was not diluted as it would

---

[20] Norman H. Nie, Sidney Verba, and John R. Petrocik, *The Changing American Voter*, p. 83.

have been had one voter response to the Great Depression simply been voter alienation from (or apathy towards) the electoral process.[21]

Nevertheless, it must be questioned whether, by itself, this can account for the inability of the Republicans to do better than they did after 1938 in presidential elections. Even in the 19th century, when there were few floating voters and internal cohesion was the main problem facing parties, coalitions were never so tight that a party could find itself frozen out of power for long. Furthermore, all the evidence suggests that by the 1930s, voters' links to their parties were much weaker than in the 19th century; thus, the notion that the Democrats had a lock on a majority of the electorate – because of their advantage in party identification among voters that made it impossible for the Republicans to compete effectively – is implausible. Indeed, as we saw at the beginning of this chapter, the Republicans actually did well in gubernatorial elections – a level of politics where it would be expected that party identification would count for more than at the presidential level.

One crude way of testing whether declining Republican identification affected the party's performance is to examine whether the share of the total vote the Republicans received in each presidential election is correlated with the proportion of Republican identifiers in the electorate in each of those years. For the period 1920–64, it is clear that there is some kind of relationship; there is an r square of .069 on the Pearson coefficient. However, the relationship is too small to provide the basis for much of an explanation as to why the Republicans lost presidential elections in the 1940s. A more plausible argument might be that it was *at the margin* that party identification really did matter. The argument might proceed as follows: Because levels of education and income were generally higher among Republicans, and it is known that these attributes are positively correlated with a propensity to vote, in elections with lower turnouts – such as in mid-term years – the Republican Party was not at a disadvantage with the Democrats. This could account for Republican success in many gubernatorial contests, for example. However, *all things being equal*, the higher the turnout, the greater the proportion of Democratic identifiers who would actually vote. Although, with the exceptions of 1932 and 1936, the Republicans always polled a larger share of the vote than the proportion of Republican identifiers in the electorate, their

---

[21] On the respective turnout rates of pre–New Deal and New Deal political generations, see Warren E. Miller and J. Merrill Shanks, *The New American Voter,* Cambridge, MA, and London, Harvard University Press, 1996, p. 113.

ability to convert that non-Republican resource into victory would diminish as more Democratic identifiers became actual voters. Consequently, as the number of Republican identifiers continued declining throughout the 1940s, the party's task became more difficult – especially in higher-turnout elections. In addition, the defection rate among Democratic identifiers was higher than it was among Republicans, and this, too, could account for greater Republican success in controlling the governorships. Consequently, that they appeared to be at parity with the Democrats in mid-term gubernatorial contests is misleading when the party's potential in presidential contests is evaluated.

Certainly, there is something to this argument, but it can be argued that there were other factors contributing significantly to the weak Republican performance at the presidential level after the New Deal. One argument is that the party's inability to win any of the presidential elections in the 1940s was mainly the result of factors specific to each election. On this account, what really mattered was the context in which particular elections were fought, and one factor common to all these elections was that the Republicans had to face an incumbent president. In 1940, the possibility of war, and in 1944 engagement in a major war, advantaged the incumbent. Roosevelt was the first two-term president to run for a further term, and it can be argued that his election results, with national defence prominent as an issue, were better than any other Democrat would have achieved. Clearly, the Republicans believed that there was an advantage to incumbency – later in the decade they responded to the possibility of a future FDR with the 22nd Amendment. In 1948, the incumbent they faced had not been elected to the presidency, but he was campaigning in the light of a booming domestic economy. In addition, ineffective campaigning by Thomas Dewey – "Dewey insisted on a sober, dignified and vaporous campaign"[22] – could be cited as a factor enabling Harry Truman to turn seemingly certain defeat into victory. Then, the first time the Republicans faced a non-incumbent since 1932 they won (1952). That incumbency benefits the party of an incumbent president has been demonstrated by Herbert Weisberg, who argues that since 1952 there has been "an overall 6.4 percent incumbency effect".[23] If there had been a similar incumbency effect in the three elections in the 1940s, the Democrats' ability to hold onto the presidency would have been much reduced in the absence of an incumbent.

---

[22] Ed Cray, *Chief Justice: A Biography of Earl Warren*, p. 190.
[23] Herbert F. Weisberg, "Partisanship and Incumbency in Presidential Elections", *Political Behavior* 4 (2002), 352.

The experience of 1948 suggests, however, that there was another factor complicating any attempt to turn the kind of Republican electoral strength that was being revealed in gubernatorial elections into presidential majorities. This was the tension between the orthodox wing of the party that was dominant in Congress and moderate Republicanism. American parties have no difficulty in coping with candidates of different ideologies running for different offices; especially with state governorships, they can play to the different values and sentiments prevalent in different states, so that in 1942, a conservative like John Bricker could win in Ohio while Dewey was winning New York. It is a little less easy, but perfectly feasible, for a party to run a campaign where the presidential candidate is of a different ideological hue from the House or Senate candidate. However, difficulties arise when the wing of a party controlling a legislature is very different from the wing of the party from which the presidential candidate is drawn. This was the problem exposed in 1948. Orthodox Republicans had no reason to doubt the record of the Republican-controlled 80th Congress, and the party could scarcely disown it, but some of its measures were an embarrassment for a moderate Republican presidential ticket. Truman was able to exploit that by "running against Congress" in his campaign. It became difficult for Dewey and his running mate, Earl Warren, to deflect attention away from a Congress that they could neither disown nor defend vigorously.

In this dilemma facing Dewey can be seen an aspect of the problem that was to bring about the downfall of moderate Republicanism, which is examined more fully in the next chapter. Pursuit of the marginal voter is the rational strategy for any candidate motivated by a desire to win. For the reasons identified earlier, it was possible for the Republicans after 1940 to nominate candidates who would do that. However, the minority status of moderate Republicans within the party would always make it difficult to reconcile some aspects of their policy agenda with that of orthodox Republicans, and that reconciliation became much more difficult during a presidential campaign in which the party controlled Congress.

To illuminate this point, it is worth contrasting the Republican position in the 1940s with that of parties at other times. For example, in the 1880s, the northern wing of the Democratic Party was a minority, and it constituted the marginal voter, but there was not a major difference on policy between it and those in the party from the South and the Border states. Accommodation was easy. The Republican Party between 1908 and 1912 became split within both its presidential and congressional wings. Accommodation was impossible, and the breakaway Progressive Party was the result. In the 1920s, the dominant conservative wing of the Republican Party in Congress also controlled presidential nominations. Divisions within the party centred on specific aspects of legislation in Congress, therefore, and did not affect the fight for the presidency. Accommodation was possible. After 1932, Franklin Roosevelt treated urban America as the marginal voter, but he was able to do so because of the much greater strength of this interest in Congress. It was not a minority in the congressional delegation – although the South exercised undue power through the consequences of the seniority system in committees – and so the congressional and presidential wings of the party could follow broadly similar agendas. Again accommodation was possible. In the case of moderate Republicanism, when their party did not control Congress, accommodation was difficult, though not necessarily impossible; once they had control of Congress, it became more difficult to present a coherent front and, as is shown in Chapter 8, it was also problematic when the party did come to control the presidency.

5. The Democratic Party in 1952

The main thrust of the argument present in this chapter has been that for all the changes FDR wrought in the party system, the limits on what he could have hoped to achieve, combined with the Republican response to his policy agenda, produced a party system that appeared to be remarkably evenly balanced. Moreover, it can be argued that there was still considerable continuity between the Democratic Party of 1952 and the Democracy of the Gilded Age. In spite of a number of important changes in the intervening 70 years, there are clear similarities between the two eras. Most especially, the Democrats remained a party that relied heavily on the South and on the Border states in order to construct a national majority. While the latter had become more competitive as long ago as the 1890s, and the Democrats could not expect to carry all of them in a close victory, they still leaned Democratic overall, and that lean had actually increased since 1932. In 1948, Truman had carried all but Delaware and Maryland, and that year the Democrats also won 86 per cent of House seats in the region; even in the defeat of 1952, the Democrats would carry two-thirds of the House seats from the Border states. One of the least-remarked-on consequences of the New Deal is that it improved Democratic electoral performances in the Border states; generally, Republicans did less well there after 1932 than they did in the quarter of a century after 1896. (For example, in their best year between 1898 and 1908, the median share of House seats won by Democrats

TABLE 7.11. *Northern Congressional Seats Held by Democrats Following Elections in 1886, 1914, and 1950, by Region (as Percentage of Total Northern Seats)*

	1886	1914	1950
Coastal states	18	15	22
Interior states	14	19	12

was 57.5 per cent of total seats, while the mean was 59 per cent of the total; when losing the presidency and the House in 1952, the party still won 67 per cent of Border seats states.) This persisting, solid base in the ex-slave states meant that comparable election results overall would continue to yield a similar share of the seats from the North. For example, the 1886, 1914, and 1950 mid-term elections produced very similar results overall, with the Democrats obtaining, respectively, 52 per cent, 54 per cent, and 54 cent of all seats; their share of northern seats was also similar – respectively, they obtained 32 per cent, 34 per cent, and 34 per cent of northern seats.

Nevertheless, there were four significant, if seemingly small, aspects in which change was evident with respect to the Democratic Party coalition's northern component, and this affects how we should interpret and compare this pattern of results in 1886, 1914, and 1950. First, the North became relatively (as well as absolutely) larger, so that being competitive in the North meant even more in the 20th century than in the late 19th century. Thus, while in 1886, 62 per cent of all House districts were in the North, this increased to 66 per cent by 1914 at which level it remained in 1950. Secondly, thanks to the impact of the New Deal realignment, the Democrats were less likely to be a minority party; they had a slightly more solid northern core (based in the cities) to complement their main area of strength nationally, and this made it more likely that they would actually win control of public offices.[24] Thirdly, the party was performing relatively better in the coastal states, the sector that now contained 54 per cent of all northern districts, than in the interior (see Table 7.11). In 1950, it won 40 per cent of the House districts in the coastal states,

---

[24] For example, between 1880 and 1890 (inclusive) the party gained House majorities on four of six occasions, between 1910 and 1920 they did so on three occasions, and between 1940 and 1950 this was achieved on five occasions; the median share of seats they received in House elections in these three periods was, respectively, 54.4 per cent, 50.9 per cent, and 54.9 per cent.

whereas it won only 27 per cent of seats in the interior states that year. The long-term move of the Democrats into the Northeast and the West Coast, which was to become so important to their presidential coalition building after the 1960s, had begun with the impact of the New Deal. The party's earlier move towards the interior states, which had been a consequence of a more general "westernization" of the party post-1896, was now being reversed. Fourthly, by 1950, Democratic strength in the North was even more heavily concentrated in urban areas than it had been in the 1880s; from 1932 onwards it was starting to become the dominant party in virtually all major urban areas. Correspondingly, the party had a much less secure base in the non-urban North in 1950, especially in the eastern half of the country, than it had had in either 1886 or 1914. That is why FDR's revolution had done no more than make many of the coastal states highly competitive; in spite of increasing Democratic dominance in the cities, the rural areas and the suburbs were providing a solid Republican base that prevented the establishment of Democratic dominance at the state level.

Consequently, in spite of the temptation to see the immediate effects of the New Deal on party coalition as being dramatic, this must be resisted. The electoral map of 1948 is not that dissimilar to that of 1916 – the West was nearly as important to Truman's victory as it was to Wilson's, and like his predecessor, Truman failed to carry major industrial states in the Northeast and the old Midwest – including New York, Pennsylvania, Michigan, and New Jersey. As has been emphasized throughout this chapter, what Roosevelt did in mobilizing a majority of first-time voters in 1932 and 1936 had a huge impact on the conduct of politics. But in the overall perspective of American party coalition building, it was not to constitute an immediate overturning of an older coalition but a modification of it. Nevertheless, in the longer term, the New Deal policy agenda had helped to create a chain reaction in terms of political demands that in the 1950s was to start undermining the entire basis of the post-1856 Democratic coalition. At the same time, the Republican Party's response to the New Deal – presidential moderate Republicans – was also to be threatened from within. This dual collapse of a political order is the subject to which we now turn.

8

The Two Parties' Coalitions Come Under Threat, 1952–1962

One of the paradoxes of the 1950s is that although it was a decade often regarded as having been dull (politically, as well as in other ways), it was one in which the first stages of major change in the party system became evident. The coalitions of both the major parties came under strain at the same time, yet the main impact of those pressures would not be felt fully until the 1960s. Consequently, despite clear evidence of continuity from the balanced post–New Deal party system that had been re-established during the 1940s, the basis of that balance became undermined. We begin this chapter by considering how the parties performed at various levels of election.

The most obvious point about presidential elections after 1952 is that the closely fought 1960 election might seem to indicate that the balance between the parties established in the 1940s had persisted throughout the decade; the Democrats won that election with a popular plurality of just 0.2 per cent of the vote. However, whilst there may have appeared to be a continuing balance, the basis of it was not quite the same as in the 1940s. In particular, the pivotal position of the coastal states in the Republican Party coalition had been much weakened in the elections of 1952–60. As can be seen in Tables 8.1 and 8.2, the coastal states now possessed only 46 per cent of the Electoral College votes in the Marginal and Democratic Marginal categories combined, whereas for the elections of 1936–48, they had accounted for 72 per cent of the total EC votes in these categories (see Tables 7.4 and 7.5). The significance of this is discussed shortly. For the moment, it is important to note that the main battleground had become a more complex arena than the one in which the parties had been fighting primarily for industrialized states on the East or West Coast. In part, this

TABLE 8.1. *Construction of Winning Republican Coalition in Electoral College, 1952–1960, in Descending Order of "Safeness" (Number of Electoral College Votes Provided by Each State Indicated in Parentheses)*

---

266 Electoral College Votes Required to Win Presidential Election[1]

Heartland States (1st–89th Electoral College Votes)

*VT (3)	IA (10)	UT (4)
NE (6)	*NH (4)	WI (12)
*ME (5)	ND (4)	ID (4)
KS (8)	WY (3)	*OH (16)*
SD (4)	CO (6)	

Intermediate States (90th–178th Electoral College Votes)

OH (9)	*NJ (16)
AZ (4)	*NY (41)*
IN (13)	
*OR (6)	

Marginal States (179th–266th Electoral College Votes)

NY (4)	*CA (32)
MT (4)	NM (4)
VA (12)	*IL (15)*
*CT (8)	

Democratic Marginal States (267th–311th Electoral College Votes)

IL (12)	MN (11)
NV (3)	
FL (10)	
*WA (9)	

States are ranked in "Safeness" by calculating the median value for the 1952, 1956, and 1960 elections of (Republican plurality over Democrats in given state) minus (Republican plurality over Democrats in all non-southern states).

States shown in italics have Electoral College votes in more than one category in this table.

* = coastal states (those on East or West Coast)

[1] For these purposes, the statehoods of Alaska and Hawaii in 1958, which increased the size of the Electoral College in 1960, have been ignored.

complexity was the result of states in the outer South becoming much more competitive at the presidential level. (Not only are Virginia and Florida in the Marginal and Democratic Marginal categories for 1952–60, but in 1960 Richard Nixon actually won Tennessee as well as these two states for the Republican Party.) However, there were also significant changes in some individual northern non-coastal states in these years; for example, the Democratic alliance with labour unions in Michigan had started to make the party far more successful there than it had been earlier.

Evidence of change was also present in gubernatorial elections, where a very different pattern of results from 1938–52 is evident. After 1952,

TABLE 8.2. *Distribution of Electoral College Votes by Type of State, 1952–1960*

Heartland States (1st–89th Electoral College Votes)
Coastal 12
Interior 77
South 0

Intermediate States (90th–178th Electoral College Votes)
Coastal 63
Interior 26
South 0

Marginal States (179th–266th Electoral College Votes)
Coastal 53
Interior 23
South 12

Democratic Marginal States (267th–311th Electoral College Votes)
Coastal 9
Interior 26
South 10

States are ranked in "Safeness" by calculating the median value for the 1952, 1956, and 1960 elections of (Republican plurality over Democrats in given state) minus (Republican plurality over Democrats in all states).

the Republicans performed much worse than they did in the 1940s. To some extent, there is a link with the changes observed at the presidential level. Consider the case of Michigan. It had been a solidly Republican state since the Civil War, and it remained Republican-leaning in spite of the effects of the New Deal. However, as the labour unions started to re-invigorate the Democratic Party organization from the mid-1930s onwards, so, too, could the party start to win elections, and they did; there was no Republican governor in the state between 1952 and 1962. However, unlike at the presidential level, overall the gubernatorial elections suggested *increasing* Democratic strength in the North – especially in the Northeast and the "old" Midwest. Whereas between 1940 and 1952 Republicans held governorships on 47.2 per cent of all possible occasions (see Chapter 7, Section 1), between 1952 and 1962 they did so on only 40.6 per cent of all occasions. Now it might be thought that this comparison reflects the distorting effect of the 1958 mid-term elections at all levels of office. Certainly, there is no question that this does account for much of the decline in Republican success. If gubernatorial terms that began in 1959 are excluded, then the Republicans occupied statehouses on 46.3 per cent of all occasions between 1952 and 1962 – only a small decrease in their success rate between 1940 and 1952. However, that is not quite the end of the story.

As was seen in Chapter 7, the Republican Party had done well in large states. If the number of Electoral College votes of a state is weighted by the proportion of the 12-year period in which the Republicans controlled the governorship, then 50.1 per cent of all EC votes would have been Republican between 1940 and 1952. If this same calculation is made for the years 1952–62 (but excluding all terms of office that began in 1959), a mere 39.5 per cent of EC votes would have been Republican. To put the matter another way, the Republicans controlled the governorships of states like Idaho, Montana, and Utah for much (or all) of this period, whereas their control of larger states like Michigan, New Jersey, Ohio, and Pennsylvania became much more restricted during the Eisenhower era. The 1958 elections thereby made a weakening situation even worse. In essence, what we see in this decade is a delayed effect of the New Deal. FDR's strategy had two effects on party competition. First, in the short term, it made for Democratic dominance between 1932 and 1938, but that was something to which the Republican state organizations could respond effectively. Secondly, though, the New Deal contributed to longer-term party building by the Democratic Party, and the effects of that (in terms of victories, such as those in gubernatorial elections) started to become apparent only in the late 1940s and early 1950s.

Nevertheless, a different pattern from this emerges if we consider the other major elections held statewide – those for U.S. Senate seats. As with the governorships, the 1958 elections saw massive Republican losses – a net loss of 13 seats that created the largest Democratic majority in the chamber since 1941–2. However, if we examine just the elections of 1954, 1956, and 1960, we see that there was a change of party control for 17 seats in total, of which 9 were switches from Democrat to Republican. Of the 8 Democrat gains, 3 were in large industrial states in the Midwest or on the East Coast (Michigan, Ohio, and Pennsylvania), while a further 2 were in another coastal state (both Oregon seats).[1] By contrast, the 9 Republican gains were largely in other kinds of states – only Connecticut and New York fell into this category. The difference in the results between the gubernatorial and Senate contests arguably reflects the fact that the temporarily "out" party in a state tended to concentrate its resources on just one contest in a state, and that contest was usually the governorship

---

[1] One of these Oregon gains was the result of liberal Wayne Morse's switching from being a Republican to a Democrat.

because of the patronage rewards that attached to the office. Senate seats were much less useful in this regard, and thus were of less importance for local and state parties. Less effort probably resulted in a lower success rate, and that might explain the difference between the Democrats' performance in gubernatorial and Senate elections in the mid-1950s. Moreover, in the 1962 mid-term elections, the Democrats were to make a gain of 4 seats in the Senate, the third-largest mid-term gain in the entire 20th century by a party holding the presidency and exceeded only by 1914 and 1934. Even though that success does not prove that the Democrats had tended to concentrate on governorships in the 1950s while their state parties became stronger, it is at least compatible with such a hypothesis. However, the important point is that as with the governorships, the Republican position was not actually improving in the 1950s, and that was extremely important for intra-party relations.

With House elections, the superficial judgement would be that the situation changed little between 1952 and 1962. With the exception of the 1958 landslide, the number of seats won by the Democrats was within the range of seats they won after 1936. Yet there are some subtle, and important, differences that point in another direction. The size of their majorities in the House after the 1960 and 1962 elections had been equalled or bettered only once since 1940 – in the presidential year of 1948. They obtained the same number of seats in 1960 as in 1948, yet the margin of the presidential plurality had been much larger in 1948 – 3.7 per cent of the total vote as against 0.2 per cent in 1960. Although many of the gains of 1958 had been wiped out in 1960, the party still had nearly 30 seats more in 1960 than after the 1950, 1954, and 1956 elections (and 50 more than in 1952). Something was changing to their advantage – and that change could be happening only outside the South.

However, at the same time, the Democratic Party was experiencing change in the South – change that necessarily hurt its coalition-building efforts. Already, evidence from presidential elections in the South was suggesting that the Republicans could start slowly to erode Democratic hegemony in that region. In the House, too, there was a slow increase in Republican representation. (In 1961, the party also took a Senate seat there for the first time since Reconstruction.) The changes in the House during the 1950s are illustrated in Table 8.3, which shows the composition of the Democratic majority after three elections that had produced similarly sized majorities for the party either side of the 1950s – 1948 (263 seats), 1960 (263 seats), and also 1962 (258 seats). (By way of setting these changes in the context of changes that occurred later, the results of the

TABLE 8.3. *Proportion of House Seats Won by the Democratic Party in Each Region, 1948, 1960, 1962, and 1992 (as Percentage of Total Number of Seats in Each Region)*

	South	Border States	North-eastern States	"Old" Midwest States[1]	Interior Western States[2]	West Coast States	United States
1948	100	86	47	47	33	36	60
1960	93	85	49	42	36	51	60
1962	90	78	50	38	35	61	59
1992	62	64	57	57	49	63	59

[1] States granted statehood before 1840.
[2] States granted statehood after 1840.

1992 election, the last one in the 20th century when the Democrats had a majority in the House, are also included; in 1993 the party had exactly the same number of seats as it had in 1962.)

Of these two counter forces acting on national Democratic Party strength, it was developments in the North (and especially on the West Coast) that were the stronger in the years up to 1962. While Democratic dominance in the South and in the Border states was weakening only slightly, there was a dramatic shift in party strength on the West Coast. Nearly all of this was due to political change in California, of which there were three main components. There was a continuing massive increase in the state's population, which increased the state's importance in national coalition building. Then, after 1958, the unique cross-filing primary system was abolished – this was a system that had tended to benefit Republican incumbents in the immediate post-war years. Finally, and this point is discussed again in Section 5, reapportionment of electoral districts in 1961–2 failed for the first time to provide a Republican advantage.[2]

How should this change in the composition of the House be understood in the context of longer-term change in the party system? Table 8.4 shows the percentage of House seats won by the Democrats in each region at different periods. Three of the elections (1888, 1916, and 1952) each produced a narrow Republican plurality (the Democrats won, respectively, 47.2 per cent, 48.2 per cent, and 48.9 per cent of all seats), and thus they show the core support for the Democrats in each period. The other three

[2] On the roles of Jesse Unruh and Phil Burton in the California reapportionment, see John Jacobs, *A Rage for Justice: The Passion and Politics of Phillip Burton*, Berkeley, University of California Press, 1995, pp. 87–90 and 116–22.

TABLE 8.4. *Proportion of House Seats Won by the Democratic Party in Each Region in Three Periods (as Percentage of Total Number of Seats in Each Region): Late 19th Century (1888 and 1882), Progressive Era (1916 and 1910), Mid–20th Century (1952 and 1962), and Early 21st Century (2002)*

	South	Border States	North-eastern States	"Old" Midwest States[1]	Interior Western States[2]	West Coast States	United States
1888	89	72	32	37	8	29	47
1882	91	86	46	53	28	86	62
1916	97	77	25	31	28	26	48
1910	97	77	43	56	18	8	58
1952	94	67	37	28	20	29	49
1962	90	78	50	38	35	61	59
2002	41	44	58	39	31	64	47

[1] States granted statehood before 1840.
[2] States granted statehood after 1840.

elections (1882, 1910, and 1962) were close in time to the first three, and produced similarly sized but relatively large Democratic majorities. (The Democrats won 61.5 per cent, 58.3 per cent, and 59.3 per cent of all seats, respectively, at these elections.) Not surprisingly, in most cases and in all the regions except the South, the Democrats show increases in the numbers of their seats between the narrow defeats and the comfortable victories.[3] In that sense, all regions usually contributed to that kind of victory. However, even in the elections that they won comfortably in earlier years, the Democrats did not usually secure as many as half the seats in a region – except in the Border states and, of course, the South. The exceptions are illuminating. In both 1882 and 1910, the party won more than half the seats in the old Midwest (Illinois, Indiana, Michigan, and Ohio).[4] By contrast, in the period after 1952 it was the two coastal areas – the

[3] Presenting the data in the way that is done in Table 7.4 does have some disadvantages, of course. The Congress elected in 1910 was the only one in that era in which the Democrats had a similar majority to the ones it obtained in 1960 and 1962. However, using it in conjunction with 1916 has the disadvantage that an election in which a "western" strategy (1916) was employed is juxtaposed with one in which it was not (1910). Thus, the larger majority of 1910 had seen the Democrats elect a much smaller proportion of House members in both of the newer parts of the West (the interior and the West Coast) than was to occur in 1916. Nevertheless, it does help to illuminate the changing importance of the two coastal regions for the Democrats in the 1950s.

[4] The Democrats also won 86 per cent of seats in the West Coast states in 1882, but since there were a total of seven seats at stake there, this is of relatively little interest when national coalition building is considered.

Northeast and the West Coast – where the Democrats could win half the seats in the region in favourable election years. In the decades after 1962, those two regions would gradually come to form the core of the Democratic coalition. In the 1950s, the old Midwest was no longer a region in which the Democrats reached parity with the Republicans in House elections. The significance of this point is that it adds further weight to the argument that the battle for the coastal regions – the marginal region in presidential elections in the 1940s – was being won by the Democrats. In doing so, the nature of the "margin" would change, and that would have a major effect on optimal party strategies.

Finally, we turn briefly to state legislatures. As with other types of election, the Republicans had narrowed the gap between themselves and the Democrats after 1938, and following the 1952 election, the party had virtually the same share of these seats nationally as the Democrats. (From 1942 to 1948, and again from 1950 to 1954, the Republicans controlled more state legislatures than the Democrats.) Thereafter, the gap opened up again in the 1954 mid-term elections, but more importantly, it did not close at the time Eisenhower was winning re-election in 1956. The significance of this is that it exposes once more the fallacy of any claim that the Republicans' problems began with the 1958 landslide (when the party won only 35 per cent of all state legislature seats). Certainly, that landslide was a major blow to the party of the incumbent president, but then the Democrats had suffered a similar defeat in 1946. What is interesting about 1958 is that, first, it was preceded by the failure of Eisenhower to generate any coattails for the party in 1956 and, secondly, it was followed by a narrow presidential defeat in 1960 when once again the party generally lagged well behind its presidential candidate. Thus, while Nixon was winning 49.5 per cent of the popular vote, the Republicans were obtaining less than 40 per cent of state legislature seats. By the early 1960s, the Republican Party was starting to resemble a minority party – in terms of the building blocks available to it from which to construct a national majority – something that it had not been in the 1940s.

Consequently, although the evidence from different levels of election does not point incontrovertibly in the same direction, one point is clear – except in winning two presidential elections, the Republicans were certainly not doing better in the 1950s than they did in the 1940s. Indeed, in gubernatorial and state legislature elections, they were in a much worse position by the early 1960s than they had been a decade earlier. Moreover, by no means can all of their worsened position be attributed to the effects of the 1958 landslide. Not only is there some evidence that the party's electoral strength was weakening before then, but the party also failed to make the kind of recovery after the landslide that, for example, the Democrats had managed between 1946 and 1948. This was important for the intra-party tensions that were threatening to tear the party apart by the end of 1962, and which are discussed in more detail in Sections 3 and 7. However, at the same time as the Democrats seemed to have improved their position vis-à-vis the Republicans in the northern states, so also was their traditional base in the South coming under threat. So why was the seemingly stable, and evenly balanced, pattern of party competition established between 1938 and 1952 collapsing on both sides? To answer this question we turn again to the framework of analysis introduced in Chapter 2 and deployed previously in Chapters 4 and 6. This enables us to separate the different factors that might account for changes in the capacity for a party to build a national coalition.

1. Had the Interests Within Either Coalition Become Incompatible?

Unquestionably, the tensions within the Democratic coalition stemmed from the issue of race – and that was a matter involving incompatible interests. The party could not both represent the interests of white Southerners, who wished to maintain all aspects of racial segregation, and solicit the votes of African Americans in the northern cities. This had not been a problem for the party years before, and to understand how the conflict had emerged, it is necessary to examine how black migrants to the cities earlier in the 20th century had related to the Democratic Party.

Republican attitudes, and more especially policies, towards slavery in the mid–19th century had the result that most African Americans became Republican voters. Or rather, they became Republican voters when both of two conditions were met. First, racial discrimination did not result in their disenfranchisement; before the Civil War even the small number of "free" blacks in the South could not vote, and that had also been a problem in many parts of the supposedly "free" North during that era. (During Reconstruction, black voting rights were generally enforced in the South, though informal pressures on African Americans not to vote increased in the 20 years after 1876.) Secondly, in some parts of the rural South, where illiteracy levels were high and white landowners could exercise power in their communities, the black vote could be delivered for the Democrats by these landowners. To the extent that the southern black population had both a minimum level of information and freedom to go to the polls, they voted Republican; the much smaller number of black people in the North also supported the Republicans. As Paul Kleppner notes of the Gilded Age period: "Racial self-consciousness probably led black voters everywhere to cast a majority of their ballots for the party of the Great Emanicaptor".[5] On policy matters of concern to African Americans, the Republicans generally provided reasons for that support to continue – at least they did so until about 1890. By then, division within the Republican Party – on issues such as the Lodge Bill that would have provided for scrutinization of elections, and the Blair Bill that would have provided aid for public education (and have been of benefit mainly to African Americans) – ended the effectiveness of its support for black interests.[6]

At the same time as the Republican Party was becoming divided over its approach to its African American constituency, Democratic Parties in the South were moving to disenfranchise the black electorate. Within a decade, this had largely been achieved. By the early 20th century, the major electoral component of the southern Republican Parties during Reconstruction became unimportant actors in the two-party battle nationally, and the Republicans responded by becoming much less attentive to black interests than they had been earlier. As Desmond King says of the first decade of the 20th century, "the neglect of Black Americans' interests by Republicans was significant, and indeed Theodore Roosevelt 'reduced the number of Negro officeholders [in the federal government]'".[7] To the extent that there now was a black electorate – and this was a relatively small electorate – continuing attachment to the Republican Party stemmed mainly from a combination of sentiment and the fact that while the Republicans were now indifferent to black interests, much of the Democratic Party was still openly hostile to them.

This would have been a stable solution for the parties but for the first wave of mass migration of African Americans from the South – a migration that started in the years immediately before the First World War. These populations tended to be concentrated geographically within cities, and potentially they were a resource for a party that was willing to mobilize them. As we have seen, to the extent that an urban party was

---

[5] Paul Kleppner, *The Third Electoral System, 1853–1892*, p. 180.

[6] Michael Perman, *Struggle for Mastery. Disfranchisement in the South, 1888–1908*, Chapel Hill, University of North Carolina Press, 2001, pp. 39–42.

[7] Desmond King, *Separate and Unequal: Black Americans and the U.S. Federal Government*, Oxford, Oxford University Press, 1995, p. 7; the passage King quotes is from George M. Frederickson, *The Black Image in the White Mind*, Hanover, NH, Wesleyan University Press, 1987, p. 301.

relatively safe from a challenge from its opponents, little might be done by them to incorporate new groups into the party's coalition. However, when a party had an incentive to improve its position, African American voters would be a tempting target – for urban Democrats as well as for some Republicans. One of the more interesting examples of this strategy was in Missouri, and it is interesting because it might be expected that in a Border state, an appeal to black voters in the cities could provoke difficulties with the rural Democratic electorate. However, after an electoral debacle in 1924, the Democratic Party did adopt the strategy. As Franklin Mitchell argues:

> The efforts of Democrats to capture a large share of the colored vote in St. Louis and elsewhere . . . was . . . revolutionary, especially when contrasted with the party's attitude towards the Negro voter in 1924. The most readily observed change took place in the party platform. In 1926 . . . the Democratic planks not only included a program for Negroes, but, unlike the G.O.P. plank, stipulated that all public institutions for colored persons should be directed and staffed by their own people . . . their plank placed the party on record as a friend of the Negro.[8]

It is against this background of some state Democratic Parties having moved to embrace black voters, driven by the need to improve their party's position in the cities, that the impact of the New Deal should be understood.

It is a much-repeated comment that the pattern of African American voting shifted towards the Democrats with the New Deal. Most of the black electorate that did so was, of course, a non-southern one, given continuing widespread disenfranchisement south of the Mason-Dixon Line. Evidence suggested that its behaviour was like other northern urban groups in 1932 – a Democratic vote was a vote against a Republican administration, rather than being a vote for anything specific that Democratic candidates claimed they would do for African Americans. While African Americans had hoped to participate in the New Deal, they did not, as King notes: "Black Americans did not benefit proportionately from New Deal programmes, as the NAACP complained to Eleanor Roosevelt".[9] Yet FDR could not retreat to an earlier Democratic policy of open hostility to black interests. Many of the urban Democrats elected into the House in 1932, and thereafter, had black voters in their own coalitions, and it was these members, along with senators from large industrial

---

[8] Franklin D. Mitchell, *Embattled Democracy: Missouri Politics, 1929–1932*, Columbia, University of Missouri Press, 1968, p. 98.
[9] King, *Separate and Unequal*, p. 31.

states, who were to constitute a main source of pressure within the party for opposition to the politics of segregation. Thus, despite doing little for its interests as a group, FDR's policies from 1933 tended to tie the African American electorate to his party. Thus, the 1936 election consolidated change in the party that had started in the 1920s, and that meant that a tension between the interests of African Americans and white Southerners would lie at the heart of the party for more than four decades.

Nevertheless, Franklin Roosevelt had no intention of letting the South slip into the hands of the Republicans. His attempt in 1938 to remove conservatives from Congress was an attempt to remove opponents of his economic policies, rather than an overt turning against the southern elements in his electoral coalition, and not all of the conservatives he targeted were Southerners. Indeed, the one attempt he made outside the South to replace an influential incumbent – New York Congressman John J. O'Connor – was a rare success for the campaign. Moreover, the South did elect some rabid New Dealers in the 1930s – Florida Senator Claude Pepper being an obvious example – as well as moderates who were willing to go along with much that their president proposed. However, the centre of opposition within the Democratic Party to his programmes was in the South, and it was a region to which policy concessions would have to be made if it were to continue to be part of the Democratic Heartland. To that end, Roosevelt did little to encourage black political leaders that his administration would be sympathetic to them. For example, in 1938, the administration withdrew its support from yet another effort to pass federal anti-lynching legislation.

The approach paid off. The states that had abandoned his fellow New Yorker, Al Smith, in 1928 had not only returned to the Democratic fold in 1932; they stayed there throughout the Roosevelt years. With one seemingly minor exception, during the period 1932–44 the states in the region were about as Democratic (when compared with the nation as a whole) as they had been in the Bryan and Wilson years. The one exception was Virginia in 1940 when Roosevelt ran only 4 per cent ahead of his national vote share, whereas in that state, pre-1928 Democratic presidential candidates had consistently run more than 30 per cent ahead of the national vote share. Although 1944 was a better year for the Democrats in Virginia, 1940 had provided early evidence of the problems the party would encounter in the region from 1948 onwards.

Pressure to promote racial policies that would surely alienate the white South grew steadily during the Roosevelt years, and became worse after his death. They emanated from within the party and from outside it. As just noted, the internal pressure resulted from the very success of some Democratic Parties in the northern cities in attracting black voters during the 1920s. The major turning point was 1936, when for the first time, most black voters voted for the Democrats; essentially, black voters were responding to the New Deal in the way that many poorer urban whites were. However, once African Americans were in the party, Democratic members of Congress representing these voters came under increasing pressure to support the causes of particular salience to their black constituents. Obviously, these causes included civil rights legislation and other measures (for southern blacks) that would put that sector of the party into direct conflict with southern Democrats.

The party was now trapped. More African Americans migrated from the South during the war – with the economic boom providing an important incentive – and even more did so after 1945, when improvements in agricultural technology greatly reduced the need for a rural southern workforce. Thus, during the 1940s and early 1950s, "pull" followed by "push" in the labour market produced the greatest internal migration of African Americans ever. The population patterns of many northern cities changed radically, and in doing so increased further the pressure inside the Democratic Parties in the North to promote the demands of political leaders in the black communities. The number of northern Democratic politicians who were willing to let southern whites run politics in their own region entirely in the way they wanted shrank rapidly. Only 12 years after the party had abolished one of the devices that had helped protect the white South (the two-thirds rule for presidential nominations), it formally adopted in 1948 a platform committing the party to a policy of civil rights. In this switch of direction, the role of Roosevelt's successor had been important. Both sides of Harry Truman's family were from Kentucky and had sympathized with the South in the Civil War; he was brought up in another border state (Missouri) and might have been expected, therefore, to be sympathetic to southern interests.[10] But his political mentor had been the Pendergast machine in Kansas City, and it was that machine that had been at the forefront in recruiting African Americans into the state party in the 1920s. Truman was an urban-oriented, rather than a southern-oriented, Democrat; it was his administration that initiated the desegregation of the federal government that the Wilson administration

---

[10] On the Civil War sympathies of the two sides of Truman's family, see Alonzo L. Hamby, *Man of the People: A Life of Harry S. Truman*, New York, Oxford University Press, 1995, pp. 4–5.

had segregated more than 30 years earlier.[11] Furthermore, the 1948 party platform began the section on civil rights by commending Truman "for his courageous stand on the issue of civil rights". In response to Truman and the 1948 platform, some politicians in the Deep South bolted from the party and ran their own candidate, who won four states that year.

The external pressures on the party were just as great as the internal ones. The northern migration of black Americans did not merely create difficulties for Democrats in Congress and in the White House; it also provided resources for those pursuing other forms of political action. That action included legal suits, and later (in the 1950s), direct but passive resistance modelled on the approach of Mahatma Gandhi. Moreover, during the 1941–5 war, many African Americans had served abroad in the U.S. military. That experience not only helped to fuel claims that military service for the country constituted grounds for an entitlement to a certain minimum level of civil rights, but it also exposed many black Americans to the experience of countries that did not provide legal discrimination on grounds of race. Later, the advent of television, which could transfer images immediately to living rooms, provided another resource for those who could use publicity skilfully to further their cause. The campaign against racial segregation intensified after the *Brown* decision in 1954, for this removed the judicial rationale for many of the South's practices. (Implementing those decisions would be a long process, of course, and one that inevitably intensified the tensions within the Democratic Party.) Furthermore, America's leadership of the Western allies during the Cold War changed the importance of the race issue to federal administrations. Before 1945, there were hardly any foreign policy implications to the official condoning of segregation and discrimination in the states that wanted to practice it. After 1947, Soviet propaganda could point to the hypocrisy of a regime that supposedly advocated freedom for other countries, but which failed to protect certain freedoms within its own borders. An essentially domestic issue now had external dimensions.

In response to these demands for changed Democratic policies on race, the white South rapidly lost its status as the most loyal part of the Democratic coalition. It began with the 1948 bolt and the formation of a States' Rights Party that chose Strom Thurmond, the South Carolina governor, as its presidential candidate. Despite Truman's eventual success that year, the dangers of pursuing the strategy followed in 1948 were evident. For the next three presidential elections, the party deliberately sought to placate

[11] See King, *Separate and Unequal.*

the white South without repudiating overtly the claims of black political leaders. It was a difficult balancing act, and even that strategy did not prevent significant shifts in support away from the Democratic Party nationally. If the party was no longer uniquely placed to protect the South, then the incentive for supporting the national ticket was much reduced. Moreover, economic development in much of the outer South (including West Texas, which culturally was not part of the South at all) was expanding the size of social classes that might well be attracted to Republican economic policies.[12] Consequently, in the four elections between 1948 and 1960, there was a significant change in the relative electoral security offered to the party. The crudest measure of this is to look at the states lost by the Democrats in each election. In 1948, they lost four states to the States' Rights candidate (Alabama, Louisiana, Mississippi, and South Carolina). In 1952 they lost four completely different states (Florida, Tennessee, Texas, and Virginia) to Republican Dwight Eisenhower, while the latter won all those states and Louisiana in 1956. Despite losing the election of 1960, the Republicans still won three southern states that year (Florida, Tennessee, and Virginia). The Solid South was no more.

More revealing, though, is the party's *relative* performance in the southern states. In the states of the Deep South, the party's share of the vote in the median election had been more than 40 per cent higher than the party's share nationally during the four election years of 1932–44. In descending order of Democratic dominance, these states were South Carolina (+78.5 per cent), Mississippi (+77.5 per cent), Louisiana (+58.0 per cent), Alabama (+54.5 per cent), Georgia (+53.0 per cent), Texas (+51.5 per cent), and Arkansas (+44.0 per cent). In those years, the lean towards the Democratic Party in the four states of the outer South had been significant, though not as substantial as in the Deep South. The difference between the party's share of the vote in the state and its national share was +29.5 per cent in Florida, +24.5 per cent in North Carolina, +17.5 per cent in Virginia, and +14.5 per cent in Tennessee. In the four succeeding elections, the Democratic "lean" in the median election reduced dramatically in most of the Deep South. The smallest decline was in Georgia, where the "lean" went from +53.0 per cent to +43.5 per cent; in Louisiana, though, it went from +58.0 per cent to 13.5 per cent, while in Texas, it dropped from +51.5 to +3.0 per cent. Similarly diverging results were

---

[12] On the long term impact of this development on the parties in Congress, see Nelson W. Polsby, *How Congress Evolves: Social Bases of Institutional Change*, New York, Oxford University Press, 2004.

evident in the outer South, too. In North Carolina, the decline was modest (+24.5 per cent to +17.5 per cent), as it was in Tennessee (+14.5 per cent to +9.0 per cent), while in both Florida (+24.5 to +0.5) and in Virginia (+17.5 to –0.5) it was much greater. However, the important point is that every southern state experienced a decline.

Moreover, the Democrats' problem was not just that there had been a major shift in voter support from 1932–44 to 1948–60, but that within the latter period, the Democrats' relative appeal in the South was continuing to decline. In 8 of the 11 states (Arkansas, Florida, Georgia, North Carolina, South Carolina, Tennessee, Texas, and Virginia) the Democrats' share of the vote (in relation to the party's national share) was lower in 1960 than in any preceding election since the end of Reconstruction. In two other states (Alabama and Mississippi), the result was (relatively) the second-worst performance for the party since 1876 – the worst being in 1948, when the States' Rights Party had drawn votes disproportionately from the Democrats. Only Louisiana, where the Democrats did relatively better in 1960 than in 1948, 1952, and 1956, failed to conform to this pattern. That it was a Republican president who had appointed Earl Warren, the architect of the *Brown* decision, to the Supreme Court, and that it was the same president who had sent troops to Little Rock to enforce a desegregation order, did little to reverse the declining lean of southern states to the Democratic Party in presidential elections. The equivocation of both Adlai Stevenson's and John Kennedy's campaigns on civil rights matters could do little to reverse the growing tendency of some sections of the southern electorate to vote Republican in presidential elections. The problem was seen at its most extreme, perhaps, in Texas, where in 1960, Lyndon Johnson appeared on the ballot twice – once as the running mate of John Kennedy and once as the U.S. Senate candidate. He won the latter election with a plurality of nearly 17 per cent of the total vote, whereas the Democrats won the presidential election by a mere 3 per cent of the vote.

The party was in danger of being squeezed from both ends by its attempt to keep African American voters and the white South within the coalition. Following the desegregation efforts of the Truman administration, 83 percent of black voters in 1952 had voted for Adlai Stevenson. In 1956, only 68 per cent of them did so, while Kennedy did only a little better in 1960, obtaining 72 per cent of the black vote.[13] However,

---

[13] Robert Axelrod, "Where the Vote Comes From: An Analysis of Electoral Coalitions, 1952–1972", p. 89.

the continuing popularity of the New Deal agenda, and the robustness of Democratic organizations in many urban areas, meant that for the time being, the black vote was still mainly a Democratic vote. However, whether the Democratic Party in the long term could maximize loyalty among that sector of the electorate would depend on its ability to offer more than the Republicans on issues of direct concern to black voters. The relationship between the party and black America was far from being cemented in the 1950s.

The cementing of that relationship began in 1962 when the Kennedy administration finally found itself outmaneuvered by the civil rights movement into supporting direct federal intervention in the South for the protection of civil rights workers. With this intervention, the previous Democratic strategy since 1948 simply collapsed, and with it any hope the party might have of reversing the erosion of its support in the region. There was a serious risk that in the 1964 election, the party would lose considerably more states in the presidential election than they had in 1960, so that success would depend on doing even better outside the South than they had then. In the event, Kennedy's assassination transformed the party's short-term prospects, though, even if his visit to Dallas in November 1963 had ended differently, the Kennedy administration might well have been saved in 1964 by a parallel crisis in the Republican Party.

The conservative activist movement that brought about the candidacy of Barry Goldwater in 1964 marked the end of the era in which moderate Republicanism was the dominant force in presidential politics. Unlike the Democratic divisions, though, the split in the Republican Party was not brought about primarily by fundamental incompatibilities between different interests that the party was attempting to aggregate. As was argued in Chapter 7, many moderate Republicans could find much on which to agree with their orthodox Republican colleagues. The main exceptions were the New York liberals, nearly all of whom were based in New York City.

The peculiarity of New York City was the entrenched position of the regular Democratic organization, still sometimes known as Tammany Hall. In many other cities, liberals, labour unions, and various other kinds of reformers had been able to devise effective structures within (or allied to) the Democratic Party with which to compete for power with the regular organization. The very strength of the regular Democrats in New York City meant that these other political actors had had to move outside the party – creating structures such as the Liberal Party and also running for office as Republicans. The New Deal did not completely change this situation, so that in the 1940s, there were in the city Republicans who "bought into" virtually the entire New Deal policy agenda. Their antagonism to the Democrats was a local antagonism, but it meant that they were operating within a national party that was largely hostile to many of their political beliefs.

These kinds of liberal Republicans were rare, however. Many of their moderate or moderate-to-liberal colleagues were much less sympathetic to mainstream, urban-oriented Democratic policies than were the likes of New York's Jacob Javits. For example, in spite of a large increase in labour union membership after 1945, California Governor Earl Warren refused in 1947 to veto a bill on secondary boycotts that the unions had demanded that he veto.[14] Moreover, it was not the extreme, urban liberals, such as Javits, that had been the key power brokers in Republican presidential politics. Rather, it had been the more moderate figures like Dewey, and later Nelson Rockefeller, who had had this role. Consequently, with respect to the interests the party was trying to aggregate into a coalition, there was no reason why agreement could not be reached on a presidential agenda by the various sectors of the party. Theirs was not a situation akin to the Democrats, where two powerful, and opposing, interests could not possibly agree on an agenda in the longer term.

2. Had the Two Parties' Coalitions Become Too Disparate?

The short answer to the question of whether the Democratic Party had too disparate a coalition is that it was too disparate, but that while this was likely to lead to the collapse of the party's New Deal coalition in the long term, it was not the immediate cause of the coalition's fragmentation in the 1960s. Ultimately, race was the cause of the Democratic coalition being too broad-based, just at it was the direct cause of elements in the coalition being incompatible. It was race earlier – and, in particular, the fear in the 1890s that one's political opponents might use black voters against one's own interests – that had led to the successful efforts to restrict the franchise and to make it difficult for organized opposition to the Democrats to form. Whether it was the white Bourbons who initiated this, or their opponents (the white populists), and that matter has long been contentious, the result was the same: One party, albeit a party in name only, became the vehicle through which political power was contested in each

[14] Ed Cray, *Chief Justice*, p. 179.

southern state.[15] The result was that by the 1950s, southern Democratic politicians came in all forms. There were a few, like Claude Pepper, who had been enthusiastic supporters of New Deal economic intervention; there were some economic populists, like the Texan Wright Patman, who continued to worry about the economic and political power of eastern financial institutions. More numerous, though, and constituting about two-thirds of the southern House membership, were conservatives who were concerned about continued federal interventionism, partly because they subscribed to an older Democratic ideal of "small government" and partly because they saw such interventions as devices that undermined the ability of the southern states to hold the line on racial integration. What united nearly all these politicians was public opposition to racial integration, but that aside, they formed a group that was conspicuous by its diversity.

Except in relation to issues of race, this diversity did not affect adversely the party's ability to construct a coalition to win presidential elections. The universalist ideology on which Democrats campaigned after 1948 was not the subject of contention within the party at the presidential level.[16] Diversity had also been managed reasonably well by senior Democrats – at least, it was following Roosevelt's failed attempt to purge opponents of the New Deal in the 1938 mid-term elections. The post-war economic boom, and techniques of macro-economic demand management, made it possible for conservative and liberal Democrats to reach accommodations with each other on many aspects of economic policy. Moreover, within Congress, the greater ability of southerners to accumulate seniority (thanks to the absence of serious opposition in general elections) gave them a degree of influence on the legislative agenda that made it worthwhile for them not to provoke too much confrontation. The post-war era was also one in which Democratic congressional leaders who prided themselves on their ability to effect compromises (especially Sam Rayburn and Lyndon Johnson) could keep the many elements of the party together when legislating.

However, in the long term, and even if the racial conflict within the party had not torn apart the New Deal coalition, there were both social and institutional factors working against its continuation. On the one

---

[15] For example, see the opposing views of C. Vann Woodward, *The Strange Career of Jim Crow,* Third Edition, New York, Oxford University Press, 1974, and Albert D. Kirwan, *Revolt of the Rednecks: Mississippi Politics, 1876–1925,* New York, Harper and Row, 1951.

[16] On this ideology, see John Gerring, *Party Ideologies in America, 1828–1996,* Chapter 7.

side there was economic development. If the southern economy became richer and more complex, it would be increasingly difficult to represent satisfactorily all the social and economic cleavages in the region within one party. The "Eisenhower Republicans" in Virginia and Florida in 1952 and 1956 were an early manifestation of the social economy of the South becoming more complex. It was not just a matter of the South being carried along in a national economic boom; technological change was also important. As Nelson Polsby has argued, the air conditioner made the South inhabitable.[17] Americans had long had suitable and efficient means of making themselves warm in winter; it was not until after the Second World War that they had similar means of keeping themselves cool in the summer months. Once it became possible to control in summer the internal climate of work and home environments, the South became a far more attractive place in which to live. In addition, for employers faced with higher levels of wages, thanks to successful unionization in the North, the South offered the prospect of a low-wage economy – and it was an economy that in the mid-1950s was starting to be better linked to the rest of the United States by an extensive inter-state highway system. Certainly, its history of race relations had contributed to the under-development of the southern economy in the past, but many factors were pushing towards its expansion in the post-war years. With that expansion, the complete political monopoly previously enjoyed by the Democrats had to come under threat.

Alongside economic transformation, there was an institutional threat emanating from congressional opposition in the North to the terms of their coalition arrangement with the South. The inability of the large northern majority to get its way after the 1958 landslide set in motion a number of changes in Congress (including the formation of the Democratic Study Group) that a decade and a half later would lead to congressional reform, including the weakening of the application of the seniority system in the selection of committee chairs. While there can be no doubt that the various aspects of the North–South split on the race issue contributed to those institutional pressures on the Democratic coalition in Congress, the pressures would have been there anyway. From the perspective of the Northerners, it was they and certainly not the Southerners who were the "marginal voters" that gave the party its majority; if they were not getting the full rewards that should come with being in a majority party, then the rules of that particular game would have to be changed.

[17] Nelson W. Polsby, *How Congress Evolves*, pp. 80–2.

The first battle in this campaign was in 1961 when, by expending much political capital, John Kennedy was able to assist the Democratic House leadership in expanding the size of the Rules Committee – one of the main ways in which southern conservatives had controlled the flow of legislation to the chamber itself. In the long term – and in this case that meant several decades – the incentive for those who were conservative on economic issues to operate within the Democratic Party would decline. Of course, that is precisely what happened.

In the case of the Republican Party, the breadth of the coalition was not really a problem. Those liberal Republicans who embraced not only the entire New Deal agenda but also the interests of labour unions were a small minority within the party. Moreover, as noted in the previous section, they were not the main players in the presidential-selection process on the party moderates' side. There were a number of issues that divided Republicans both in Congress and outside – support for civil rights legislation being one – but the party did not enjoy the kinds of electoral monopolies that could produce incoherence within a coalition.

3. Did Either Party Suffer a Decline in Its Resource Base?

Decline in its resource base was not relevant in the case of the Democrats, but, along with the problem of disproportionate power being exercised by one group of leaders (Section 8), it was important for the widening of divisions within the Republican Party. In theory, if both parties in a two-party system are seeking consistently to attract the marginal voter, and if all political actors are operating under conditions of good information, then the result will be close elections that on each occasion are a "toss-up". Neither party has cause to regret its strategy because neither could have improved on its performance by doing something different. In practice, and given imperfect information, party politicians are likely to judge a strategy by its immediate results: "Did the party actually win the last election, or how many recent elections has it won?" are the critical questions likely to be asked in this context. It is not enough to get as close to winning as the party possibly could; it is winning that is important. In the 1950s, the moderate Republicans faced the problem that their electoral success was insufficient to satisfy those politicians and activists who supported conservative causes. The party needed control of public offices to show that everyone was benefiting from following the policy agenda of that relatively small minority in the party – the moderates. After 1952 that control was largely absent.

While the 1952 elections had been a genuine party triumph – producing a Republican president, party control of both houses of Congress, and control of more than half the governorships and a majority of state legislatures – no election subsequently produced that result. The year 1956 was a personal triumph for Eisenhower, but the Democrats retained their majorities in Congress, and Republican successes in the large states in gubernatorial contests were running at lower levels than in the 1940s. The huge losses in 1958, and the relatively modest recovery from those losses in 1960, merely added weight to the argument of those who claimed that a moderate Republican strategy was not working for the party. The person who was to become the leader of the rebellion against that strategy was Barry Goldwater. Having been largely supportive in the Senate during the Eisenhower administration (in Senate votes in 1955 and 1956 he had supported the administration on 66 per cent of occasions), after 1956 he moved to distance himself from it. As Robert Alan Goldberg argues:

[F]or some time Goldwater had chafed under Eisenhower's leadership of the party and nation. He had grown impatient with the president over patronage issues and the administration's affirmation of New and Fair Deal programs. Eisenhower's short coattails in 1956 only confirmed for Goldwater that the White House had neglected political responsibilities.... With Ike in his last term as president, Goldwater became less hesitant. His support of the administration on the Senate floor dropped to 57 per cent in 1957 and 1958 and then to 52 per cent in the last two years of the Eisenhower presidency.[18]

Had the Eisenhower administration been able to deliver more electoral success, it would have been much more difficult for Goldwater (and others) to distance themselves from the party in this way. Thus, relative lack of electoral success, and the resources that success brings, contributed to the opening up of a fissure within the party.

4. Were Newly Enfranchised Interests Being Mobilized by Either Party?

As we have seen, the lack of success by the Republicans after 1932 can be largely attributed to the Democrats' mobilization of first-time voters. Is there any evidence of similar mobilization in the 1950s that could have contributed to a fundamental change in the balance between the parties?

The main change in the electorate occurred in the late 1940s and early 1950s with the large influx of African Americans from the South, where many of them had been disenfranchised, to the northern cities,

[18] Robert Alan Goldberg, *Barry Goldwater*, p. 118.

where most, when they voted, were Democrats. This had consequences for both parties. For the Democrats, it increased the pressure on northern politicians to do something about black interests, and those difficulties increased during the 1950s. Balancing these claims against those of the white South was more difficult for Kennedy in 1960 than it had been for Stevenson in 1952 and 1956. Thus, to prevent a white southern backlash, he waited until two days before the election to release a letter, through black ministers, showing that the family of Martin Luther King, Jr., had expressed their gratitude to Kennedy for his sympathy during King's recent imprisonment. However, this change in the composition of the electorate in the cities also had adverse consequences for the Republicans – it was increasing the Democratic vote in those cities and in the states in which they were located. That is one of the reasons why the Republicans' electoral advance of the 1940s appeared to stall in the 1950s.

The other main change in the 1950s was that migration by Northerners into both Florida and Virginia was making it easier for the Republicans to win presidential contests, even while, at other levels of public office, Democratic dominance survived. This was to be a harbinger of social change throughout the South that would transform that region after the 1960s.

5. What Was the Influence of Changes in External Political Structures?

Until 1962 there were no such changes, but that year there was a significant institutional reform, the effect of which would have been to put further pressure on moderate Republicanism – even if the campaign to run Barry Goldwater as the presidential candidate in 1964 had been beaten back by the moderates. The balance between the parties in the House of Representatives in the 1940s was the product of two countervailing biases. The Democrats benefited from the absence of effective Republican opposition in the South, so that they had a much larger share of seats there than they would have had in anything resembling a competitive party system. On the other, electoral malapportionment in the North gave a pro-Republican bias there that was worth about 20 seats to the party in the years between 1946 and 1960.[19] The *Baker v. Carr* decision of 1962 swept away the foundations of that bias. However, this decision

---

[19] Gary W. Cox and Jonathan N. Katz, *Elbridge Gerry's Salamander: The Electoral Consequences of the Reapportionment Revolution*, Cambridge, Cambridge University Press, 2002, p. 59.

must be placed in context. The increased success of the Democrats in a few coastal states in the 1950s had meant that they had been able to eradicate the bias there even before the Supreme Court decision. According to Gary Cox and Jonathan Katz:

The Republican advantage in the North begins to erode noticeably in 1962, when California, Massachusetts, and Pennsylvania replaced Republican plans with Democratic or bipartisan/radical plans. With the entry of the courts into the redistricting process, the number of Democratic and bipartisan/radical plans further increased and, by 1966, the Republican advantage was largely gone.[20]

Thus, the seemingly small advances made by the Democrats in the coastal states in the 1950s had a payoff after redistricting in 1961, and that is why Table 8.3 indicates that the party was improving its position further in the House in this region between 1960 and 1962. However, even if those advances had not been made, the Republican bias would have been eliminated by the courts and the Republicans faced with a far more demanding task in winning the House than the one they had had in 1952. That would have increased tensions within the party. For that reason, it can be argued that Goldwaterism might well have resurfaced after 1966 – even if it had been repelled during 1962–4 – so that the days of moderate Republicanism were probably still numbered.

6. Loss of Fluidity in the Electoral Market?

In general, as voters continued to become less attached to parties, the possibility of capturing votes that might otherwise go to the other party increased. However, while there was greater "fluidity" in the electorate generally, at the same time in some states one party was building up organizations that had previously been weak, thereby making it more difficult for its opponent to continue winning regularly. This was one of the delayed effects of the New Deal that was starting to bring benefits to the Democrats in the 1950s, and it helped to reverse the recovery made by the Republicans after 1938. There were three states in which this effect was especially noticeable. Pennsylvania was one. In Philadelphia, regular Republican activists switched to the Democrats in the hundreds in the early 1950s, thereby helping to make yet more competitive a state that had been one of the most Republican of all up to 1932. In Michigan, it was the labour unions that helped to bring about a similar result in a state that

[20] Ibid., p. 60.

had also been Republican-leaning earlier. In Minnesota, the Democrats merged with the largest state-level third party in the United States (the Farmer-Labor Party) after the Second World War, and this union again increased party organizational strength in a way that would harm the Republicans.

7. Was There an Absence of Potential Leaders in the Party?

Unlike the problem faced by the Democrats between 1896 and 1912, and to a lesser extent in the 1920s, a lack of potential leaders in the party was not a factor in weakening the capacity of either party to build coalitions in this period. Indeed, the increased prominence given to international affairs in post-1945 America, combined with the advent of television coverage, meant that the Senate became a far more plausible arena from which to recruit presidential candidates than it had been earlier, and that increased the pool of potential candidates to both parties.

8. Was Either Party Controlled by Just a Few Interests?

Having the party under the control of just a few interests was not a factor in the break-up of the Democratic coalition, but it was for the Republicans. One difference between the two parties was the composition of each activist base. The data of Herbert McClosky et al. from the late 1950s showed that Republican activists were much further to the right of their party than were Democratic activists to the left of theirs.[21] This would not matter if party leaders merely had to take the activists' views into account, rather than having decisions about candidates and party platforms determined by the activists. Up to and including 1960, it was the former balance of power that prevailed. To put the matter crudely, there were three sets of Republican actors, and they could be located on a traditional left–right political spectrum. Towards the centre of the spectrum was the relatively small band of coastal-based moderate leaders, whose position as the marginal voters in the presidential election system had made them so powerful in determining the party's approach to those elections. To their right was the main core of the party's elected public officials, the orthodox Republicans. Many of them would prefer a Robert

---

[21] Herbert McClosky, Paul J. Hoffman, and Rosemary O'Hara, "Issue Conflict and Consensus Among Party Leaders and Followers", *American Political Science Review*, 54 (1960), 406–27.

Taft to a Dwight Eisenhower as a presidential candidate, but a sufficient number of them recognized the logic of electoral competition and were always willing to accept a candidate and a programme that could win – providing it did not involve a complete sell-out to the New Deal agenda. Then to the right of the orthodox politicians were a handful of "true believer" public officials and a large army of party activists. For them, the failure to nominate Taft in 1952 was a sell-out by the party, and in the future they looked to nominate a candidate who better reflected their views. As of the early to middle 1950s, their prospects of doing that appeared limited, since most orthodox Republicans in public office would accept a conservative as the party's presidential candidate only if it was clear that such a candidate would win. For the most part, the latter were worried that that kind of candidate could not win, and that their own political careers might be endangered.

During the course of the 1950s, however, the marginalization of the conservative activists in the party was reduced by two developments. The first, which was discussed in Section 3, was that moderate Republicanism was not only failing to deliver conservative policies but also providing less electoral success for the party than it had in the 1940s. Although many orthodox Republican politicians would remain suspicious of a radical departure from the party strategy of recent decades, there was increasing discontent among the most conservative members of that group with the failure of the strategy to "deliver". The second development was the reinforcement of conservative activist ranks by newly mobilized members. This movement, which began in the South and Southwest of the country, was to take root in communities that "shared an older regional identity that defined itself against northeastern power, a model of growth based on 'clean development', a socially homogeneous group of highly skilled, affluent inhabitants, and, often, the presence of defense and military".[22] As Lisa McGirr notes in her study of Orange County, California, the first place in which these new activists were evident:

[T]heir posture as outsiders enabled them to build a self-conscious movement to develop a critique of liberal elites. The world of the New Deal state...first marginalized, then reshuffled, and eventually reinvigorated American conservatism. By the 1960s, conservatives had organized a cohesive movement with institutions, networks, and a broad grassroots following.[23]

---

[22] Lisa McGirr, *Suburban Warriors*, p. 14.
[23] Ibid., p. 17.

Even if their opponents in the party had recognized the threat much earlier than they did, and even if their leaders had coordinated their opposition to the efforts by these activists to impose Barry Goldwater on the party in 1964, the long-term prospects for the survival of the old coalition were poor. Had Goldwater been stopped that year, there were still two respects in which the new activism was already weakening the basis of the party's post–New Deal coalition. First, as the overall number of conservative activists increased, so did the number of moderate Republicans in public office decline – especially on the West Coast. On the East Coast, moderate Republicanism would stagger on for another decade or so – its symbolic end perhaps being the switch in the 1970s of the liberal Republican mayor of New York City, John Lindsay, to the Democratic Party, following his earlier defeat in the Republican primary. (He won that re-election bid in 1969 as the Liberal Party candidate.) Secondly, orthodox Republicans now had to pay more attention to the demands of conservative activists; the deals that had sustained the position of moderate Republicanism in presidential politics were much less possible after 1960.

Given that moderate Republicans could no longer claim that the coastal states were the undisputed marginal voter in presidential elections, the whole basis of an electoral strategy centred on that wing of the party started to collapse in the 1950s. A Nixon victory in 1960 – which would likely have been accompanied by continuing Democratic majorities in Congress – would not have slowed down the process that much. Concessions to the likes of Nelson Rockefeller, of the kind that Nixon himself had made in advance of the 1960 national convention, would be seen as an unacceptable price to pay for a prize that was of decreasing value – to those who held orthodox or more conservative views in the party. For that reason, by the early 1960s, the Democrats stood poised to enhance their position in those parts of the North in which moderate Republicanism had helped to keep them at bay.

The new conservative activism among Republicans did not yet dominate the party in the early 1960s, but its "exclusivism" had already added a new dimension to American party politics. That dimension was a reduced willingness to compromise in the pursuit of a national political majority. The effect was the same as if the party had been controlled by just a few of the interests it had always tried to mobilize. Unlike the western progressives in the 1920s, the moderates could not devote their attention to pushing their agenda through Congress – because there were too few of them there. Theirs had always been a presidential orientation, and the new conservatism wanted to deny them influence there, as well as in all other party arenas. There was little place for moderate Republicanism in the transformed Republican Party.

9. Changes in the Rules for Selecting Presidential Candidates

While changes in the rules for nominating presidential candidates were to be a factor hindering the efforts of the Democrats in constructing a national coalition a decade or more later, it was not a factor putting either party under stress in the years up to 1962.

10. The Democratic Party in 1962

By the end of 1962, the Democratic Party was facing the biggest change in the structure of its electoral coalition since the Civil War. At the heart of its problem was an incompatibility between two of the major interests it was seeking to aggregate, together with, in the South, too great a range of interests that it embraced within its coalition. The new commitment to federal intervention in support of civil rights would certainly reduce the party's prospects of winning in 1964, and thereafter, even in the eight southern states that the party had managed to retain in 1960. The real question facing the party was whether "damage limitation" was possible, so that some Electoral College votes from the region would remain in the Democratic camp. On the other side, their prospects in the North were much improved, both because of their own growing organizational strength in various states and because of the stresses placed on the Republican Party coalition – stresses that meant that a strategy based on moderate Republicanism could not continue much longer.

The defeat of Richard Nixon in the California gubernatorial contest in 1962 seemed not only to provide evidence of the Democrats' new position in the northern states but also to mark the political exit of the most powerful possible challenger to John Kennedy's re-election. Yet a year later, Kennedy had to visit Texas in an effort to shore up electoral support in a state that had gone for him in 1960 only because Lyndon Johnson was his running mate. What would have happened if he had returned alive from that visit is a matter of considerable debate. The likely new political configurations were complex – and they were made that much more complex not just by the Kennedy assassination but also by the continuing civil rights revolution and later by the Great Society programmes and the Vietnam War. Consequently, in the absence of some or all of these additional factors, it is impossible to work out whether the Democrats would have emerged better off than they were in relation to the size of their previous coalition or whether they would still have ended up at their actual post-1972 position. That is, would they still have become what they did – a majority party in the nation for all offices save the presidency – a level of office for which individual Republican candidates could often rely on southern voters to carve out victory for themselves?

There are many possible alternative (and plausible) answers. For example, while Barry Goldwater is usually credited with moving the Republicans towards a southern strategy, it could be argued that factors such as the reapportionment revolution (and its consequent impact on Republicans in the House) might have pushed many orthodox Republicans to move in that direction later in the 1960s. On the other hand, the success of the Democrats in largely reuniting the South behind Jimmy Carter in 1976 points to the role that southern moderates might have played earlier in stabilizing the Democratic majority – had events post-1962 been different than they actually were. The problem is that while it has been possible to delineate the long-term change in the years up to 1962, the interaction of that change with the many contingencies that affected party politics in the 1960s makes it far more difficult to explain the likely consequences of those changes absent the various contingencies. What is indisputable, though, is that irrespective of events after 1962, the Democratic coalition was going to change; the post–New Deal era of party coalitions was over. The party was becoming, and also had to become, a far more northern dominated party than it had been in the past.

9

Conclusions

The six preceding chapters have sought to outline the different phases of the Democratic Party's attempts after 1876 to maintain a sufficiently strong base in the North so that it was capable of winning presidential elections and obtaining congressional majorities. But how did the party do overall in this effort during the entire period between 1877 and 1962? There are two quite distinct parts to any answer to this question. The first concerns whether the Democrats *could* win enough individual states in the North to be in a position to construct a majority coalition. The second concerns their ability to make the constituent parts of a potential coalition cohere, and thereby create a coalition. Being competitive enough in some northern states was a necessary condition for winning a national majority, though it was not a sufficient condition. In the first part of this concluding chapter, we resume the discussion started in Chapter 2, Section 4, as to how the Democrats were placed in relation to individual northern states, before turning to summarize the factors that affected the party's ability to aggregate certain northern states into a national coalition.

It was shown in Chapter 2 that for the entire period 1877–1962, Democratic strength in relation to the winning of state governorships varied little until the middle to late 1950s when it started to increase. Nevertheless, if, as in Table 2.3, we seek to control for the type of election being contested, and assume that all four periods featured one of each type of election, a slightly different pattern emerges (see Table 9.1). The Democrats were doing worse in 1911–31 than in 1877–89, then recovered to their earlier level of performance post–New Deal, while their gains after 1958 appear much smaller. How should this be understood? Turning first to the change between the first and second periods, all is not quite as it

TABLE 9.1. *Northern State Governorships Weighted by Number of Electoral College Votes Attached to Each State: Median Share of Total Votes Held by Democratic Party in the February of Years Following Presidential Elections or Mid-term Elections for Selected Periods, 1877–1973, and by Type of Election (as Percentage)*

	After Democratic Candidate Wins Presidency	After Mid-term Elections During a Republican Presidency	After Republican Candidate Wins Presidency	After Mid-term Elections During a Democratic Presidency	Mean for All Four Types of Election
1877–89	52	46	23	30	38
1911–31	44	38	18	30	33
1939–57	39	51	35	24	37
1959–73	54	52	30	42	45

might seem from Table 9.1. It was argued in Chapter 3 that one of the main features of party competition in the late 19th century was the ability of the Democrats to win in some safe Republican states in mid-term years because of the tendency of winning Republican presidential coalitions to fragment in non-presidential election years. One of the changes that occurred after the early 1890s was that further party consolidation, particularly in Michigan and Pennsylvania, put the governorships there even further beyond the reach of the Democrats. Because of its size, and because it was one of the few states that had four-year terms for governors in the 19th century, Pennsylvania has a distorting effect on the data. In fact, the single Democratic victory in 1882, when the Republican coalition fragmented, accounts for nearly all of the seeming decline in Democratic penetration of the North between 1877–89 and 1911–31. If Pennsylvania is omitted from all data for these periods, the Democrats' performance in the two eras is remarkably similar (Table 9.2). There was a slight decline over time, but it was only slight, and certainly too small to be compatible with a "system of 1896" model.

The other interesting aspect of the data in Table 9.1 is that the Democratic advance in the North after the late 1950s appears to be much less pronounced than was evident in the earlier tables. Weighting governorships by the size of a state's Electoral College vote, and then controlling for the type of election contested, makes the differences among all four periods seem much smaller. Under similar electoral conditions nationally, the Democrats appear to be not that much more of a northern party by the

TABLE 9.2. *Northern State Governorships (Excluding Pennsylvania) Weighted by Number of Electoral College Votes Attached to Each State: Median Share of Total Votes Held by Democratic Party in the February of Years Following Presidential Elections or Mid-term Elections for 1877–1889 and 1911–1931, and by Type of Election (as Percentage)*

	After Democratic Candidate Wins Presidency	After Mid-term Elections During a Republican Presidency	After Republican Candidate Wins Presidency	After Mid-term Elections During a Democratic Presidency	Mean for All Four Types of Election
1877–89	46	46	26	34	38
1911–31	49	43	20	34	37

1970s than they had been either 50 or nearly 100 years earlier. At least, that is the conclusion that must be drawn when examining gubernatorial elections. However, there are two related disadvantages to relying just on this level of office when assessing the changing state of the building blocks available to the Democrats when constructing a national coalition. One disadvantage is that personal attributes of candidates for a higher-profile office such as a governorship might distort the extent of party strength in particular states, even though the distortion is much less than with presidential elections. The other disadvantage is that although gubernatorial elections were held more frequently than presidential elections, there were still a relatively small number of instances to be considered for any given year, and that, too, could create a distortion. For that reason, it is useful also to consider the pattern of Democratic success at another level of office within the states – such as the lower chamber of state legislatures. Extreme caution must be exercised in interpreting patterns of results in such elections, though. Malapportionment of electoral districts in some states can misrepresent party strength at a particular time, and changes in the extent of malapportionment over time will similarly mislead us about changes in party strength. Nevertheless, with that important caveat, it is useful to examine whether the patterns evident in gubernatorial elections are also evident in state legislature elections.

As can be seen in Table 9.3, from 1877–89 to 1911–31 a broadly similar pattern is evident in the lower chambers as in the governorships – there was little change between the two periods. On 14 per cent of all possible occasions between 1877 and 1889, the Democrats won at least 50 per cent of the seats in the lower chambers, while between 1911 and 1931, they

TABLE 9.3. *Occasions on Which Democratic Party Had More Than 50 Per Cent of Seats in Lower Chambers of State Legislatures in Northern States for Selected Periods, 1877–1973 (as Percentage of Total Number of All Possible Occasions)*

	All Northern States	All Northern States Except Rocky Mountain States and Pacific Coast States	Illinois, Michigan, New Jersey, New York, Ohio, and Pennsylvania
1877–89	14.0	12.1	21.4
1911–31	13.8	9.1	12.1
1939–57	25.0	9.4	6.6
1959–73	42.3	36.6	47.9

did so on 13.8 per cent of occasions. (That the Democrats were winning a much smaller proportion of all available seats in the later period was due mainly to the fact that they were now winning even fewer seats in several states that had leaned Republican in the earlier period.) However, after the New Deal a different pattern emerged. Democratic success in controlling these chambers nearly doubled (to 25 per cent of all possible occasions) between 1939 and 1957 and increased again (to 42.3 per cent) for the last period, 1959–73. The surge after 1959 was to be expected in the light of the gubernatorial election results, but the improvement in 1939–57 is not. The party seemed to be doing much better in controlling state legislatures than would have been predicted on the basis of their success in gubernatorial elections in the two periods. Nevertheless, this disparity is not quite what it appears at first sight.

All the Democratic improvement in the legislature elections from 1939–57 is accounted for by their success in just two regions – in the Rocky Mountains and on the West Coast. If data from these two regions are excluded from consideration for both 1911–31 and 1939–57, the success rate of the Democrats is the same – the Democrats controlled lower chambers on a mere 9 per cent of all occasions in both periods. Two points are worth noting. The first is that this provides evidence of the persistence of FDR's original 1932 coalition, one based partly on the western states, well beyond the early New Deal years. The small states in the Rocky Mountains region, many of which had moved towards the Democrats in the 1890s, continued to be a bedrock of support for the party. After the New Deal they were joined by the three West Coast states – states where the Democrats had largely become weak after the 1890s. The second point is that, generally, the states in these regions had had their party organizations dismantled to a much greater degree in the Progressive Era than had happened in the states on the East Coast and in the old Midwest.[1] In states with a more individualistic style of politics, we would expect the Republican recovery after 1938 to be less evident. In regions with more effective party organizations, the Republicans could mobilize their long-standing organizational resources – it would count for much more – so that "across-the-board" electoral successes by them would be more evident. That is precisely what we find. With the exceptions of Massachusetts and Rhode Island, the Democrats' advance was largely reversed outside the Far West after 1938 – in spite of FDR's success in mobilizing new urban electorates.

This is one of the paradoxes of party change in these years. Roosevelt's public policies attracted new urban voters to the Democratic Party, and in both presidential and congressional elections their presence shifted the long-term balance between the parties nationally. But many of the voters he was attracting lived in states where party organizations were traditionally strong, and where, despite the new electoral mobilization by the Democrats, Republicans could themselves mobilize successfully to retain control of governorships and state legislatures. The popular image of the New Deal "revolution" is that it delivered party control in the big industrial states of the East and the Midwest to the Democrats – but it did nothing like that. Consider together six of the largest states – Illinois, Michigan, New Jersey, New York, Ohio, and Pennsylvania (Table 9.3). The Democrats held more than 50 per cent of lower chamber seats on no more than 7 per cent of all possible occasions between 1939 and 1957; between 1911 and 1931 they had done so more frequently – on 12 per cent of all occasions. Of course, some of this difference might be explained by an increasing malapportionment bias against the Democrats in these states. However, it cannot conceal the main point that party organization mattered in the post–New Deal era. It mattered because it meant that irrespective of his successful electoral strategy in the urban areas, Roosevelt could not immediately dislodge the Republicans in many states where he had made his party more competitive nationally. It would take two decades for the full effects of his strategy to be evident.

That the underlying Democratic position – the building blocks in the states from which they could hope to construct a national majority – had changed less than we might expect in nearly eight decades after 1877 is

[1] See Martin Shefter, "Regional Receptivity to Reform: The Legacy of the Progressives", *Political Science Quarterly*, 98 (1983), 459–83.

TABLE 9.4. *Proportion of Border State Governorships Held by Democrats in the February of Years Following Presidential Elections or Mid-term Elections, 1877–1973 (as Percentage of Total Border Governorships)*

1877	100	1903	40	1929	33	1955	67
1879	100	1905	60	1931	33	1957	50
1881	100	1907	60	1933	83	1959	67
1883	100	1909	33	1935	67	1961	100
1885	100	1911	33	1937	83	1963	83
1887	100	1913	50	1939	100	1965	83
1889	80	1915	50	1941	67	1967	67
1891	80	1917	83	1943	67	1969	17
1893	100	1919	83	1945	67	1971	50
1895	80	1921	33	1947	67	1973	50
1897	40	1923	33	1949	100		
1899	40	1925	50	1951	83		
1901	40	1927	50	1953	67		

interesting. It is so because over that entire period, the Democrats had every reason to attempt to increase their penetration of the North; if they did not, their overall underlying position in relation to the Republicans would surely decline. That is, they would have relatively fewer building blocks with which to construct a majority, and there would have been two causes of that decline. The first was that the population of the North grew faster than the rest of the country during this period; since they were the larger party in the North, the Republicans would likely be the beneficiaries, all things being equal. The second cause was the demise of the Border states as a wholly loyal contributor to the Democratic coalition. Viewed strictly from the viewpoint of the building blocks, the Democrats needed to be stronger in the North, if only to compensate for declining solidity in the Border states.

One of the curious aspects of the Border states is that they are the only region that conforms to the conventional view about the fate of the Democratic Party between the 1870s and the 1960s. With respect to gubernatorial elections, a period of stability until the 1890s was followed by one of much-reduced Democratic success – a situation that lasted until the New Deal (see Tables 9.4 and 9.5). Subsequently, there was a much higher rate of Democratic success than there had been in the years 1911–31. Moreover, this is not just a manifestation of greater Republican competitiveness in the smaller states in the region; a similar pattern is observable when the size of states is taken into account (see Tables 9.6 and 9.7). (However, while this pattern of success does fit the traditional account,

TABLE 9.5. *Median and Mean Proportions of Border State Governorships Held by Democratic Party in the February of Years Following Presidential Elections or Mid-term Elections for Selected Periods, 1877–1973 (as Percentage of Total Number of Border Governorships in Each Year)*

	Median	Mean
1877–89	100	98
1911–31	50	48
1939–57	67	74
(1939–53)	(67)	(77)
1959–73	67	65

TABLE 9.6. *Border State Governorships Weighted by Number of Electoral College Votes Attached to Each State: Proportion of Total Held by Democratic Party in the February of Years Following Presidential Elections or Mid-term Elections, 1877–1973*

1877	100	1903	53	1929	30	1955	76
1879	100	1905	80	1931	30	1957	65
1881	100	1907	80	1933	95	1959	78
1883	100	1909	27	1935	80	1961	100
1885	100	1911	27	1937	86	1963	84
1887	100	1913	68	1939	100	1965	84
1889	87	1915	68	1941	68	1967	63
1891	87	1917	95	1943	67	1969	24
1893	100	1919	95	1945	75	1971	61
1895	94	1921	30	1947	75	1973	44
1897	43	1923	30	1949	100		
1899	43	1925	52	1985	85		
1901	53	1927	52	1953	76		

it does not mesh with the usual explanation of the origins of the change. Increasing Republican competitiveness was evident from the early 1880s, and was not a manifestation of the political upheavals of the 1890s [see Chapter 4, especially Table 4.2]). Not surprisingly, the same general trend was also evident with respect to control of state legislatures (see Table 9.8). However, for our purposes, this growing competitiveness in the Border states from the late 19th century made it that much more important for the Democrats to improve their position in the North, and yet their under-lying position, as evidenced by their success in gubernatorial elections, changed relatively little over many decades. Why?

TABLE 9.7. *Border State Governorships Weighted by Number of Electoral College Votes Attached to Each State: Share of Total Votes Held by Democratic Party in the February of Years Following Presidential Elections or Mid-term Elections for Selected Periods, 1877–1973 (as Percentage)*

	Median	Mean
1877–89	100	98
1911–31	52	58
1939–57	76	79
(1939–53)	(76)	(81)
1959–73	71	67

TABLE 9.8. *Occasions on Which Democratic Party Had More Than 50 Per Cent of Seats in Lower Chambers of State Legislatures in Border States for Selected Periods, 1877–1973 (as Percentage of Total Number of All Possible Occasions)*

	All Border States	All Border States Granted Statehood by 1877
1877–89	97.1	97.1
1911–31	64.1	58.5
1939–57	78.9	74.5
1959–73	91.1	88.6

Second column excludes Oklahoma (granted statehood 1907).

From one perspective, the Democrats' failure to open up the North in the first half of the 20th century might seem odd. After all, it is widely recognized that the peculiarly close ties between voters and their parties that had characterized the period from the 1830s to about the 1890s became weaker in the 20th century. Yet the Democrats made remarkably little progress against the Republicans at the state level in the North. There were four main factors that explain why they did not. In the first place, party institutionalization from the end of the 19th century made it much more difficult to turn short-term advantage into long-term domination of elective office. Nowhere is this better illustrated than in the later Republican revival, after six years of the New Deal. In spite of the fact that the New Deal helped city and state parties by channelling federal money in the states' direction, the resilience of the Republican organizations was evident in the extent of their electoral success (especially in the Northeast and Midwest) after 1938. Moreover, the more hierarchically organized and efficient urban organizations had largely come into being during the near decade and a half before 1909 when the Democrats were out of power in most non-southern states. While a state like Pennsylvania was exceptional in the extent to which it converted short-term advantage at that time into long-term supremacy, there is no doubt that the Democrats were harmed by being split at a period of greater centralization in party structures. Before the 1890s, governing party organizations were much less resilient in the face of short-term splits or unpopularity, and that provided opportunities for the minor party – mostly the Democrats in the North – to win. Those opportunities diminished after the 1890s, and it was not until the rise of candidate-centred politics in the 1960s that the impact of party organization on the state building blocks would be weakened substantially.

The stabilization of party organizations after the 1890s, though, was only one factor limiting the prospects for Democratic efforts to "break into" the North. Another factor was the absence of resources by which a governing party at the state level could hope to establish groups of party loyalists on the basis of its own policies. There could be no equivalent of the "interest group liberalism" that FDR ushered in at the federal level because the states lacked the tax bases with which to enact programmes that could establish voter dependency. Indeed, it was that lack of resource autonomy that helped to make variants of moderate Republicanism so successful at the state level. In a sense, state politics could become a matter of managerialism – a question of which party could better manage programmes that were initiated and largely funded by the federal government. It did not take a Democrat to manage such programmes; a Republican who did not overtly reject all the New Deal agenda might claim to be just as effective in delivering them. In the absence of their own programmes, as well as dependent client groups, most state Democratic parties found it difficult to sustain success – except on the back of especially popular individual politicians. One indicator of just how little electoral success state-level Democratic *Parties* had after the New Deal is revealed by considering the occasions on which one Democrat succeeded another as a governor following an election – that is, excluding cases where succession was the result of the predecessor's death or resignation. In the 20 years after 1938, this happened on just 8 occasions in 31 states, while on 11 occasions, a Democrat attempting to replace a retiring Democratic incumbent failed to do so. Indeed, if the cutoff date is taken as 1940, rather than 1938, on the grounds that this excludes all the immediate effects of the New Deal, then the Democrats' position appears even worse; only 4 Democrats succeeded Democratic incumbents, while 9 challengers failed in the attempt to do so.[2]

The pattern with the Republicans was very different. Between 1940 and 1956 inclusive, there were 44 instances of Republicans succeeding a Republican incumbent at an election, with only 13 cases of a Republican challenger failing to succeed an incumbent. (If the 1940 election is excluded, the respective figures are 41 and 12.) Of course, this exaggerates the strength of the Republican *Party* because a number of these states leaned heavily to the Republicans. Eight states (Iowa, Kansas, Maine, Nebraska, New Hampshire, North Dakota, South Dakota, and Vermont) might be removed from consideration on these grounds.[3] This reduces the number of "successions" from one Republican to another to 15.[4] However, this is still greater than the number of "failed" successions, of which there were 11.[5] Whereas incumbency was very important for the Democrats in helping retain control of governorships, it was less so for Republicans – even when states where they were dominant are excluded from consideration. As a crude estimate, it can be said that after 1938, only on about one occasion in three could the Democrats retain control of a state when the incumbent did not run again, while in similar circumstances, their Republican counterparts won on nearly 60 per cent of all occasions. As an indicator of underlying Democratic Party strength in the North, this suggests that as late as the mid-20th century, the Democratic

---

[2] A Democrat replaced an incumbent Democratic governor at an election in Arizona (1940), Colorado (1956), Indiana (1940), New Jersey (1940), New Mexico (1942 and 1946), Rhode Island (1950), and Utah (1940); Democrats failed to succeed a retiring Democratic incumbent in Colorado (1950), Illinois (1952), Indiana (1944), Nebraska (1940), New Jersey (1942), New Mexico (1950), New York (1942), North Dakota (1944), Ohio (1956), Washington (1940), and Wyoming (1950).

[3] This is a tough restriction to impose. For most of this period, Nebraska was probably no easier for the Republicans to hold than it was for the Democrats to retain control of Arizona and New Mexico. If both of these states were to be excluded from the data just cited in the main text the number of occasions between 1940 and 1956 inclusive on which the Democrats would have retained control of the governorship in the absence of an incumbent would be 5, while they would have failed to do so on 10 occasions.

[4] Colorado (1942), Connecticut (1946), Idaho (1950 and 1954), Indiana (1956), Michigan (1946), New Jersey (1946), Oregon (1942), Pennsylvania (1942, 1946 and 1950), Utah (1956), Wisconsin (1950 and 1956), and Wyoming (1954).

[5] These cases are Colorado (1946 and 1954), Indiana (1948), Massachusetts (1944 and 1956), Michigan (1940), New Jersey (1953), New Mexico (1954), Ohio (1944), Pennsylvania (1954), and Washington (1956).

Parties in the northern states were often deficient by comparison with the Republicans.

A third factor limiting the prospects for the Democrats in building a majority party at the state level was intra-party factionalism. In two-party systems, coalitions are necessarily rather broad, so that the range of interests that have always had to be accommodated is broad. Franklin Roosevelt had created a (relatively) new national party because he went outside the already loose national party structures; his doing so meant that the wing of the party that had supported Al Smith rapidly became irrelevant. In state parties, though, it was usually much less easy for a new governor, or anyone else, to ignore intra-party divisions in quite the way that FDR could. Where state parties could be redefined around a newly mobilizing interest in the party, it tended to be in states where the Democratic Party had been relatively weak before. One such example is Michigan, where the labour unions re-vitalized, and re-shaped, the party from the 1930s onwards. Elsewhere, party building that lay outside the shadow of the national party and its agenda was relatively uncommon.

Finally, a fourth factor making it more difficult for the Democrats to construct a majority coalition at the state level, effective after 1920, was the enfranchisement of women. The first "Michigan School" surveys in the 1950s indicated that women were 3 percent to 5 per cent more Republican than men.[6] Unlike arguments made about later gender gaps, these authors argued that there was no specific gender component to the difference in voting behaviour, and the gap related to aggregate differences in other social characteristics between men and women. Thus, women were more heavily represented among elderly voters (who were more Republican), and vote turnout among women declined even more heavily than among men within the least-educated sectors of the population. For our argument, the causes of the "gap" are of no concern – except one. Women were less likely to vote than men in the South, so that the likely gap between 1920 and 1962 in the North was probably much closer to 3 per cent than 5 per cent. However, even this kind of gap would have cost the Democrats offices. For example, in the election years in which the Republican recovery began in 1938 and 1940, Republicans had pluralities in five gubernatorial contests of less than 1 per cent of the total vote, another plurality of less than 1.5 per cent and yet another plurality of just

---

[6] Angus Campbell, Philip E. Converse, Warren E. Miller, and Donald E. Stokes, *The American Voter*, p. 261.

over 2.0 per cent.[7] All things being equal, we might assume that most of the governors elected in these states would have been Democrats but for the enfranchisement of women. Consequently, the Democrats' record in office holding after 1920 would surely have been rather better but for the admission of women to the electorate, and when comparing its relative performance before and after 1920, some account should be taken of that. Clearly, though, the admission of women to the electorate created a further incentive for the Democrats to improve their position in the northern states.

To what extent, then, is it justifiable to conclude that the varying performance of the Democrats nationally between 1877 and 1962 can be explained in terms of their ability to develop or maintain support (that is, their building blocks) at the state level? With two important qualifications, the answer is "not that much"; their varying performance has much more to do with the ability of leaders to construct a coalition from the available building blocks (and keep it together) than with the presence or absence of strength at the state level. Given the great variability in the Democrats' performance in national elections over this period, it is interesting just how little variation there was in the building blocks available to them in the form of evident electoral strength in the states. However, as has just been noted, there are two important qualifications to this point. First, the much-increased competitiveness of the Republicans in the Border states in the 50 years between 1880 and 1930 undoubtedly hurt the Democratic Party, and is a factor that can help explain some of the Democrats' poor performance nationally – especially after the mid-1890s. Secondly, the New Deal did make a difference – especially in the longer term; by the mid-1950s, the Democrats were starting to do much better in state elections in parts of the North than they had done in the 15 or so years after 1938. The Republican counter-offensive was now much less effective, and it was these years that saw the Democratic Party reap the rewards of the electoral realignment that the New Deal policies had effected; in much of the North after 1958, the party went from being just competitive to being dominant within many states.

The emphasis placed here on the similarity in the level of the resources available in the states to the Democrats nationally over more than eight

---

[7] The states where Republican pluralities were less than 1.0 per cent were Connecticut (1938), Kansas (1940), Massachusetts (1940), Missouri (1940), and Washington (1940). In New Hampshire (1940) the plurality was 1.4 per cent, while in Montana (1940) it was 2.1 per cent.

decades does not mean, of course, that there was not significant change within individual states during this time. In the 1920s and 1930s, Indiana, for example, moved from being one of the most competitive states to a Republican-leaning state. However, for the most part, and in the long term, many of these shifts tended to cancel each other out. This argument runs contrary to the claim associated with "realignment theory", which sees significant shifts in the balance between the parties as being the product of changes in their underlying position. In brief, the claim advanced in this book is that it was not so much the building blocks available to the parties that changed over time, but rather the constraints and opportunities they faced in constructing a majority coalition from the "blocks" that seemed to be available to them. The focus here, though, has not been on success or failure at *particular* elections, when highly specific factors might well have come into play, but rather on more general factors that might apply across different election cycles. In fact, during the course of the book, six main factors have been identified that affected how successful the Democrats were in aggregating the potential members of a coalition into an actual coalition. We re-examine each of these factors in turn now.

1. Longer-Term Effects of Short-Term Electoral Change

One of the main problems of coalition building is that particular strategic choices made for an election at time t can affect the conditions under which strategy at $t+1$ (and even later) can be effected. That is, short-term shifts in electoral behaviour can affect the competitive balance between parties even when there is no long-term shift in electoral behaviour. As we have seen, there appears to be no evidence of an electoral realignment after 1896, yet one effect of that election was to make coalition building much more difficult for the party for the next 14 years. Left as it was with few leaders to challenge the unelectable Bryan, the Democratic Party suffered a succession of major presidential defeats from which it could only partly recover in mid-term elections, and it could not do so sufficiently to generate new leaders who were capable of providing a credible alternative to Bryan. Then, again, there are the medium-term consequences of the 1912 election, following which the party failed to follow a sufficiently aggressive progressive agenda that might have helped it consolidate its position in the West. The Democratic Party did relatively well in the presidential election in the eastern states that year. However, although the Wilson administration pursued progressive legislation and policies, these were insufficient to woo western Republicans to the party, and they also did nothing to satisfy the more conservative eastern voters. It was not until after the 1914 election produced major losses in the East that the party accepted the logic of following a more thoroughgoing western electoral strategy. But by then it was too late to make common cause with potential Republican allies. Less success in the East in 1912 might have led the party more firmly to adopt a "western" strategy – one that might have enabled it to consolidate itself in that region.

On the other hand, obviously, there were some elections from which the Democrats could benefit later from the performance of their opponents. After the 1946 mid-term landslide, the Republicans had congressional majorities in both houses, but they were majorities that were dominated by orthodox Republicans. Their policy agenda in 1947–8 made it much more difficult in 1948 for the moderate Dewey-Warren ticket to withstand the indirect attacks Truman was able to make on them through his criticisms of the Congress.

2. The Complexity of the Potential Coalition

Two-party politics places an incentive on both parties to construct relatively large coalitions; the ability of one of them to do so depends partly on the coalition-building strategy of the other. If the one has constructed a majority coalition that embraces both a relatively narrow range of interests and is also "connected" (in the sense that there are obvious links among all members of the coalition), the more difficult it is likely to be for the other party to fragment that coalition in attempting to construct a majority of its own. From 1877 until about the end of the 1880s, coalition building more closely resembled this kind of model than it would later. The Democrats, united by an ideology of non-state interference, was strong in the ex-slave states and could build a national majority by winning a small number of (mainly) medium-size or large states – most of which were located in just two regions (the Northeast and the old Midwest). No more than between five and seven states were truly competitive at that time, and those states were the key to success for either party.

The political turmoil that began at the end of the 1880s, and which lasted until after the 1896 election, made coalition building far more difficult, especially for the Democrats, in the succeeding six decades. Neither party could have fully incorporated the demands of western primary producers without risking defection by other members of their coalition. Ignoring these western interests cost the Republican Party the 1892 election, while placing them at the heart of their own coalition in 1896 could not save the Democrats from defeat in that election. However, after 1896, there could be no straightforward return for the Democrats to the simpler strategic world of the 1870s and 1880s. Not only did seven new western states join the Union in the 1890s, but the western-oriented election strategy of 1896 had longer-term consequences for the party. With the exception of California, the Democrats had been relatively weak in the West until the 1890s. One effect of Bryanism was to transform some of the states in that region into contestable territory for the party. While, in a sense, this could be said to constitute an opportunity for the party, it made coalition strategy more difficult. As the evidence in Table 4.5 demonstrates, both for 1908–20 and 1920–32 the Democrats' most winnable states in presidential elections were a much more heterogeneous group than they had been in 1880–92. In constructing a majority from their most winnable states before 1892, the Democrats required just 19 states, all of which had achieved statehood before 1860; to do this in 1908–20 required winning 27 states, 9 of which attained statehood after 1860, while the same feat in the years 1920–32 involved 28 states, 7 of which were western, post-1860 additions to the Union.[8]

Of course, reconciling western interests with those of other parts of the country was not a uniquely Democratic problem. It was to re-emerge as one of the main sources of division in the Republican Party during Taft's presidency, and it lingered on (after the formal split in 1912) as a source of internal Republican division in Congress until the end of the 1930s. Nevertheless, until the 1936 nomination reform, it tended to hurt the Democrats more often than the Republicans at the presidential level of coalition building because of the party's super-majoritarian selection procedures. It was much less easy to override or control minority interests in the Democratic Party, so that open conflict within the party was more likely to break out. By the 1930s, though, the West's distinctiveness as a region was declining, and this meant that incorporating the western element into the party coalition produced much less conflict than it had earlier.

During the later 1940s, however, it was another aspect of coalition complexity that was starting to cause difficulties for the party – the

---

[8] Strictly speaking, the total number of new states is 10 for the 1908–20 period and 8 for the 1920–32 period, because West Virginia did not attain statehood until 1863. However, since it is not in the West, and its territory was part of a state before 1863, it has been excluded from consideration here.

demands of the segregated South. As increased African American migration to the North put pressure on northern politicians to confront the race issue, so white Southerners sought to prevent desegregationist policies from being implemented. With increasing evidence of southern voting defection in the 1950s, the relatively brief interlude in which the complexities of building a national coalition had eased came to an end. Once again, the Democrats were trying to hold together potentially conflicting interests in a single coalition; their main hope in counteracting the impact of this attempt lay in their growing strength in the North in the 1950s – the delayed impact of the political effects of the New Deal were starting to shift the balance there to their advantage.

3. Internal Conflict and Its Resolution Within a Coalition

The obvious problem posed by the increased complexity of a party's potential coalition was that one component might "exit" at a particular election – it would fail to support the party's presidential candidate actively, or might even throw its support to another candidate or party. Such disagreements were essentially short-term, though. More devastating to a party's electoral chances was the possibility that different components of the potential coalition might be engaged in active conflict with each other because of an underlying lack of respect for the principles or values for which its opponents stood. Difficult though the relations were between the progressive and orthodox wings of the Republican Party between about 1910 and 1916, they lacked this characteristic. By contrast, the Democrats did experience that kind of separation in the "culture war" of the 1920s. It was an era in which the party did disastrously in three successive presidential elections, and yet its performance, in gubernatorial or U.S. Senate elections, for example, demonstrated that the Democratic Party still had a potential national coalition that could be constructed. United though they often were against Republicans in their own states or regions, Democrats were also at odds with each other – not just over specific policies but also over the respect they accorded each other.

The key to the construction of a national coalition under these circumstances lay in four factors. First, the party had to be competing in a presidential election in conditions where the economic radicalism associated with its western wing was not at a disadvantage; the high prosperity of the 1920s, for example, were poor conditions for that kind of economic interventionism to prosper. Yet there was never much prospect that the conservative, eastern economic strategy associated with Al Smith would be able to mobilize voters in many other parts of the country. Thus, it was only through some revival of the Bryanite-Wilsonian approach that it would be possible to link enough elements of the party together, and that could be undertaken only if the economy did not seem to be booming. Secondly, there had to be a marked shift in public support away from prohibition, so that the Smith-Raskob strategy of combining economic conservatism with an anti-prohibition stance could be undermined. That became possible after 1926 with a clear shift in public support away from prohibition. Thirdly, there had to be available a plausible political entrepreneur who could make the seemingly impossible alliance between western economic radicalism and anti-prohibition credible – thereby transcending the divide between the party's two cultures. The only strategy for uniting the elements in the coalition that could possibly work would be one that would somehow fuse the conflicting elements of a western, radical, and dry sub-culture and an eastern, conservative, and wet one. Fourth, having won power, it was then necessary to devise public policies to unite the party over policy goals, and thereby buy time to weaken the long-standing antagonisms over fundamental social values between the competing sub-cultures in the party.

With these four factors, the ending of the culture war – a conflict that had its roots in the rapid transformation of American society through industrialization and mass immigration – was possible. However, it took time for the coincidence of an ending of prosperity, public shifts in attitudes to prohibition, and the partial discrediting of the electoral viability of the major public officials associated with the "war" (Smith and William Gibbs McAdoo) to create the opportunity for the "transcending" electoral strategy to succeed. Until that opportunity arose, the Democrats would be unable to resolve the internal conflict that had become so pronounced by the end of the Wilson administration. Changed attitudes towards prohibition from about 1926–7, the onset of the Great Depression in 1929, and the availability, in Franklin Roosevelt, of an economic radical who was willing to abandon prohibition made it possible for the Democrats to re-unite the two wings of the party. However, it was to take the New Deal to make those earlier divisions irrelevant.

4. The Inertia Created by a Fragmented Governmental System

Broadly speaking, political parties can generate loyal followings among voters in one of two ways. The first is through the defence of particular social identities; parties arise from sub-cultures that are under threat or feel under threat in some way, and a party subsequently reinforces that association by a whole variety of symbolic means. This is how most parties developed links with mass electorates in Europe and North America during the 19th and early 20th centuries. Although those identities often persisted from one generation to another, various changes in social arrangements usually resulted either in their becoming weaker or in the link with a specific political party becoming weaker. In the absence of some means of reviving party-voter ties, party coalition building would necessarily become more difficult. The second way of developing loyal electorates is by implementing public policies that are of benefit to a group of voters and by reinforcing a belief that other parties are less committed to the sustenance of those policies because they represent interests that have a stake in curtailing them. This generation (often re-generation) of loyal voter support is a means of developing links to parties when the effects of social identities on voting behaviour have been reduced. However, to be effective, it is necessary for a party to control the policy-making process, and in the United States the dispersion of power among different political institutions makes that unusual.

It is not just the separation of powers between president and Congress, nor the presence of a strong second chamber in the legislature; it is also how power is distributed within the chambers that hampers the systematic building of long-term support for a majority party through the use of public policy initiatives. Consequently, once the links between the parties and specific social identities started to weaken from the late 19th century onwards, maintaining party coalitions, or re-invigorating them, became far more difficult. The New Deal era was a unique period in American party politics, one in which a president was able to re-structure his party's electoral coalition, and what made it possible was not just large congressional majorities that lasted for six years, but also the deference his congressional party displayed to the president during Roosevelt's first four years. It is more usual for incoming presidents to find that the fragmentation of power creates a tendency towards policy inertia after their first year or so in office, and this means that there is insufficient time to use the party's control of government for the purpose of re-building longer-term support within different sectors of the electorate. Despite the fact that party-voter links had been weakening since the end of the 19th century, the more centralized control of political institutions evident in the New Deal era yielded a brief re-invigoration of partisanship in America.

The uniqueness of the New Deal period in 20th century American party politics was well captured by Silbey's comments (made in 1991):

> The revival of partisanship, powerful as it was for some years after 1933, was only a deviation from the long-range pattern of party collapse. A new political era dawned in the decade after 1948. The decline of political parties resumed at an even faster pace as the New Deal began to fade from popular memory, while other, extraparty elements became even more firmly entrenched on the landscape. Party control of the electoral process continued to weaken.[9]

In this environment of weakening political parties, and with continuing fragmented party control of the political institutions that affected public policy, coalition building became increasingly difficult for parties to control – except in the very short term, that is, in particular election years.

5. Leadership Attitudes Towards Coalition Transformation

Democratic presidents displayed different approaches to the possibility of restructuring their party's existing coalition, with most seeking to preserve ways of aggregating the various interests that had supported the party in the past. Grover Cleveland rejected any attempt to appease western interests in the depression of 1893, and linked his administration to a hard-line approach on currency. From one perspective this made clear sense. In the past Democrats had won by uniting a solid South with parts of the Northeast and the Midwest – with the latter occupying the key position of the marginal voter. However, with the possibility of some form of alliance with the Populists in 1896, the strategic position changed. After the success of the Populists in the West in 1892, those Democrats from districts (especially in the South) that would benefit from a less rigid stance on the gold question could see the possibility of a kind of coalition with populism – the very coalition that actually was to form in 1896. For them, there was now less need to respect the power of the previous marginal voter, because there now seemed to be a "new" marginal voter available – with whom alliances would be made. Cleveland's policies ignored the new strategic considerations for his party, and in doing so arguably he made the split in the party over silver that much more damaging than it might have been.

Woodrow Wilson, too, was cautious in not moving quickly towards building a new coalition. One of the criticisms made of him by Theodore

---

[9] Joel H. Silbey, *The American Political Nation, 1838–1893*, p. 241.

Roosevelt and other Republican progressives was that he was not pursuing the full progressive agenda. Moreover, he supported the highly partisan approach to legislation adopted by the Democratic Party in Congress. As a result, any opportunity of linking his party to the western Republicans was lost. Later, John Kennedy was to prove equally timid with respect to racial desegregation. It was not until violence directed against civil rights demonstrators and organizers forced the hand of the administration that Kennedy gave up his attempt to appease the white South. (As a non-elected incumbent whose party had suffered major mid-term losses in 1946, Truman after 1948 could merely seek to consolidate the New Deal coalition, and so he can be excluded from consideration here.)

Alone among the Democratic presidents who had an opportunity to restructure the party's coalition, Franklin Roosevelt actually tried to do that – and he did so successfully. Having been elected in 1932 by the older, western-oriented Democratic coalition, Roosevelt was then able to have his administration devise public policies that would prove attractive to previously unmobilized voters in northern cities. This improved the competitiveness of the party in states that had not been a central component of the 1932 coalition, turning the major industrial states into the real battleground for the presidency for the next 20 to 30 years. Undoubtedly, two factors facilitated this. First, the sense of a national emergency meant that Congress and other political actors deferred to presidential leadership for a few years to a degree that was unusual. Secondly, the size of the Democratic victory in 1932 meant that there was an influx of new members to the Democratic caucus – members who represented urban districts. They wanted policies that would help them consolidate their position as incumbents, and the New Deal did just that. However, there can be no question but that it was Roosevelt's particular response to the economic crisis that enabled him to transform what had hitherto been essentially western support for economic intervention by government into support that was now firmly grounded in the large cities.

6. Changes in the Composition of the Electorate

The process of political socialization placed limits on the ability of either party to make frequent and major changes to the kinds of coalitions they tried to construct: Members of succeeding generations would bring with them political values and opinions that had been learnt within families and communities. Moreover, patterns of population migration created opportunities that were likely to be of much more benefit to one party than the other. For example, that it was people of mainly Yankee descent who moved into Northern Plains states (such as North Dakota) while it was Southerners who moved into Oklahoma meant that the Republicans had advantages mobilizing in the former while the Democrats had advantages in the latter. In general, before the 1890s, the Republicans benefited more from westward migration and the creation of new states there, while after the 1890s, that advantage was partly nullified. However, the population migrations that had the greatest potential for changing the competitive balance between the parties were, first, that from continental Europe (in the decades up to the 1920s) and, secondly, the northern migration of African Americans in the 20th century. In both cases, the northern cities were the main centres of migration.

As was seen in earlier chapters, and contrary to conventional wisdom, the 1890s did not witness a major shift in political domination of the large cities from the Democrats to the Republicans. There was a change from a Democratic advantage before that decade to a Republican advantage from the 1890s until the 1930s, but the latter was much smaller than has usually been believed. That urban party consolidation coincided with a period of difficulty for the Democrats helps to explain the Democratic Party's inability to build on their earlier strength in those places. However, the important point is that neither party had political organizations that proved capable of "reaching" all of the new immigrants, and that was one reason why voter turnout declined so much in the early decades of the 20th century. It was these sorts of "unmobilized" voters whom FDR could attract into voting for a new kind of Democratic Party, thereby swinging a much larger proportion of the urban vote to his party than the Republicans had been able to do in the preceding decades. This was the basis of the most fundamental change in the nature of the Democratic Party coalition in the eight decades covered by this study.

The migration of African Americans was significant in a different way. Both periods of migration (in the first two decades of the 20th century and in the 1940s) occurred after the Republican Party had ceased to be much concerned with the interests of African Americans in the South. In the northern cities, the Republican Party, therefore, was no longer the "natural" party for the new black voters. To the contrary, local initiatives in mobilizing black voters there in the 1920s, followed by the New Deal, helped to forge links between African American communities and the Democratic Party that expanded the party's electoral coalition. Certainly, after the New Deal, alienating black voters in the North would have been a dangerous strategy in states that were now highly competitive, and on which the results of presidential elections depended. Unfortunately for the Democrats, courting the African American vote inevitably involved internal party pressure for civil rights in the South, and that in turn threatened a key element of the party's coalition-building strategy since the 1850s. The prevarication on the issue of civil rights by Democratic presidential candidates in the 1950s and early 1960s was viable only so long as the persistence of racial segregation was not directly threatened; once it was, the entire basis of the party's coalition-building strategy had to change. Growing Democratic strength in the northern states meant that there could be no question of reverting to a southern-oriented strategy, but it also meant that there were now greater opportunities in the North for the party to compensate for the collapse of its southern monopoly. The key question, though, and it was the question that was central for Kennedy until his death, was how to manage this transition in the party. His successor, Lyndon Johnson, was to opt for a much bolder approach in dealing with civil rights than Kennedy had ever shown. Together with the Republican candidacy of Barry Goldwater in 1964, it served to speed up the process of coalition change.

Nevertheless, the central point being made here is that population migration acted essentially as an exogenous variable on the circumstances in which parties made choices about their electoral coalitions. The opportunities for, and the restrictions on, changing an earlier coalition were shaped not just by political institutions and the choices made by political leaders, but also by changes in American society. This meant that how easy or difficult it was to construct the Democratic Party coalition varied considerably over time, and in ways that did not always mesh with the effects of other factors. For example, the opportunity to mobilize the new urban electorate in the 1920s depended on winning the presidency first, and that could not occur until circumstances were present in which the effect of the party's culture war could be neutralized.

Final Thoughts

How then should the Democrats' ability to put together a national coalition be assessed overall? The party held the presidency for a little under half the time between 1877 and 1962 – a total of 38 years – but from 1876 it won more votes than the Republicans in 11 of the 21 elections. There can be no question that it benefited, for up to two decades, from being out of office at the onset of the Great Depression, but equally it had been harmed for a decade and a half, during an era of party consolidation, by being in office during the economic depression that began in 1893.

By comparison with the Republicans, the party suffered from three major disadvantages as an aggregator of different interests. First, as the party that won the Civil War and was then in office at key periods later in the 19th century, the Republicans had been able to create new states in territories that leaned Republican so that the Democrats had more difficulties in turning national majorities into presidential victories. Secondly, the party's more decentralized nominating system (until 1936) made it more difficult for it to aggregate the various interests that were possibly at its disposal into effective coalitions. Especially between 1896 and 1912, this hurt the party with respect to finding suitable presidential candidates, and it also exacerbated the problem of the party's internal divisions in the 1920s. The Republicans, too, had their divisions, but their more centralized national structure enabled the party to relegate those disputes to the congressional level – where their potential for adversely affecting presidential coalition building was reduced. Thirdly, the homogeneity of the states in the Democrats' core region of support – linked as they were by a distrust of the federal government, out of a fear that it could endanger the entire basis of a segregated society – made it more difficult for the party to extend its coalition in the North. The Republican Party was capable of rather more flexibility – as was demonstrated in the party's move towards moderate Republicanism in the two decades after 1940. Given that the coastal states constituted the marginal voter, those states had the leverage to force "moderation" on the party, but it was important, too, that they did not face a wholly intransigent opposition. By contrast, parts of the Democratic South were all too ready to "bolt" (as in 1948) in the face of concessions being made to its party's marginal voters.

For these reasons, heading "further North" than it already was in 1877 proved not to be easy for the Democratic Party, and that is why it took eight decades before it became much more of a northern party than it had been in the second half of the 1870s. To form a national majority, especially at the presidential level, it always had to improve its competitiveness in the North – not least because of its declining control of the Border states between 1880 and 1930. While there was an incentive to do just that, the party was often constrained in its efforts by factors beyond the control of its leadership. Yet the clear conclusion from this study is that the constraint facing it did not really lie in the distribution of partisans in the electorate: It was not an alleged electoral realignment in the 1890s that blighted the party's chances for a generation. Leaving aside the exceptional period from 1894 to 1910, it was not relative lack of strength vis-à-vis the Republican Party that was responsible for its years out of national office, and even its weakness in that particular period was not the result of an electoral realignment. The constraints on the party, many of them internal to the party, were mainly those associated with *aggregating* different interests, rather than its having insufficient interests at its disposal to construct a national majority. In a heterogeneous society, coalition building within the context of a two-party system is not easy, and it should not be surprising that it should fail frequently and also change in fundamental ways only slowly.

Appendix: Note on Data Sources

All data relating to state legislature seats held by the Democratic and Republican Parties were calculated from a data set collected originally by Walter Dean Burnham: "Partisan Division of American State Governments, 1834–1985", Inter-University Consortium for Political and Social Research, Study No. 16.

Data for congressional elections between 1880 and 1932 in cities with populations of more than 200,000 (and used in Tables 3.6, 3.7, and 5.1) were calculated by the author from data presented in *Congressional Quarterly's Guide to U.S. Elections*, Third Edition, Washington, DC, Congressional Quarterly, 1994. The cities comprised all those in northern and Border states, but excluded those in the 11 southern states. Cities were included in the data for the first election following a U.S. Census that revealed the city now had a population of at least 200,000. The counties that formed a congressional district were checked, and districts were included in the data when it was clear that at least 50 per cent of the electorate of that district were residents of the county containing the city of 200,000. In the case of many states, the decision as to which districts should be included, and which omitted, was relatively straightforward. There were some "difficult cases", however. A good example is New Jersey. Newark and Jersey City both warranted inclusion from 1912, but the state legislature drew district boundaries so that the cities were divided among several districts, and in no single district did those parts of the city included constitute a majority of the district. To include none of the districts would have distorted the data set overall, just as including all of them would have. Consequently, in these cases, selection proceeded as follows. The number of districts the city would have had, if seats had been allocated proportionately to the relative size of the city in the state, was calculated. That number of districts was then selected, the districts chosen being those containing the largest number of residents of that city.

Inevitably, though, some apparent anomalies arise. For example, for 1902–10, Buffalo has only one district that qualifies, while San Francisco, Cincinnati, and Pittsburgh have two each. Nevertheless, overall, the list of districts included for each period does largely reflect the relative size of each city.

For each period, the cities and congressional districts included were as follows, in order of city size at each census (except for 1922–30, when there was no congressional redistricting following the census, and the same order as for 1912–20 is used):

1882–1890 New York and Brooklyn (NY 2, 3, 4, 5, 6, 7, 8, 9, 10, 11)
              Philadelphia (PA 1, 2, 3, 4, 5)
              Chicago (IL 2, 3)
              Boston (MA 3, 4)
              St. Louis (MO 8, 9)
              Baltimore (MD 3, 4)
              Cincinnati (OH 1, 2)

1892–1900 New York and Brooklyn (NY 2, 3, 4, 5, 6, 7, 8, 9, 10, 11, 12, 13)
              Chicago (IL 2, 3, 4, 5, 6)
              Philadelphia (PA 1, 2, 3, 4, 5)
              St. Louis (MO 8, 9)
              Boston (MA 3, 4)
              Baltimore (MD 3, 4)
              San Francisco (CA 4, 5)
              Cincinnati (OH 1, 2)
              Cleveland (OH 21)
              Buffalo (NY 32)

1902–1910 New York (NY 2, 3, 4, 5, 6, 7, 8, 9, 10, 11, 12, 13, 14, 15, 16, 17, 18)
              Chicago (IL 1, 2, 4, 5, 6, 7, 8, 9)
              Philadelphia (PA 1, 2, 3, 4, 5, 6)
              St. Louis (MO 10, 11, 12)
              Boston (MA 9, 10, 11)
              Baltimore (MD 2, 3, 4)
              Cleveland (OH 20, 21)
              Buffalo (NY 35)

San Francisco (CA 4, 5)
Cincinnati (OH 1, 2)
Pittsburgh (PA 31, 32)
Detroit (MI 1)
Milwaukee (WI 4)

1912–1920   New York (NY 2, 3, 4, 5, 6, 7, 8, 9, 10, 11, 12, 13, 14, 15,
                16, 17, 18, 19, 20, 21, 22, 23)
             Chicago (IL 1, 2, 3, 4, 5, 6, 7, 8, 9)
             Philadelphia (PA 1, 2, 3, 4, 5, 6)
             St. Louis (MO 10, 11, 12)
             Boston (MA 10, 11, 12)
             Cleveland (OH 20, 21)
             Baltimore (MD 3, 4)
             Pittsburgh (PA 30, 31)
             Detroit (MI 1, 2)
             Buffalo (NY 41, 42)
             San Francisco (CA 4, 5)
             Milwaukee (WI 4, 5)
             Cincinnati (OH 1, 2)
             Newark (NJ 9, 10)
             Los Angeles (CA 9, 10)
             Minneapolis (MN 5)
             Jersey City (NJ 12)

1922–1930   New York (NY 2, 3, 4, 5, 6, 7, 8, 9, 10, 11, 12, 13, 14, 15,
                16, 17, 18, 19, 20, 21, 22, 23)
             Chicago (IL 1, 2, 3, 4, 5, 6, 7, 8, 9)
             Philadelphia (PA 1, 2, 3, 4, 5, 6)
             St. Louis (MO 10, 11, 12)
             Boston (MA 10, 11, 12)
             Cleveland (OH 20, 21)
             Baltimore (MD 3, 4)
             Pittsburgh (PA 30, 31)
             Detroit (MI 1, 2)
             Buffalo (NY 41, 42)
             San Francisco (CA 4, 5)
             Milwaukee (WI 4, 5)
             Cincinnati (OH 1, 2)
             Newark (NJ 9, 10)
             Los Angeles (CA 9, 10)
             Minneapolis (MN 5)

Jersey City (NJ 12)
Kansas City (MO 5)
Seattle (WA 1)
Indianapolis (IN 7)
Rochester (NY 38)
Portland (OR 3)
Denver (CO 1)

1932–1938   New York (NY 2, 3, 4, 5, 6, 7, 8, 9, 10, 11, 12, 13, 14, 15, 16, 17, 18, 19, 20, 21, 22, 23)
Chicago (IL 1, 2, 3, 4, 5, 6, 7, 8, 9)
Philadelphia (PA 1, 2, 3, 4, 5, 6, 7)
Detroit (MI 1, 13, 14, 15, 16)
Los Angeles (CA 13, 14, 15, 16, 17)
Cleveland (OH 20, 21, 22)
St Louis (MO 11, 12, 13)
Baltimore (MD 3, 4, 5)
Boston (MA 10, 11, 12)
Pittsburgh (PA 32, 33, 34)
San Francisco (CA 4, 5)
Milwaukee (WI 4, 5)
Buffalo (NY 41, 42)
Minneapolis (MN 3, 5)
Cincinnati (OH 1, 2)
Newark (NJ 11, 12)
Kansas City (MO 5)
Seattle (WA 1)
Indianapolis (IN 12)
Rochester (NY 38)
Jersey City (NJ 13)
Louisville (KY 3)
Portland (OR 3)
Toledo (OH 9)
Columbus (OH 12)
Denver (CO 1)
Oakland (CA 7)
St. Paul (MN 4)
Akron (OH 14)
Providence (RI 2)

Bibliography

Aldrich, John H., *Why Parties? The Origin and Transformation of Political Parties in America*, Chicago, University of Chicago Press, 1995.

Alexander, Herbert E., *Financing Politics*, Washington, DC, CQ Press, 1976.

Andersen, Kristi, *The Creation of a Democratic Majority, 1928–1936*, Chicago, University of Chicago Press, 1979.

Argersinger, Peter H., "A Place on the Ballot: Fusion Politics and Antifusion Laws", *American Historical Society*, 85 (1980), 287–306.

Axelrod, Robert, "Where the Vote Comes From: An Analysis of Electoral Coalitions, 1952–1972", in Jeff Fishel (ed.), *Parties and Elections in an Anti-Party Age*, Bloomington and London, Indiana University Press, 1978, pp. 86–99.

Barry, Brian, "Is It Better to Be Powerful or Lucky? Part II", *Political Studies*, 28 (1980), 338–52.

Barry, Brian, *Political Argument*, London, Routledge and Kegan Paul, 1965.

Bartels, Larry M., "Electoral Continuity and Change 1868–1996", *Electoral Studies*, 17 (1998), 301–26.

Bartley, Norman V., *The New South, 1945–1980*, Baton Rouge, Louisiana State University Press, 1995.

Black, Earl, "The Newest Southern Politics", *Journal of Politics*, 60 (1998), 519–612.

Black, Earl, and Merle Black, *Politics and Society in the South*, Cambridge, MA, Harvard University Press, 1987.

Brady, David W., John F. Cogan, and Morris P. Fiorina (eds.), *Continuity and Change in House Elections*, Stanford, CA, Stanford University Press, 2000.

Brown, Roger G., "Party and Bureaucracy: From Kennedy to Reagan", *Political Science Quarterly*, 97 (1982), 279–94.

Bukowski, Douglas, *Big Bill Thompson, Chicago and the Politics of Image*, Urbana and Chicago, University of Illinois Press, 1998.

Burner, David, *The Politics of Provincialism: The Democratic Party in Transition, 1918–1932*, Cambridge, MA, Harvard University Press, 1967.

267

Burnham, Walter Dean, *Critical Elections and Mainsprings of American Politics*, New York, Norton, 1970.

Burnham, Walter Dean, "The Changing Shape of the American Political Universe", in Walter Dean Burnham (ed.), *The Current Crisis in American Politics*, New York and Oxford, Oxford University Press, 1982, pp. 25–57.

Burnham, Walter Dean, "The Turnout Problem", in A. James Reichley (ed.), *Elections American Style*, Washington, DC, Brookings Institution, 1987, pp. 97–133.

Burnham, Walter Dean, and William N. Chambers (eds.), *The American Party Systems*, Second Edition, New York, Oxford University Press, 1975.

Burns, James McGregor, *Roosevelt: The Lion and the Fox, 1882–1940*, New York, Harcourt, Brace and World, 1956.

Campbell, Angus, Philip E. Converse, Warren E. Miller, and Donald E. Stokes, *The American Voter*, An Abridgment, New York, John Wiley, 1964.

Carmines, Edward G., and James A. Stimson, *Issue Evolution: Race and the Transformation of American Politics*, Princeton, NJ, Princeton University Press, 1989.

Chubb, John E., and Paul E. Peterson, *The New Direction in American Politics*, Washington, DC, Brookings Institution, 1985.

Clubb, Jerome M., William H. Flanigan, and Nancy H. Zingale, *Partisan Realignment: Voters, Parties and Government in American History*, Beverly Hills, CA, Sage, 1980.

Cole, Wayne S., *Roosevelt and the Isolationists, 1932–45*, Lincoln and London, University of Nebraska Press, 1981.

Coleman, John J., *Party Decline in America: Policy, Politics and the Fiscal State*, Princeton, NJ, Princeton University Press, 1996.

Cooper, John Milton, Jr., *Pivotal Decades, The United States, 1900–1920*, New York, W. W. Norton, 1990.

Cox Gary W., and Jonathan N. Katz, *Elbridge Gerry's Salamander: The Electoral Consequences of the Reapportionment Revolution*, Cambridge, Cambridge University Press, 2002.

Craig, Douglas B., *After Wilson: The Struggle for the Democratic Party, 1920–1934*, Chapel Hill and London, University of North Carolina Press, 1992.

Cray, Ed, *Chief Justice: A Biography of Earl Warren*, New York, Simon and Schuster, 1997.

Dahill, Edwin McNeil, "Connecticut's J. Henry Roraback", PhD dissertation, Columbia University, 1971.

Dunleavy, Patrick, *Democracy, Bureaucracy and Public Choice*, Hemel Hempstead, Harvester Wheatsheaf, 1991.

Feinman, Ronald L., *Twilight of Progressivism: The Western Republican Senators and the New Deal*, Baltimore and London, Johns Hopkins University Press, 1981.

Finegold, Kenneth, *Experts and Politicians: Reform Challenges to Machine Politics in New York, Cleveland and Chicago*, Princeton, NJ, Princeton University Press, 1995.

Finegold, Kenneth, and Theda Skocpol, *State and Party in America's New Deal*, Madison, University of Wisconsin Press, 1995.

Finegold, Kenneth, and Elaine K. Swift, "What Works? Competitive Strategies of Major Parties out of Power", *British Journal of Political Science*, 31 (2001), 95–120.

Finer, S. E., "Patronage and the Public Service", *Public Administration*, 30 (1952), 329–60.

Fleming, James S., "Oscar W. Underwood: The First Modern House Leader", in Roger H. Davidson, Susan Webb Hammond, and Raymond W. Smock (eds.), *Masters of the House*, Boulder, CO, Westview Press, 1998, pp. 91–118.

Frederickson, George M., *The Black Image in the White Mind*, Hanover, NH, Wesleyan University Press, 1987.

Fredman, L. E., *The Australian Ballot: The Story of an American Reform*, East Lansing, Michigan State University Press, 1968.

Gerring, John, *Party Ideologies in America, 1828–1996*, Cambridge, Cambridge University Press, 1998.

Giffin, William W., "The Political Realignment of Black Voters in Indianapolis, 1924", *Indiana Magazine of History*, 79 (1983), 133–66.

Goldberg, Robert Alan, *Barry Goldwater*, New Haven and London, Yale University Press, 1995.

Hamby, Alonzo L., *Man of the People: A Life of Harry S. Truman*, New York, Oxford University Press, 1995.

Huston, James L., *The Panic of 1857 and the Coming of the Civil War*, Baton Rouge and London, Louisiana State University Press, 1987.

Jacobs, John, *A Rage for Justice: The Passion and Politics of Phillip Burton*, Berkeley, University of California Press, 1995.

James, Scott C., *Presidents, Parties and the State: A Party System Perspective of Democratic Regulatory Choice, 1884–1936*, Cambridge, Cambridge University Press, 2000.

Jewell, Malcolm E., and Sarah M. Morehouse, *Political Parties and Elections in American States*, Fourth Edition, Washington, DC, Congressional Quarterly Press, 2001.

Key, V. O., *Southern Politics*, New York, Alfred A. Knopf, 1949.

Key, V. O., Jr., "A Theory of Critical Elections", *Journal of Politics*, 17 (1955), 198–210.

King, Anthony, "Political Parties in Western Democracies", *Polity*, 2 (1969), 111–41.

King, Desmond, *Separate and Unequal: Black Americans and the U.S. Federal Government*, Oxford, Oxford University Press, 1995.

Kirwan, Albert D., *Revolt of the Rednecks: Mississippi Politics, 1876–1925*, New York, Harper and Row, 1951.

Kleppner, Paul, *The Third Electoral System, 1853–1892: Parties, Voters and Political Cultures*, Chapel Hill, University of North Carolina Press, 1979.

Kyvig, David E., *Repealing National Prohibition*, Chicago and London, University of Chicago Press, 1979.

Ladd, Everett Carll, Jr., *American Political Parties: Social Change and Political Response*, New York, W. W. Norton, 1970.

Lamis, Alexander P., *The Two-Party South*, New York, Oxford University Press, 1984.

Lowi, Theodore, "The Public Philosophy: Interest Group Liberalism", *American Political Science Review*, 61 (1967), 5–24.

Lubell, Samuel, *The Future of American Politics*, Third Edition, New York, Harper and Row, 1965.

Mackenzie, G.Calvin, "The State of the Presidential Appointment Process", in G. Calvin Mackenzie (ed.), *Innocent Until Nominated: The Breakdown of the Presidential Appointments Process*, Washington, DC, Brookings Institution, 2001, pp. 1–49.

Mansberger, John W., *From Obstruction to Moderation: The Transformation of Senate Conservatism, 1938–1952*, London, Associated University Presses, 2000.

Mayhew, David R., "Electoral Realignments", *Annual Review of Political Science*, 3 (2000), 449–74.

Mayhew, David R., *Electoral Realignments: A Critique of an American Genre*, New Haven and London, Yale University Press, 2002.

Mayhew, David R., *Placing Parties in American Politics*, Princeton, NJ, Princeton University Press, 1986.

McCaffery, Peter, *When Bosses Ruled Philadelphia: The Emergence of the Republican Machine, 1867–1933*, University Park, Pennsylvania State Univerisity Press, 1993.

McClosky, Herbert, Paul J. Hoffman, and Rosemary O'Hara, "Issue Conflict and Consensus Among Party Leaders and Followers", *American Political Science Review*, 54 (1960), 406–27.

McCormick, Richard L., *From Realignment to Reform: Political Change in New York State, 1893–1910*, Ithaca and London, Cornell University Press, 1981.

McCormick, Richard L., *The Party Period and Public Policy: American Politics from the Age of Jackson to the Progressive Era*, New York, Oxford University Press, 1986.

McGerr, Michael E., *The Decline of Popular Politics: The American North, 1865–1928*, New York and Oxford, Oxford University Press, 1986.

McGirr, Lisa, *Suburban Warriors: The Origins of the New American Right*, Princeton and Oxford, Princeton University Press, 2001.

Milkis, Sidney M., *The President and the Parties: The Transformation of the American Party System Since the New Deal*, New York and Oxford, 1993.

Miller, Warren E., and J. Merrill Shanks, *The New American Voter*, Cambridge, MA, and London, Harvard University Press, 1996.

Mitchell, Franklin D., *Embattled Democracy: Missouri Politics, 1929–1932*, Columbia, University of Missouri Press, 1968.

Mulder, Ronald A., *The Insurgent Progressives in the United States Senate and the New Deal*, New York, Garland, 1979.

Nardulli, Peter F., "The Concept of a Critical Realignment, Electoral Behavior, and Political Change", *American Political Science Review*, 89 (1995), 10–22.

Nie, Norman H., Sidney Verba, and John R. Petrocik, *The Changing American Voter*, Cambridge, MA, and London, Harvard University Press, 1976.

Pegram, Thomas R., *Partisans and Progressives: Private Interest and Public Policy in Illinois, 1870–1922*, Urbana and Chicago, University of Illinois Press, 1992.

Perlstein, Rick, *Before the Storm: Barry Goldwater and the Unmaking of the American Consensus*, New York, Hill and Wang, 2001.

Perman, Michael, *Struggle for Mastery, Disfranchisement in the South, 1888–1908*, Chapel Hill, University of North Carolina Press, 2001.

Petrocik, John R., "Realignment: New Party Coalitions and the Nationalization of the South", *Journal of Politics*, 49 (1987), 347–75.

Polsby, Nelson W., *How Congress Evolves: Social Bases of Institutional Change*, New York, Oxford University Press, 2004.

Rae, Nicol, *The Decline and Fall of Liberal Republicanism from 1952 to the Present*, New York, Oxford University Press, 1989.

Reynolds, John F., and Richard L. McCormick, "Outlawing 'Treachery': Split Tickets and Ballot Laws in New York and New Jersey, 1880–1910", *Journal of American History*, 72 (1986), 835–58.

Reynolds, John F., *Testing Democracy: Electoral Behaviour and Progressive Reform in New Jersey, 1880–1920*, Chapel Hill and London, University of North Carolina Press, 1988.

Ritter, Gretchen, *Goldbugs and Greenbacks: The Antimonopoly Tradition and the Politics of Finance in America*, Cambridge, Cambridge University Press, 1997.

Rodgers, Daniel T., "In Search of Progressivism", *Reviews in American History*, 10 (1982), 113–32.

Sanders, Elizabeth, *Roots of Reform: Farmers, Workers, and the American State, 1877–1917*, Chicago, University of Chicago Press, 1999.

Schattschneider, E. E., *The Semisovereign People*, Hinsdale, IL, Dryden Press, 1975.

Schiesl, Martin J., *The Politics of Efficiency: Municipal Adminstration and Reform in America, 1880–1920*, Berkeley, University of California Press, 1977.

Schwarz, Jordan A., *The Interregnum of Despair: Hoover, Congress and the Depression*, Urbana, IL, University of Illinois Press, 1970.

Shafer, Byron E., and William J. M. Claggett, *The Two Majorities: The Issue Context of Modern American Politics*, Baltimore and London, The Johns Hopkins University Press, 1995.

Shafer, Byron E., and Richard G. C. Johnston, "The Transformation of Southern Politics Revisited: The House of Representatives as a Window", *British Journal of Political Science*, 31 (2001), 601–25.

Shefter, Martin, *Political Parties and the State: The American Historical Experience*, Princeton, NJ, Princeton University Press, 1994.

Shefter, Martin, "Regional Receptivity to Reform: The Legacy of the Progressives", *Political Science Quarterly*, 98 (1983), 459–83.

Shover, John L., "Ethnicity and Religion in Philadelphia Politics, 1924–1940", *American Quarterly*, 25 (1973), 499–515.

Silbey, Joel H., *The American Political Nation, 1838–1893*, Stanford, CA, Stanford University Press, 1991.

Silva, Ruth C., *Rum, Religion and Votes: 1928 Re-examined*, University Park, Pennsylvania State University Press, 1962.

Sinclair, Barbara, *Congressional Realignment, 1925–78*, Houston, University of Texas Press, 1982.

Stanley, Harold W., "Southern Partisan Change: Dealignment, Realignment, or Both?", *Journal of Politics*, 50 (1988), 64–88.

Stein, Judith, "The Birth of Liberal Republicanism in New York State, 1932–1938", PhD dissertation, Yale University, 1968.

Stewart, Charles, III, and Barry R. Weingast, "Stacking the Senate, Changing the Nation: Republican Rotten Boroughs, Statehood Politics and American Political Development", *Studies in American Political Development*, 6 (1992), 223–71.

Summers, Mark Wahlgren, *Party Games: Getting, Keeping, and Using Power in Gilded Age Politics*, Chapel Hill and London, University of North Carolina Press, 2004.

Sundquist, James L., *Dynamics of the Party System*, Washington, DC, Brookings Institution, 1973.

Thelen, David, *Paths of Resistance: Tradition and Disunity in Industrializing Missouri*, New York, Oxford University Press, 1986.

Tsebelis, George, *Nested Games: Rational Choice in Comparative Politics*, Berkeley, University of California Press, 1990.

VanderMeer, Philip R., *The Hoosier Politician: Officeholding and Political Culture in Indiana, 1896–1920*, Urbana and Chicago, University of Illinois Press, 1984.

Ware, Alan, *The American Direct Primary: Party Institutionalization and Transformation in the North*, Cambridge and New York, Cambridge University Press, 2002.

Ware, Alan, "The Funding of Political Parties in North America: The Early Years", in Peter Burnell and Alan Ware (eds.), *Funding Democratization*, Manchester, Manchester University Press, 1998, pp. 22–46.

Weatherford, M. Stephen, "After the Critical Election: Presidential Leadership, Competition and the Consolidation of the New Deal Realignment", *British Journal of Political Science*, 32 (2002), 221–58.

Weed, Clyde P., *The Nemesis of Reform: The Republican Party During the New Deal*, New York, Columbia University Press, 1994.

Weingast, Barry R., "Political Stability and Civil War: Institutions, Commitment, and American Democracy", in Robert H. Bates et al., *Analytic Narratives*, Princeton, NJ, Princeton University Press, 1998, pp. 148–93.

Weisberg, Herbert F., "Partisanship and Incumbency in Presidential Elections", *Political Behavior*, 4 (2002), 339–60.

Wesser, Robert F., *A Response to Progressivism: The Democratic Party and New York Politics, 1902–1918*, New York, New York University Press, 1986.

Woodward, C. Vann, *The Strange Career of Jim Crow*, Third Edition, New York, Oxford University Press, 1974.

Index